Poetic Authority
Spenser, Milton, and Literary History

Poetic Authority

Spenser, Milton, and Literary History

JOHN GUILLORY

Columbia University Press
New York   1983

Library of Congress Cataloging in Publication Data

Guillory, John D.
Poetic authority.

Bibliography: p. 191
Includes index.
1. English poetry—Early modern, 1500-1700—History
and criticism.   2. Authority in literature.   3. Spenser,
Edmund, 1552?-1599—Criticism and interpretation.
4. Milton, John, 1608-1674—Criticism and interpretation.
5. English literature—History and criticism—
Theory, etc.   I. Title
PR508. A88G84 1983   821'.3'09   82-14565
ISBN 0-231-05540-4
ISBN 0-231-05541-2 (pbk.)

Columbia University Press
New York   Guildford, Surrey

*Clothbound editions of Columbia University Press books are Smyth-sewn and
printed on permanent and durable acid-free paper.*

Contents

Preface

Authority encloses any discourse whatever within its brackets of common perception and value; it is the court of final appeal whose existence is presupposed by every utterance. The concept might seem therefore as unproblematic as an axiom of geometry. Yet this analogy gives us the peace of delusion, since it effaces the difficult prehistory of the axiom, and of every ground of consensus. The shifting of the ground disturbs consciousness at the depth where we are moved to believe not only something but someone: the human totality once known as an *auctor*. The process by which authority is acquired, by which a figure is elevated to a canon, ultimately to a life beyond life, remains largely mysterious. I am concerned here with one kind of authority—the poetic—but I have assumed the universality of the problem my argument addresses. Canonical authors are not markedly different in this respect from their contemporary workers in the medium of power; they have only chosen a strangely durable medium, the text, which has come to signify the very assurance of an afterlife.

When we have once recognized that the ground of consensus makes possible even our disagreements, the historicity of authority appears to us as a truth of skepticism (frightening perhaps), but also as nothing other than the real history of authors. They are themselves the epicenters of significant upheavals, whatever relation holds between them and historical causes. The Renaissance is notable for its self-proclaimed critique of authority, the manifestations of which are so familiar. The Reformation, the rejection of scholasticism, the "new science," are large movements; and the deposition of a king a very conspicuous event to the retrospective eye. For the student of discontinuity, however, it is an equally important fact that Charles I was a "divine right" monarch, no less modern for his absolutist claim than the regicides who declared their authority with an ax. I find this moment an epicenter analogous to the one I would like to call the emergence of "literature" (the Renaissance lacked the word, though Sidney means just this by poetry). Literature emerges when its inert relation to the sacred text of Western man, the Bible, is disrupted. I am less interested to describe the fully "secular" text (which, as an ontological category, remains dubious even today) than the resistance of certain authors to writing that is not, in effect, *scriptural*. This resistance defines the claim to authority of the two poets who, more than any others (more, that is, than Chaucer or Shakespeare), have established the literary history of England. The "line" of poetry descending from Spenser and Milton is aggressively scriptural, and it is a great irony of its success that the Bible has now been annexed in university curricula "as literature." It is no longer audacious to make this substitution since the originative reversal—"literature as scripture"—has for very long been the ground of poetic authority. I cannot hope to describe for all texts the theology of this transubstantiation, but I do intend to fill in one significant segment of the history. The possibility of distinguishing unequivocally between sacred and profane (consider Titian's famous painting and its ambiguities) is contingent at the least upon a program of radical purification, and finally upon the invocation of transcendent origins. Authority, we know, makes recourse to what is ancient; but the closure of the biblical canon, while it restricts both religious and poetic possibilities, simultaneously enjoins a more extreme defense of authority than any institution undertook through the instrument of tradition. This defense, which is in its own way as absolutist as "divine right," renews the life of an ancient figure: inspiration. The Protestant poet, whose authority must be wrested from the tradition, from the history of error, returns by means of this archaizing movement to the fountain of the Reformation, to *prophetic* history. Authority is by this means contracted to the bounds of the sacred text, the paradigmatic force of which is subversively increased. The Royalist defenders understood that the new inspiration reared itself in alliance with that other, most detested consequence of the Reformation, "enthusiasm." *Paradise Lost* is arguably the *terminus ad quem* of this development, an apocryphal scripture for a "church of one."

Although inspiration asserts the authority of the poetic text by invoking the participation of divinity in its production, it can be regarded from another, contemporaneous point of view as a regressive delusion. Some Renaissance writers (Mazzoni, Scaliger, Sidney in some moods, Hobbes always) demytholgize the inspirational pretensions of the literary text, and the name they give for the origin of this text is "imagination." They do not mean by this word the completely mystified normative term so current in our discourse of "creativity." On the contrary, they mean a modest recalcitrance to the composure of reason. The rule of imagination would be for them anarchy itself. This study describes an end and a beginning: the end of inspiration and the beginning of imagination. However, I do not identify this beginning with the origin of the secular text, or this end with the end of the sacred text. My hypothesis is that the authority of the imagination (which is almost never questioned by post-Renaissance critics) is completely implicated in the efflorescent death of inspiration; and this death, paradoxically, makes possible the survival of "scripture," always at the end of its era. The continuance of scripture is what we must now try to understand, as it is finally more important than the event announced in literary history as the internalization of the muse.

Poetic authority is ideally attained by a successsful persuasion, a rhetoric within the text, but it is by no means clear what end is achieved by success. No reader is compelled to interpret a "literary work" as a persuasion to a particular belief or action, but rather to contend with that language in its design upon him. The distinction of sacred and secular is one such design. My reading of Spenser and Milton is largely an elucidation of each poet's dialogue with the represented sources of poetic authority. This dialogue is a rhetoric more interior still, by which the poet persuades himself of his authority. If the "something of divinity" lingering in the poems of Spenser and Milton reflects not the waning of biblical authority but its brief intensification, the availability of a psychology of imagination coexisting with the retrograde motion of Protestant hermeneutics (a conjuncture attested by the *Leviathan*) eventuates in a paradox, a leap of semantic electricity across a gap in terminology. Not until the notion of inspiration becomes philosophically untenable does it become possible to place poetry under the regime of imagination—but only because the motive behind the reassertion of inspiration attaches itself to this new object. The peculiar twist in the catena of literary history is reflected by the fact that both Spenser and Milton polemicize against the imagination. Neither poet tracks his poetic origins to the door of Phantastes' chamber. And yet the post-Miltonic imagination no longer names an exclusively secular origin (as it did for Mazzoni or Bacon) but a further remystification of the same imagination. The polemic of Spenser and Milton is simply forgotten as

their names become, for Addison, for Johnson, for Wordsworth, signatures of imaginative power. Between the birth, then, of a putative "secular"
text, and the later triumph of the imagination, there is an interesting hiatus.
This book describes the hiatus.

   Poets do not usually preface their works with acknowledgments of their
poetical "teachers," as critics are impelled to do by the conventions of their
genre. But Dryden has given us this famous testimony: "Milton has
acknowledged to me that Spenser was his original." I do not think it would
be easy to say what Milton is acknowledging, although I would argue that
his statement is not substantially different from those ritual formulas with
which most works of criticism begin. The argument of this book is
structured about just those places in the poems of Spenser and Milton
where something or someone is being acknowledged (either openly, or by
the more oblique means of allusion and echo). The concept of acknowledgment can be usefully distinguished from "influence" in literary history, a
figure inaugurated most splendidly in Jonson's praise of Shakespeare. It
will be evident to readers of this book that I am not concerned to write the
story of Spenser's influence on Milton, but of their respective acknowledgments. I am interested in those maneuvers of invocation and recognition
by which an author becomes an *auctor*. Poets certainly do confront each
other as psyches in the course of literary history, as the notion of influence
proposes, but these disembodied egos are also to be conceived as allegorically laden figures of *prosopopeia*. If the critical or climactic moments in the
careers of my two poets are often those in which the *auctor* is acknowledged
(Chaucer in the *Mutabilitie Cantos*, Spenser in *Areopagitica*—there are many
others), these first-order phantasms conceal behind their empty sleeves
other more spectral sources (Ovid for Spenser, Shakespeare for Milton),
who in turn gesture toward the groundless origin, the imagination itself.
By deferring, in particular, the question of Spenser's influence (that would
be another, and different, book) I am led to consider the complicity of
imagination in the construction of that fiction which is the "line" of
Spenser and Milton. The adjacency of Shakespeare to this line has everything to do with the fortunes of fantasy, and by recognizing this fact, we
should be able to recover a literary history less deformed by linear genealogy. *Prosopopeia* appears to function in this history as the trope of the
chosen origin, and therefore need not even present the figure of a poet.

The recognition of Galileo in *Paradise Lost*, the culminating acknowledg-ment in the series reconstructed in this book, veils no earlier literary figure (except, most ironically, the Milton of the prose tracts), but Galileo does focus in his specular instrument both Milton's visionary expectations in the triumph of the Commonwealth and his final disillusion with prophetic history. What are we to make of such an acknowledgment? It has been my purpose to show that the psychomachia of literary history constitutes not only the genealogy of poets, but also, and more truly, the contest of literature and history. The disinclination of Spenser and Milton to ac-knowledge the imagination tells us how much faith they possessed, or desired to possess, in providential history. In this light, the resistance set up by the imagination points obliquely if unambiguously to the problem of Satan, whose birth is here marked (his revolution is for Milton the beginning of cosmic history), just as his death will later become "a tragedy for the imagination."

Satan's own failure to acknowledge his Creator is associated by Milton with the sense of debt ("The debt immense of endless gratitude, / So burdensome still owing, still to pay"). Satan is the son in whom the Father is not well pleased, but could we say that Milton's acknowledgment of Spenser would necessarily have elicited the father's delight in what Dryden called the "poetical son"? We cannot assume such approval, any more than we are willing now to claim the license of our teachers for every venture of our critical intelligence. Hence we acknowledge our debt but confess that the faults are our own. "Debt," in fact, is the one word the reader of criticism is certain to find in any preface, and upon reflection, this is most surprising. Is there any sense in which our debts are *discharged* by public acknowledgment? The ethos of debt defines precisely the realm of the *private*. It would seem that intellectual debts are never discharged but their payment only postponed by the protestations of a "grateful mind."

The metaphor of debt is itself a difficult acknowledgment of the impos-sibility of a "full disclosure." Failures of acknowledgment can be very painful, but they are not finally a matter of law (not even the laws of genre). Rather, such failures are nothing other than the lived problems of philoso-phy—or perhaps only the *one* problem of "other minds," about which Stanley Cavell has written these fine sentences:

> The claim of suffering may go unanswered. We feel lots of things—sympathy, *Schadenfreude*, nothing. If one says that this is a failure to acknowledge another's

suffering, surely this would not mean that we fail, in such cases to *know* that he is suffering? It may or may not. The point, however, is that the concept of acknowledgment is evidenced equally by its failure as by its success.[1]

It is as "Satanic" to deny one's origins as it is inhuman to doubt the pain of the other. But such inhumanity, as Cavell would say, is a response of which only humans are capable. If solipsism is the transcendental version of skepticism, then inspiration must give us the analogous claim of poetic authority. The "muse" evades the human origin. That we are capable of forgiving such claims is a most compelling fact of literary citicism. We know that the "human interest" (the lack of which in *Paradise Lost* Dr. Johnson lamented) is all that can or need be recovered from literature, that the parade of "daemonic agents" in Spenser, of gods and more-than-men in Milton, only temporarily obscures the figure across the way, whom we recognize at last. Poets cannot fail to evidence the authority of their origins, by which we really mean that authority is only made manifest in the act of acknowledgment. Authority has not even the voice of pain to make itself known. I am not sure that it matters, then, whether acknowledgment takes Angelic or Satanic form; it might be that the best teachers are witnessed by the heretics they create. Is this not just the relation that holds between Milton and his "better teacher[s]"? Such relations are the interest of poetry, the repayment of its debt, and so, too, it should be clear from our need to acknowledge, the interest of criticism. In Spenser's gentler, though ambiguous words, it is better "That good should from us goe, then come in greater store."

Here, then, are my own *auctors*, who have preceded me in researching the dissevered body of truth. My reflections on authority and literary history had their origin in Hannah Arendt's essay, "What is Authority?"— which spoke, it seemed to me, to the mysterious gaps in E. R. Curtius' "golden chain" of literary greatness. Harry Berger, Jr., William Kerrigan, and Angus Fletcher have bequeathed to me the Spenser and Milton whom I recognize and love. I am aware that other poets go by these two names, but it is not for me to speak of them. I owe to my first "better teacher," A. Bartlett Giamatti, the source of my Spenserian project, and to John Hollander, guidance in the completion of my Protestant Reformation. To Leslie Brisman and to Harold Bloom, I offer this book in partial repayment for having learned to take literature seriously. Whatever remains of scholasticism in my work is no fault of theirs. A number of friends and colleagues have read this book, at earlier or later stages of composition, and they have given me advice and encouragement without which I could not have continued. I thank especially Jean-Pierre Mileur, Margaret Ferguson, Maureen Quilligan, and Donald Cheney. I have found in these and all my *auctors* not the comfort of system, but a means to that severity which is yet "in true filial freedom plac't; / Whence true autority in men."

CHAPTER ONE

The Genealogy of Imagination

"You can't hear God speak to someone else, you can hear him only if you are being addressed."—That is a grammatical remark.

Wittgenstein, *Zettel*

1. *The Imagination as Origin and the Origin of Imagination*

There is a remarkable continuity in the writings of philosophers and literary figures before the Renaissance on the subject of imagination, or "fantasy."[1] Despite the minor disputes and the multifarious distinctions generated by the categorizing minds of classical and medieval thinkers, no single development may be said to have permanently altered a body of thought defined for almost two millennia by Aristotelian psychology.[2] The imagination possesses an irreducible and relatively trivial meaning: it is that capacity of the mind to represent images to itself in the absence of sense perception. How, then, has the imagination come to occupy so esteemed a position in the discourse of post-Renaissance man? Philosophers have for the most part neglected the term, no doubt because it is used in such vague and honorific senses; but there are more interesting reasons for this neglect, which it is the burden of this chapter to explore. Whatever one might wish to say about the true nature of imagination, the very vagueness of the term is the first indication of its historical significance. The term begins to become important as soon as it wanders from its basic signification. The increasing vagueness allows the imagination to become attached to a complex of ideas that seem to bear no intrinsic relation to the root meaning. At this point imagination enters the discourse of literature and permanently changes its character. I propose to offer here nothing like a segment in the history of ideas but rather a discussion of what happened when this term began to "wander."

Within the framework of faculty psychologies, and most of the other anatomical divisions of mind that prevailed before and during the Renaissance, the imagination is seen to mediate between sense and reason. Other axes of division are possible, but the fantasy maintains its function as mediator between the percept, liberated from the object of perception, and the higher faculties of mind. Bacon calls the imagination the *nuncius*, messenger.[3] From our historical vantage point, the possible connection between imagination and art is suggested at once by their common ground in mediation, but with rare and inconsequential exceptions, this association is not advanced seriously until the Renaissance. The imagination only strays outside the confines of faculty psychology to form a tenuous but recurrent connection with vision and inspiration. The divinely inspired prophet sees images in his mind as opposed to actual percepts. The Neoplatonists (or Plotinians) are particularly interested in exploring this connection,[4] and the idea survives into the Renaissance as the single extension, or breach in a closed structure, by which the imagination will liberate itself from its restrictive past, a liberation that includes the disentanglement of imagination from inspiration itself. The faculty that mediates will soon begin to form bridges between areas of thought that were, in the opinion of many writers, better kept separate; and as the persistence of these new meanings can no longer be ignored, the imagination's power is acknowledged in the intensely negative reactions it provokes.

We might begin with a less troubled statement of the relation between fantasy and vision in the *Summa Theologica* of Thomas Aquinas, whose confident assertion of a hierarchy of revelation may be taken as representative of what became increasingly uncertain in the Renaissance: "Hence it follows that prophecy whereby a supernatural truth is seen by intellectual vision, is more excellent than that in which a supernatural truth is manifested by means of the similitude of corporeal things in the vision of the imagination."[5]

Nowhere in Aquinas (nor, for that matter, in Aristotle) are we told that this vision of the imagination is responsible for poetry—and this, despite the fact that invocation has become a commonplace of poetic practice. It seems plausible that the *poetic* fantasy remained dormant simply because no one thought specifically in terms of a "psychology of composition." Theology may have appropriated the language of psychology or any number of other disciplines, but the borrowed language remained enclosed within the sacred categories, sanctified but also immobilized. When the literary critics of the early Renaissance employed a more naturalized psychology to describe poetic activity, the stratified order of medieval discourse was shattered (Panofsky calls this phenomenon "de-compart-mentalization").[6] It became possible for defenders of poetry (Boccaccio is a good example)[7] to claim that poets *are* theologians; such statements, whether or not they are so intended, have a destabilizing effect. The great Dante controversy of the sixteenth century may be summed up in one question: Was Dante a theologian or a poet, or both? And it is no accident that the controversy focused on the phrase "All'alta fantasia qui manco possa" at the end of the *Paradiso*.[8]

For the moment we may allow these events and concepts to remain suspended in their historical solution while the significance of one more fact is considered. E. R. Curtius writes, in *European Literature and the Latin Middle Ages*, that the Platonic doctrine of inspiration "lived on through the entire millennium which extends from the conquest of Rome by the Goths to the conquest of Constantinople by the Turks."[9] By the end of the Renaissance the idea of *furor poeticus*, related to, though not exactly identi-fied with, the inspiration of the prophets, loses whatever validity it may once have had in poetic theory. Curtius notes a few instances of survival, in the Florentine Neoplatonists and in the "Protestant Muse" of John Milton; yet he offers no reason for the degeneration of the idea into a weak metaphor. Elsewhere in his book Curtius discusses the concept of "creative imagination," which he believes to emerge first in the writings of Goethe. "Antiquity," he says, "lacked this concept."[10] But did the Renaissance? This three-hundred-year hiatus in poetic theory lends a strange but fascinating structure to Curtius' study, for the imagination seems to arise from no-where; it has no history, and yet it marks both an end and a beginning, since Goethe also defines for Curtius the end of the classical-medieval era and the beginning of modernity; he is the last undeniably great writer in Western literature. Does the inception of creative imagination with Goethe perhaps have more to do with this end-beginning than with any actual historical origins? And is this why Curtius sees no relation between the appearance of imagination and that other end, the end of inspiration? Writing within the *Dämmerung* of Western civilization Curtius proposes one last myth, a myth of origins, and like all such myths the origin of the myth itself is necessarily obscured. From Henri Bergson, Curtius appropriates a metaphysical evolutionism that sees the imagination as a human extension of the "fonction fabulatrice" that Nature displays in producing her multiform species.[11] The awakening of man to his true nature is the self-awakening of imagination, a myth in which we still participate and which has had the effect of placing imagination beyond analysis. The "fonction fabulatrice" transcends history because it is the meaning of history. It is not surprising, then, that Curtius should combine Bergson's evolutionism with his own darker feeling that history is somehow over. It is as if the inner workings of history were suddenly exposed, imposing upon us the burden of still believing in the myth while contemplating its naked mechanism. If we are to understand how this idea of imagination entered the discourse of poetry, we must bring together the two ideas that were held apart in Curtius' book: imagination and inspiration. The renewed contact between these two estranged ideas will allow us to pursue a genuinely historical study of imagination, and this study will of necessity demythologize its subject (as all historical explanation strives to oppose myth). The imagination is the heart of our modern mythology, the myth of the "creative" man who arrogates to himself the power to speak "In the beginning..."

Theories of poetry are perennially grounded in the concept of mimesis, which has been seen, from Plato onward, to coexist uneasily with the concept of invention or fiction. It would not be inaccurate to say that poetic theory addresses first and last this problem, so simply stated but ramifying endlessly in the discourse of Western criticism. Dante's uncompromising assertion of his poem's mimetic status understandably troubled his successors, because, if accepted, it challenged the easy hierarchy of sacred texts. Paradoxically, it is the nonexistence of the category of literature that makes possible the dispersion and authority of apocryphal scripture in the Middle Ages, or the sacralization of pagan texts (the medieval *Aeneid*). These texts become sacred *by association* with the Bible. Eventually the arrow of categorization will point the other way: texts will become secular by an increasingly careful and anxious *distinction from* the sacred text. It is inevitable that Dante's *Commedia*, situated at the hinge of this reversal, should seem problematic for the critics of the sixteenth century; either Dante *feigned* his poem, in which case its pretensions to theological certitude might possibly be dismissed; or, he really saw everything he said he saw, an alternative that stretched the credulity of even the most ardent believers.

Dante's "allegory of the theologians," so finely explicated by Singleton, resurrected a poetic stance so old it was new.[12] Poetic inspiration, distinguished from the idea of *prophetic* inspiration, survived into the Renaissance (with the exceptions noted by Curtius) as metaphor. Dante seems to have conflated the two types, as they had been indistinguishable in the mythical past of poetry, thus precipitating the quarrel over whether a poetic text might yet be "sacred." Boccaccio saw the implications of both the distinction and the conjunction of these concepts when he decided that the pagan poets could not have been inspired but rather generated their verse out of a *vi mentis*.[13] Such a phrase, with its potential for reductive meaning, afforded the basis of an explanation alternative to the sacral one, for any writer who cared to dispute *contemporary* claims to inspiration. My intention is not to summarize the subsequent Dante controversy, which has been adjudicated by Hathaway, Weinberg, and others, but to draw attention to the elegant determinism of this historical fact. It is as though the entire inky debate were meant to give a name to this anonymous "energy of mind," a name authorized by Dante himself: *fantasia*. The disputant who most lucidly recapitulates the results of the controversy is Jacopo Mazzoni, in Book I of his *On the Defense of the Comedy of Dante* (1587):

> I say, then, that the phantasy is the power of the mind for dreams and for poetic verisimilitude. But because my adversaries express no doubt of what I also believe, namely that the phantasy is the power on which dreams depend, something Aristotle has often said and his followers have often repeated, it will therefore be well to demonstrate that poetic verisimilitude is also founded on the same power of mind. The verisimilitude, then, sought after by the poets is of such a nature that it is feigned by them according to their wish...Then of necessity the power fitted to generate is the fantastic power called by the Latins *Imaginative*. All that we have just said was first set forth by Aristotle in the second of *De anima*...
>
> We clearly see, then, if I am not wrong, that phantasy is the true power over poetic fables, since she alone is capable of those fictions which we of ourselves are able to feign and put together. From this of necessity it follows that poetry is made up of things feigned and imagined, because it is founded on phantasy.[14]

The subordination of dream to the power of fantasy is necessary within the context of this discussion, not only because Dante's poem is a dream vision, but also because the adversaries to whom Mazzoni refers (foremost among them, Bellissario Bulgarini, in his *Alcune considerazioni* of 1582) had placed the dream outside the explanatory apparatus of faculty psychology. As Hathaway concludes, a position like Bulgarini's really holds that Dante's high fantasies must mean "visitations upon us of powers outside of ourselves, not the workings of our own minds."[15] In short, they are *inspirations*. Bulgarini's interpretation of Dante's *fantasia*, which we are now inclined to see as correct (however inimical Bulgarini is to Dante's intentions) returns the imagination to its subordinate function as the mere transmitter of images that are perceived, either naturally or by supernatural implantation. When Dante says, then, that his "lofty fantasy" failed, he means that he has crossed some boundary beyond which he sees no *mental* images. Mazzoni is willing to deny Dante this vision, and hence to misinterpret the lines from the *Paradiso*, because he sees very clearly the enormously inflated claims that might result from a fully inspirationalist poetic. Proceeding from the premise that Dante is a poet and not a theologian, Mazzoni attempts to preserve this distinction by advancing what he believes to be the true defining feature of poetry: the imagination as an autonomous power of mind. The historical originality of this idea is an ironic consequence of a tangle of circumstances; Mazzoni's deepest impulses are conservative, and this conservatism, as we are now able to demonstrate, contributes toward the naturalization of Renaissance conceptions of poetry.

In the passage quoted above, Mazzoni pleads his reliance upon no lesser authority than Aristotle: "All that we have just said was set forth by Aristotle in the second of *De anima*." But where in this treatise is a relation established between poetry and imagination? In fact, Mazzoni's conception of a poetic fantasy is derived not from *De anima* but from Plato's *Sophist*, where a distinction is drawn between eicastic and fantastic imitation.[16] Elsewhere Mazzoni has many things to say about this distinction, much more than is warranted by the Platonic text. Plato's dialogue is permeated by an irony that has always rendered its interpretation problematic, but it is at least fair to say that the concept of fantastic imitation—describing literally the process by which a sculptor creates a statue that *appears* to, but does not exactly copy an object[17]—cannot be dissociated from the opprobrium Plato heaps upon the Sophist. The category of fantastic imitation is devised to trap the offending figure in his net of deception, his involvement in the mere *species* of things. The fact that Mazzoni again misinterprets his primary text is less important, however, than the meaning he thinks he is deriving. The poet (about whom Plato does not write in the *Sophist*) is "he who adopts fantastic imitation and who consequently has the false and the lie for subject."[18] Pressured by his need to find an authority and an authoritative term for a process he believes to be the distinction of poetry, Mazzoni allows Plato's fantastic imitation to stand in a synonymous relation to the activity of *feigning*. And the *phantasia* itself, bringing with it the basic Greek meaning of image-making, determines that this feigning is to mean *feigning images*. Thus the poetic imagination is born: "And poetry will be in its genus the fabricating art, and a maker of the image. . ."[19]

The reader must bring to such an argument an appreciation of the fact that the sequence of misinterpretation by which the psychology of Aristotle is reconciled to the finely ironic categories of the *Sophist* is the peculiar contribution of sixteenth-century poetics. We can scarcely recover a state of mind in which it is possible to think about art without thinking of the imagination, but only by thinking this relation back to its beginning can we free ourselves to write a less mythologized history. The dissemination of the idea will concern me shortly, though for the moment we need to return Curtius to the stage and question this omission from his history. And we discover that in the Epilogue on "Imitation and Creation" he has already answered our question in a comment on the Aristotelians of the sixteenth century:

> By much interpretation, it has been thought possible to make the tortured text yield the meaning of "creative vision." But does this square with Aristotle's intention? We shall leave the question unsettled. But it is certain that no critic of Antiquity so understood him. Cinquecento Aristotelianism too could turn and twist the basic concepts of the *Poetics*, but imitation remained imitation. Aristotle remained Aristotle.[20]

Curtius obliquely points to the kind of "misinterpretation" whose significance I have just argued, suggesting that Renaissance writers are often most original where they seem to be most unreliable. The distinction between Mazzoni's imagination and "creative vision" is hardly considerable. Scaliger, Sidney, Castelvetro, and Puttenham evolved similar conceptions, the latter most explicitly in his famous comparison of poets to "creating gods," who, like God himself, "without any trauell to his divine imagination made all the world of naught."[21] I have taken Curtius as a representative figure, not because the error of omission in any way vitiates his great work of literary history, but rather to pose the question of why critics remain incurious about the origins of the poetic imagination. It should be possible now to determine the historical significance of imagination's birth, and to do that we shall have to return to the idea whose end coincided with this beginning.

It would not be true to say that the idea of imagination is used in the sixteenth century to confront and dismiss the notion of inspiration. Not even Mazzoni saw all of the implications of his conception, and those of his contemporaries who emphasized the idea of feigning in poetry did not always, as a consequence of this idea, reject traditional conceptions of the poetic furor. On occasion, however, they did state their disbelief in the older notions, leaving the reader to surmise the reasons.[22] And yet the merest touch of naturalistic psychology immediately brings the two notions into conflict. The inspired vision is constituted as images, and as soon as that vision is subjected to an epistemological questioning it becomes possible to "explain" these images as the product of the mind alone. Whatever is not truly inspired is only imagined. This train of thought seems so inescapable today because this is exactly how we have come to naturalize the supernatural.[23] The gods have not died, they have merely been internalized as powers of mind—so "genius" in the Renaissance migrates from the supernatural plane into the mind of man, the daemon simultaneously mutating into mental faculty. One understands, of course, that there must have been a tremendous resistance to this process of naturalization, and some of that resistance is felt in the enforced separation of imagination from inspiration.

The issue that remains submerged in Mazzoni (and to a lesser extent in Sidney) is directly confronted by Tasso, who is interested in preserving the "something of divinity" in poetry so important to both Spenser and Milton: "And Mazzoni is even less right in saying that the most perfect poetry is phantastic imitation. Such imitation is of things that are not and never were..."[24] Still relying on the currency of the terminology derived from the *Sophist*, Tasso goes on to assert the superiority of the eicastic poet (for Tasso this means "historical," a sense quite removed from Plato's text), offering in response to Mazzoni's interpretation of Dante's "alta fantasia" a reading more compatible with his basically mimetic principles: The fantasy is an intellectual vision, "the power which is like light in illuminating things and revealing itself."[25] Tasso's return to the position that "poets are theologians" is inevitable, and he finally aligns himself with the mythic and authoritative "original" poets, Linus, Orpheus, and Musaeus. In short, he returns to the figure of the *vates*, the inspired poet.

At this point it would perhaps be wise to acknowledge the fictions of my own history, since I am claiming for my genealogy of imagination nothing like a sudden and revolutionary transformation of *theories* of poetry. Rejections of the *phantasia* are far more common than celebrations, but also no less important in the progress of the idea. Neither is it particularly important to demonstrate the influence of Mazzoni in subsequent texts on the subject. The invention of the poetic imagination is a process in which Mazzoni participated, but it seems as inevitable as the mathematical calculus, simultaneously "invented" by Newton and Leibniz. We are as yet a long way from understanding this process in causal terms, and certainly the "history of ideas" can provide us no comfortable answer. A more exclusively semantic history is all that can be attempted here, as we turn to the English tradition, and to Sidney's *Apology for Poetry*.

The baffling diversity of influences upon Sidney's text is less important finally than the fact that these influences are primarily Italian, and that the new feeling about imagination is here enlisted in a defense of poetry against a tradition that is endemically suspicious of this faculty.[26] Sidney's appropriation of continental ideas is thus colored by his response to the moral objections of his contemporaries, and his theory inaugurates the ambivalence that we will see in both Spenser and Milton. Speaking of the distinction between eicastic and fantastic, for example, Sidney translates the terms into moral counters, misinterpreting Plato again, and even more interestingly, dissociating the fantastic from his own understated approval of imagination: "For I will not denie but that mans wit may make Poesie (which should be *Eikastike*, which some learned have defined, figuring foorth good things) to be *Phantastike*: which doth, contrariwise, infect the fancie with vnworthy obiects."[27] This mixing of moral and aesthetic categories results in what appears to be an attitude like Tasso's in the later *Discourses on the Heroic Poem* (1594), but Tasso's definition of the term fantastic ("imitation of things that are not and never were") is exactly like Sidney's definition of the poet: "For these third [poets] be they which most properly do imitate to teach and delight, and to imitate borrow nothing of what is, hath been, or shall be: but range, onely rayned with learned discretion, into the diuine consideration of what may be, and should be."[28]

This, Tasso would say, *is* fantastic imitation. No continuities can be established merely on the basis of the terms chosen by a given writer, and if we are to understand what is really being said about imagination, we must account for the unacknowledged wandering of quasi-technical terms from the fields in which they originate. This divergence of meanings is most in evidence at those points in a text where ambivalence leads to a sudden qualification of an otherwise very positive assertion, a divergence that may be illustrated in these sentences of Sidney's on the Idea or "fore-conceit" of the poem: "And that the Poet hath that *Idea* is manifest, by deliuering them forth in such excellencie as hee hath imagined them. Which deliuering forth also is not wholie imaginatiue, as we are wont to say by them that build Castles in the ayre."[29]

The distinction between the "imagined" and the "wholly imaginative" somewhat obscures Sidney's equation of the Idea or fore-conceit with the image. Thus qualified, the language of imagination becomes the continual recourse of the *Apology* whenever Sidney's subject is the *poet* rather than the *poem*. We become aware at different points in the essay of the divergent polemics for poet and poem when Sidney himself becomes aware of the discrepancy, reiterating as a consequence his intention to speak of poetry, not poets ("yet say I, and say again, I speak of the art, and not of the artificer"). There follows from these abrupt self-reminders a return to a more conventional view of poetry as a kind of moral mimesis. This theory, which it is easy to believe is at the center of Sidney's oration, is actually never reconciled to the idea of image-making, a disunity attested by the very reluctance with which the mimetic theory is introduced:

> Now let vs goe to a more ordinary opening of him, that the trueth may be more palpable: and so I hope, though we get not so vnmatched a praise as the Etimologie of his names wil grant, yet his very description, which no man will denie, shall not iustly be barred from a principall commendation.
> Poesie therefore is an art of imitation...[30]

It is certainly a mistake to think Sidney unaware of the difficulty of integrating the two conceptions of feigning and mimesis in one theory. The only thing the poet imitates, in Sidney's view, is his own Idea, and this Idea is created *ex nihilo*; it is the golden world that never was. My reading suggests that the more fundamental aim of Sidney's essay is to moralize the imagination; and he cannot state this aim because, given the climate of opposition within which he writes, he cannot admit that imagination *needs* to be moralized.

Shortly after the more "ordinary" opening of his subject Sidney pauses to classify poets into three types: the first type, "they that did imitate the inconceivable excellencies of God," are the ancient poets, the Hebrew prophets and the Greeks and Romans; they are the *vates*, inspired poet-priests, and their verse is inseparable from the sacred function they fulfill in their societies. The second type of poet is the "philosophical," whom Sidney admires while leaving the question of whether these men are really poets undecided. The third type, for which he gives no name, are those who, in the words already quoted, "borrow nothing of what is, hath been, or shall be."[31] Remembering the point later in the text at which Sidney specifically denies the doctrine of inspiration ("he [Plato] attributeth unto Poesy more than myself do, namely, to be a very inspiring of a divine force"),[32] may we give a name to this third category of poets and call them *secular*? The originality of Sidney's *Apology* perhaps lies in just this intuition: he must redeem poetry from its fallen state, its secularity, without returning, as Tasso did, to the mystified notion of the inspired poet. The imagination enters upon the English scene uneasily allied to a view of poetry emptied of divinity, and that is the stage upon which Spenser and Milton will play out the anxieties of the religious poet. It remains for us now to finish this preliminary apparatus by drawing out some of the implications for literary history of the secular, autonomous fantasy.

2. *The Messenger and the Usurper*

The imagination is perceived, almost from the beginning of its importance in faculty psychology, under the category of mediation. Bacon finds a place for poetry and rhetoric, as imaginative expressions, within the "Art of transmitting."[33] From the perspective of a semantic history, however, the term has begun to drift away from its empirical base. The association of the fantasy with art is not a logical necessity; rather, the psychological term is extended by analogy to explain the origin of the poem in the poet's mind. The analogical extension subverts the basic meaning even while carrying that meaning into a new field, and the final result of this process of contamination is a new idea: the autonomous imagination.

Granted the mechanics of this history, a question is immediately raised about the relation of mediation to the new meaning: how does autonomy react upon mediation? Bacon addresses just this question in the *Advancement of Learning*: "Neither is the Imagination simply and only a messenger; but is invested with or at leastwise usurpeth no small authority in itself, besides the duty of the message."[34] The idea of usurpation hints at a political analogy, which Bacon at once develops by attaching his argument to the traditional idea of the soul as a governmental hierarchy. The mind, or reason, is intended to preside over the imagination, Bacon says, like "*a magistrate...over a free citizen.*" Some autonomy is granted, and hence the possibility of abuse, of usurpation. The failure of imagination to deliver proper sense impressions to the reason, or sometimes its blockage of the reason's commands, is a frequent complaint in Renaissance texts on the subject (the younger Pico's *De Imaginatione* is a good example).[35] But these worries are lent a particular urgency by Reformation and Puritan writers, and the special vehemence with which this faculty is deplored requires some explanation. Sidney understood that the contemporary attack on poetry implicated a faculty of mind that, in itself, ought to be morally neutral—but such was the barrage of complaint laid down against both poetry and the fancy that the question of where the corruption originated was hopelessly confused. Even as late as *Paradise Lost*, Milton is able to represent Satan tempting Eve through "the organs of her fancy" without offering even a casual distinction between the fancy in its moral and aesthetic functions. The imagination as usurper is to have enormously important consequences in literary history, but for the moment we need only emphasize the provenance of the idea in the analogical extension of terms from the psychological sphere into the aesthetic. Two questions now need to be answered: What precisely does the imagination usurp? And why is the idea so antithetical to the Protestant impulse?

The first question may be rephrased as: What kind of mediation is interrupted by the usurping messenger? Bacon is again the most perceptive guide to the way in which these connections are made in the discourse of his age, his relegation of poetry to a lesser role within the scheme of knowledge having much to do with his sense that imagination is so difficult to keep in its place. Since he shared the rationalism, though not the enthusiasm, of his Puritan contemporaries, he too was inclined to suspect the lawlessness of the fancy: "Poetry is a part of learning in measure of words for the most part restrained, but in all other parts extremely licensed, and doth truly refer to the imagination, which, being not tied to the limits of matter, may of pleasure join that which nature hath severed, and sever that which nature hath joined, and so make unlawful matches and divorces of things."[36] And make *monsters*, Bacon might have said, since Renaissance writers tirelessly exploit just this fact about the imagination: it is the maker of such creatures as the centaur, of the hybrid, hyphenated creature.

Bacon's insight is even deeper, however; he argues that poetry works "by submitting the shows of things to the desires of the mind."[37] (Spenser's habitual play on the two meanings of "fancy" anticipates this intuition.) The imagination is nothing other than the mask of desire; it inhabits the space between the way things are, and the way we wish them to be. This truth might have only the most banal significance, if the theory of mimesis were not continually called into question by the relentless pressure of desire. Eros is a kind of mediator who unites or disunites as he wills, and it is his complicity in the imagination which makes poetry vulnerable to a moral critique. Not only mediating but moving against mediation, the imagination sets up its own creation, which answers to nothing in the realm of the true.[38] The "message," then, is not the one it was originally given to deliver, but a false message, a fiction, which it has invented out of nothing and which has no origin but itself. The mind discovers itself as origin, capable of a kind of self-begetting. And the fictions generated by this faculty are necessarily constituted as images that have displaced other "truer" images, either those first delivered by sense perception, or—and here the whole thrust of the Prostestant tradition turns agains the *phantasia*—by God.

Theological commentary, accommodating itself to the psychology of the age, speculated that the place of revelation must have been the mind itself, by means of an internal vision. Only in the revelations to Moses (the *gradus Mosaicus*) did the Bible seem indisputably to warrant a belief in a vision constituted by sense perceptions. Later prophets see "phantasms," or as the Cambridge Platonist, John Smith, was to write in his discourse "On Prophecy," the prophetic scene is "enacted upon the stage of the imagination."[39] The intrinsic relation between imagination and inspiration, so innocuous to a former age, becomes crucially important to those few poets, writers of "sacred" poetry, who resist the secularity of literature, in a way, resist literature itself. The possibility of sacred poetry, which Spenser tests by means of allegory and Milton assumes at various stages of his career, depends upon settling the place of imagination as mediator of supernatural truth. The messenger who usurps the authority of the message is the figure whose existence must be denied, or whose autonomy must be forfeited. The continued association of imagination and inspiration, after the former term has begun to accumulate its powerful new meanings, results in the demythologizing of inspiration—not necessarily, we should emphasize, the inspiration of the ancient poets and prophets, but the revival of the archaic invocation of deity by radical Protestantism. The reduction of the supernal vision to the mere image, denounced by the Counter-Reformation Tasso, means even more to the Protestant poet: it means the usurpation of vision, the displacement of God's word by the fallen word of man, and the substitution of a human authority and a human origin for that of the divine author.

This historical situation is further complicated by the ambivalence Protestant reformers themselves display in their attitude toward "special revelations" from the deity. Calvin argues very vigorously against the possibility of such revelation in his own age, betraying his uneasiness only by the intensity of his rejection.[40] He understood, as Luther perhaps did not, that the problem standing behind all such claims was one of authority.[41] Needing to offer more than a rational basis for reformation, and at the same time fearing the probing that claims to divine inspiration might provoke, the original reformers restricted the *Wort Gottes* to the Bible, a finished revelation that is only extended into the present by the act of reading. The subtlety of this revisionary revolution—prophets become interpreters— did not survive the sectarian eruption of the sixteenth century, and the chaos that one may discern so carefully contained beneath the elegant logic of Calvin's text becomes the spiritual landscape of the seventeenth century—the age of enthusiasts and churches of one.[42] And yet it is arguable that the deepest impulse of Protestantism expressed itself in this very *reductio ad absurdum*, because the question of mediation could (perhaps) be decided only by living through the consequences of a radical assertion of unmediated perception. For the present, we will postpone an answer to that question (if it has ever been answered) and allow the issues to be defined more precisely by the historical opposition, the royalist Sir William Davenant, in his Preface to *Gondibert*:

> Yet to such painfull Poets some upbraid the want of extemporary fury, or
> rather inspiration, a dangerous word which many of late successfully us'd; and

inspiration is a spiritual Fitt, derived from the ancient Ethnick Poets, who then, as they were Priests, were Statesman too, and probably lov'd dominion; and as their well dissembling of inspiration begot them reverence then equal to that which was paid to Laws, so these who now profess the same fury may perhaps by such authentick example pretend authority over the people, it being not unreasonable to imagine they rather imitate the Greek Poets than the Hebrew Prophets, since the latter were inspired for the use of others, and these, like the former, prophecy for themselves. But though the ancient Poets are excus'd, as knowing the weak consitution of those Deities from whom they took their Priesthood, and the frequent necessity of dissembling for the ease of government, yet those, who also from the chief to the meanest are States-men and Priests, but have not the luck to be Poets, should not assume such saucy familiarity with a true God.[43]

Davenant shrewdly pointed to the real ambition at the heart of many claims to divine guidance, and his exposure of contemporary pseudo-prophets perhaps explains their own reluctance to admit the problem of authority into their discourse. We may be less inclined now to doubt the genuine religious feeling being expressed in the explosion of sects, though the extent to which this feeling can be (or was) the motive for poetic composition remains at issue.

When Hobbes wrote his "Answer to Davenant," he reiterated in more sardonic tones the accusations of the Preface, but he also took the precau-tion of completely naturalizing poetry: "Time and education begets Ex-perience; Experience begets Memory; Memory begets Judgment and Fancy; Judgment begets the strength and structure; and Fancy begets the Ornaments of a Poem."[44] This "genealogy" of poetry explains very little but excludes a great deal. Hobbes intends the progress from Time to Fancy to be reductive, although the Fancy still retains more power than the "decayed sense" the *Leviathan* calls "imagination."[45] Despite his extravagant praise for Davenant's poem, Hobbes is really interested in circumscribing the language of poetry, and for that reason he further reduces the Fancy to a power of illusion, whose intensity is the result of self-reflection: "So that when she [fancy] seemeth to fly from one Indies to the other, and from Heaven to Earth...the voyage is not great, her self being all she seeks."[46]

Thus deflated, this fancy is very usefully employed in the demythologiz-ing machine of the *Leviathan*, where the authority of the Bible itself suffers a demotion similar to poetry's. Hobbes applies the strong solvent of epistemology to the credulous dependence of believers upon mere testi-

mony: "For if a man pretend to me, that God hath spoken to him super-
naturally, and immediately, and I make doubt of it, I cannot easily perceive
what argument he can produce, to oblige me to believe."[47]

The reader of the *Leviathan* may wonder how the biblical prophets
themselves can be exempt from such a stricture. Hobbes' concession to the
truth of revelation fails to efface this doubt, as his nervous contemporary
readers well knew. Instead, the Hobbesian machine calls into question
everything it brings within its ken, reducing the visionary experience ("the
pretence of private inspiration") to the phantasms of the self-provoked
imagination ("they take their own Dreams, and extravagant Fancies, and
Madnesse, for testimonies of God's Spirit").[48] And since we cannot distinguish by any empirical means the divinely inspired phantasm from those
originated in the mind, the authority of the state is offered as the only
recourse to the anarchy of individual revelation.

Some years later, Spinoza published his *Tractatus-Theologico-Politicus*
(1670), which, though it stands outside of the literary-political milieu I am
describing, brings the interplay of Renaissance and Reformation ideas to a
conclusion and a new beginning.[49] The conclusion need only be noted:
Arguing from the Renaissance conception of imagination Spinoza completes the process of demythologizing begun more than a century before.
Less crude than Hobbes in his subordination of the Bible, he is finally no
less subversive in the naturalism of his principles. The new beginning is
not so much discontinuous as inevitable; we may call it a mutation in the
nature of textuality itself: "Words gain their meaning solely from their
usage, and if they are arranged according to their accepted signification so
as to move those who read them to devotion, they will become sacred, and
the book so written will be sacred also."[50] What Spinoza declares is the
possibility of an original sacred text, one which, from its author's point of
view, is also a fiction. The *Tractatus* leads us outward to larger historical
issues that need be pursued no further, but also inward, to the more private
confrontations of literature with history. English literary history achieves
a certain continuity (the "line" descending from Spenser and Milton) in its
struggle to produce a poetic text that is both original and sacred.

3. *Dark Mediums and Literary History*

That the possibility of an unmediated perception of the non-phenome-
nal world seems to lie at the heart of the Protestant longing is everywhere

confirmed in commentary on imagination, although the more interesting thinkers must be credited with having glimpsed in the nature of humanity itself something deeply antagonistic to their quest. So John Smith, writing in his *Discourses*, produces this somewhat equivocal assertion: "Our own imaginative powers, which are perpetually attending the highest acts of our souls, will be breathing a gross dew upon the pure glass of our understandings, and so sully and besmear it, that we cannot see the image of the Divinity sincerely in it."[51] The dismissive tone may be typical but the imagination is also seen as an attendant of the soul who cannot be dismissed; and if he were, would we see God himself or only "the image of the Divinity"? Smith goes on to celebrate that day, that glad day Spenser before him longed for, when we "shall no more behold the Divinity through the dark mediums that eclipse the blessed sight of it."[52] Alas, all "mediums" are dark, and poetry, though it may deny its nature from time to time, is nothing more than a medium.

Spinoza conceived of allegory in these modest terms when he assigned the writings of the prophets to this category, assuming the distance of the allegorical image from the visionary experience. The prophets, he says, "clothed spiritual truths in bodily forms, for such is the usual method of imagination."[53] In more explicitly theological terms, John Smith writes that "Divine truth becomes many times in Scripture incarnate, debasing itself to assume our rude conceptions."[54] The model for all such mediation is the Incarnation of Christ, and the existence of this association lends to imagination itself a possible theological legitimacy one might not otherwise expect it to have. But the imagination does not become sanctified in the early Protestant tradition and this fact raises some questions about the analogy of incarnation. The most aggrandizing text on the imagination in Renaissance literature is surely the famous speech of Theseus in *A Midsummer Night's Dream*. There, the incarnative function is located wholly within the categories of the aesthetic and psychological:

The lunatic, the lover, and the poet
Are of imagination all compact.
One sees more devils than vast hell can hold:
That is the madman. The lover, all as frantic,
Sees Helen's beauty in a brow of Egypt.
The poet's eye in a fine frenzy rolling,

Doth glance from heaven to earth, from earth to heaven;
And as imagination bodies forth
The form of things unknown, the poet's pen
Turns them to shapes, and gives to airy nothing
A local habitation and a name.

(*MND* V, i, 7-17)[55]

Most interesting, perhaps, is the fact that imagination has been super-imposed upon the much older conception of the *furor poeticus*. Shakespeare's "poetic," very mediated indeed in the mouth of the unimaginative Theseus, casually acknowledges its limitations while still making some claim for the bodying forth of things unknown. For the poet is only in part like the lover and the madman: he allows the usurpation of reason and then brings that frenzy under control of his pen. The "conscious will," to borrow Coleridge's formulation, intervenes to halt the usurpation and turn the un-created (nothing) into a creation (a local habitation and a name). Neither Spenser nor Milton would have been able to agree with Theseus' analysis, which is not to say that they deny the operation of the will but that they see its greatest act as one of submission, a yielding to the "muse" or to what Milton calls in *Comus* a "superior power." (It may be useful to recall here how problematic is the relation of election or grace to the human will in Protestant theology.) The belief of the sacred poet must be that each choice dissolves into the inevitability of the already chosen; no choice is successful except the emptying of the will before God, the choice not to choose for oneself but to be the instrument of the providential will. Spenser is obviously less committed than Milton to a poetics of enthusiasm, but, as the inwardness and self-consciousness of his art increases, it is also given over to greater self-doubt and self-subversion. Milton's conception of choice (almost always renunciatory) wards off the doubt about his own election, or forces him to express this doubt covertly (for example, in the very subtle analogies between the poet and Satan in *Paradise Lost*).

What does Milton renounce? My argument points to the imagination itself as the power renounced in exchange for a power gained. We may begin to see this turn away from the autonomous fancy as early as the poem "On Shakespeare," where the praise of the opening lines is qualified in the final two couplets as somehow "too much."

What needs my Shakespeare for his honor'd Bones
The labor of an age in piled Stones,
Or that his hallow'd relics should be hid

Under a Star-ypointing Pyramid?
Dear son of memory, great heir of Fame,
What need'st thou such weak witness of thy name?
Thou in our wonder and astonishment
Hast built thyself a livelong Monument,
For whilst to th'shame of slow-endeavoring Art,
Thy easy numbers flow, and that each heart
Hath from the leaves of thy unvalu'd Book
Those Delphic lines with deep impression took,
Then thou our fancy of itself bereaving,
Dost make us Marble with too much conceiving;
And so Sepulcher'd in such pomp dost lie,
That Kings for such a Tomb would wish to die.[56]

The poem works toward its climax by opposing the fluid motion of Shakespeare's verse to the condition of stasis he induces in his hearers, and upon that abstract foundation Milton builds his conceit of the audience as monument. But much more is at stake in the poem than a clever conceit, for the condition of arrest or paralysis is everywhere morally suspect in Milton's poetry. This Shakespeare possesses the paralyzing magic of the enchanter, Comus.[57] The elegiac lines take an ironic turn when the reader discovers that "our fancy" is the object of which we are bereaved. The implication that the Shakespearean plenitude may be "too much" is more easily argued in the context of *Comus*, whose numerous Shakespearean echoes are drawn into the penumbra of the tempter's magical power. Here I want only to suggest that Milton propagates the myth of a natural, innocent Shakespeare, warbling his native woodnotes wild, in order to dissociate himself from that figure. "Fancie's child," as he is called in "L'Allegro," remains with Milton even as late as *Paradise Lost* where an interesting echo of the passage from *A Midsummer Night's Dream* occurs:

But know that in the soul
Are many lesser faculties that serve
Reason as chiefe; among these Fansie next
Her office holds; of all external things
Which the five watchfull Senses represent,
She forms imaginations, aery shapes. . .
(*PL* V, 100–5)

Milton arrives at the phrase "aery shapes" by excluding precisely the word that is centrally important in Shakespeare's line: "Turns them to shapes and gives to airy nothing." By confusing the madman's hallucination with the poetic image Shakespeare hints that what precedes this image, what occupies its space, is nothing. The idea of preliminary decreation as a constituent of the act of creation will not become a commonplace until much later than the Renaissance, but some kind of undoing, some confrontation with an abyss or a chaos, must be acknowledged as a phase in the act of creation (as it was in God's original creation). This primordial chaos is the *materia prima* of poetry as well. By denying to the imagination this preliminary act of undoing, Milton succeeds in keeping this faculty wholly distinct from his own idea of creation, a fact that we shall have to remember when Satan crosses the "abrupt abyss" to confront the "second thoughts" of God. Milton's abyss is not a void, though it sometimes seems to be both empty and full; and God's revisionary creation, we are persuaded to believe, only looks revisionary. Milton's strategy in this passage allows him to throw the weight of his condemnation against the figure of the usurper, whose function is strictly limited in the following lines:

> . . . aery shapes,
> Which Reason joyning or disjoyning, frames
> All what we affirm or what deny, and call
> Our knowledge or opinion, then retires
> Into her private cell when Nature rests.
> Oft in her absence mimic Fansie wakes
> To imitate her; but misjoyning shapes,
> Wilde worke produces oft, and most in dreams,
> Ill matching words and deeds long past or late.
> (*PL* V, 106–14)

Neither are we surprised that Milton should see the awakening of Fancy to a dangerous autonomy as the failure of mimesis, for his epic, like Dante's, makes large claims as a poem of almost pure mimesis. Hence he never associates his own poetic activity with the fancy, despite (or because of) the precedent of Shakespeare. The poet is for him the perfect mediator who usurps nothing because the authority of the message is absolute, a sacred text.

Milton's curious relation to the Renaissance imagination is illuminated by setting the conflict within the context of literary history. At the moment in which the poet doubts his own inspiration, his election, he wonders "if all be mine," and the specter of the autonomous imagination is conjured. The poetic fantasy is under repression in Milton (to a lesser extent, in Spenser also) because it means usurpation to him, the intervention of the human into the divinely originated process of mediation. At the same time, however, this usurpation is very deeply desired, because it is the means by which every poet makes his origin, his place of beginning. The imaginative act is initiated by the opening of an absence, by emptying the present of sensation so that the emptiness may be filled with the image. An analogous event governs the movement of literary history as well, where the relationship between poets can range from an identification, by means of which an origin is found, to a usurpation, by which an authority is displaced; and these two concepts define, respectively, Milton's relation to Spenser and Shakespeare.

I have associated Milton's rejection of imagination with a turn away from Shakespeare, and in the course of this study the multiple meanings of this rejection will be considered. The names "imagination" and "Shakespeare" define Milton's "negative" stance in literary history, his interest in finding an origin in a "heavenly" muse and not in any process of mind, or tradition of "secular" poetry. In this sense the authority claimed by a poet like Shakespeare is much nearer to Sidney's meaning than to any self-conception of either Spenser or Milton. Contrasting poetry with history, Sidney credits the poet with "having all, from Dante's heaven to his hell, under the authority of his pen."[58] So the poet, ranging the zodiac of his wit, or traversing the limits of a literary cosmos, refrains from asserting the coincidence of his fictive structure with the contours of God's created universe. This abstention becomes a kind of liberation, freeing the poet from the demands of a rigorous mimesis and reestablishing his authority as absolute within the unreal precincts of the fiction. The intrinsic secularization implicit in this conception of authority is intensely resisted by Spenser and Milton, although the form their resistance takes ironically assures the triumph of "literature," for they both need the usurper to establish themselves as origins; and the expression of that need permanently alters the literary history of England. The authority both poets felt they had to displace was the *secular itself*, or the established authority of Renaissance literature. So Spenser displaced secular romance into sacred quest (investing Ariostoan narrative with the moral seriousness of Tasso) and Milton displaced Shakespearean drama into dramatic narratives of

Protestant eschatology (turning blank verse into sacred epic).[59] Romance and drama are "sublimed" in Spenser and Milton, elevated to the category of the numinous. We are prepared now to understand why one major line of continuity in literary history descends from Spenser and Milton while Shakespeare dwells apart, inimitable on his poetic Olympus. Milton chooses Spenser as his "original," eclipsing with his dark medium the Shakespearean sun. This displacement, the greatest usurpation in literary history, marks the new origin Milton finds for himself.

It has become customary in recent years to speak of a "visionary" line descending from Spenser and Milton,[60] and if these two poets exhibit an intensely visionary longing, their desire to "see" is a movingly ironic event in literary history. Protestant iconoclasm is uneasily allied to a poetics of vision. The breaking of images marks the end of Spenser's *Mutabilitie Cantos*, and possibly the end of his poetic career. Milton is always an iconoclast, programatically a breaker of images, although it does not seem to me that he is recompensed for his blindness with an experience that is truly visionary. Both poets acknowledge the failure of the visionary quest. The "imagination" names for the post-Miltonic poet an "internal vision," a source of poetry, but it does not name the sacred text so much as the desire for such a text. As a name for poetic power, the word preserves both the visionary longing, and the failure of that longing. The authority of the poet is henceforth more problematic, and requires an ever more complex defense.

CHAPTER TWO

A Critique of Origins:
The Image of Source in *The Faerie Queene*

They alledge heere-with, that before Poets beganne to be in price our Nation hath set their harts delight upon action, and not upon imagination: rather doing things worthy to be written, then writing things fitte to be done. What that before time was, I thinke scarcely Sphinx can tell. Sith no memory is so auncient that hath the precedence of Poetrie.

Sidney, *An Apology for Poetry*

1. *The Floods in Generation*

Ideas of origin have always been subject to the vagaries of mystification for the reason, scarcely surprising, that imperfectly remembered origins inevitably engender mysteries. A preliminary distinction ought to be made between the idea of an origin—pure, undistorted by the act of discovery, and before which nothing comes—and the origin that is *used* to some rhetorical and pragmatic end, but such a distinction discloses that origins of the first type perhaps do not exist. Much as we may wish to purge origins of their mystery, it must be admitted that the *need* to uncover origins is never disinterested. I have already intimated that fictions of origination are involved as a form of "interest" in problems of authority, a fact to which the relation between the words *author* and *authority* is persuasive linguistic testimony. The authority of an author, even (or especially) when he is an originator, is buttressed by gestures toward a still earlier origin from which the present beginning emanates. In literature as in life it is axiomatic that what is early is more authoritative, despite the fact that this axiom is easily vulnerable to a reasoned critique. My own use of the word "genealogy" in chapter 1, in deference to the *auctoritas* of Nietzchean genealogy, suggests an even odder fact: More than any other technique of persuasion, the argument from origin can be used to subvert the pretensions of an authority that declares itself in the present, whether that authority happens to be morality or the preeminence of imagination in critical vocabulary. The precedent of the *Genealogy of Morals,* and other texts by other *auctors* traceable to those early exposers of false origins—the Reformation theologians—imposes upon even the most relentless of demythologizers the obligation to acknowledge that the negative as well as the positive argument from origin derives its authority. The difficulty of getting behind the authority of origins is perhaps insurmountable.

By way of preface I have complicated the question of origins, in order both to forestall the contemporary bias for negativity of origin, and to hypothesize that a critique of origins can be discovered in those Renaissance texts most sensitive to the anxiety of the age. Controversy was inevitably provoked by the reaffirmation of pagan literature as paradigmatic (countered by the supposition that Hebrew is the "original" language); the priority of the classical to the Christian is an anxiety writ large in the language of even the humanists. But the sophistication of a "critique of origins," as it develops in such a work as *The Faerie Queene,* is not immediately evident. It would be easy but insufficient to point to a Renaissance awareness of mythical origins as fictional constructions; nor would it serve much purpose merely to segregate the enlightened from their more mystified brethren. My hypothesis is that a true critique of origins can be formulated only upon the recognition of the virtual impossiblity of enlightenment. Let me hasten to add that I do not think good literature is defined by this recognition. Spenser's poetry undertakes a critique. Milton's does not, but precisely because Milton believes in enlightenment. The difference between the two poets here is the difference between two types of radicalism, one of which is radically conservative. With these considerations in mind, a text may now be introduced.

The passage quoted here, from Book IV, follows the long catalogue of rivers comprising the pageant that celebrates the marriage of the Thames and the Medway:

O what an endlesse worke haue I in hand,
  To count the seas abundant progeny,
  Whose fruitfull seede farre passeth those in land,

And also those which wonne in th'asure sky?
For much more eath to tell the starres on hy,
Albe they endlesse seeme in estimation,
Then to recount the Seas posterity:
So fertile be the flouds in generation,
So huge their numbers, and so numberlesse their nation.

Therefore the antique wisards well inuented,
    That Venus of the fomy sea was bred;
    For that the seas by her are most augmented.
                    (*FQ* IV.xii.1-2)[1]

The marriage of the Thames and the Medway is a Spenserian "invention,"
a myth of origination, and perhaps also one of the generative pre-texts of
The Faerie Queene.[2] The apparent hopelessness of the task set out in these
lines is belied by the fact that Spenser has already named ("contained") a
number of rivers large enough to counterfeit the infinity that he seems to
argue lies beyond the power of the artist to represent. The act of naming is
"endlesse" but very engaging because it perpetuates the beginning of
poetry in a recognition of mere naming as the aboriginal poetic achievement.[3] The function of this naming excursus is not difficult to determine:
The will to write is regenerated in a regression to archaic poetic acts, or
returns to origins.

Returning to the source in order to feed, as it were, raises an interesting
question about what we may call the "economy" of origins. As a poet,
Spenser might be said to ally himself with "antique wisards," whom he sees
as inventors of the myth of Venus. Their myth possesses a certain logic
perceived after the fact as analogous to the logic behind Spenser's own
story of the Thames and the Medway. The ocean in the Venus story
becomes identified with the infinity of the rivers or the stars, giving us an
idealized, because inexhaustible, image of source. What is taken from this
source cannot really subtract from it. At the same time, however, the
linking of the Venus story to the catalogue of rivers forces Spenser to
equate the fictionality of both tales; they are both "invented," and the
origins they are meant to discover are in fact devised for the occasion. The
choice of Venus' birth as a complement to the marriage of rivers brilliantly
defends against the inherent danger of the fictional origin by implying that
generation itself is born of that source (Spenser's *Venus genetrix*). Generation

is a self-sustaining power that, once free of its origin, can return in order to augment, not subtract: "For that the seas by her are most augmented." As I shall argue presently, Spenser usually represents origins in *The Faerie Queene* as watery sources, but the interest of this tactic lies in its relation to the economy by which energy, moral or poetic, is dispersed through the massive structure of the poem.

Hannah Arendt, in a fine essay entitled "What is Authority?" constructs a genealogy of the concept, whose roots she locates in Roman conceptions of a political order.[4] The word *auctoritas*, from which we derive our terms for author and authority, is further traced to the verb *augere*, "to augment." I introduce this etymology following upon Spenser's association of origin and augmentation not only to make a polemical point but to stress that this connection is not fortuitous. With the first words of *The Faerie Queene*, Spenser places himself within the Virgilian tradition, or at least attempts to impose upon his poetic career a Virgilian structure.[5] Whatever Virgil's *Aeneid* may actually say about the origins of the Roman nation, his epic is usually perceived as a sanctification of Roman origins, hence an affirmation of an authority (Augustus) in the present. The impulse emanates from the most entrenched beliefs of the Roman citizen:

> At the heart of Roman politics, from the beginning of the republic until virtually the end of the imperial era, stands the conviction of the sacredness of foundation, in the sense that once something has been founded it remains binding for all future generations...The foundation of a new body politic— to the Greeks an almost commonplace experience—became to the Romans the central, decisive, *unrepeatable beginning* of their whole history, a unique event. And the most deeply Roman divinities were Janus, the god of beginning, with whom, as it were, we still begin our year, and Minerva, the goddess of remembrance.[6]

The derivation of authority from augmentation leads to the conclusion that "what authority or those in authority constantly augment is the foundation." Additions or extensions must be submitted to the authorizing model of an "unrepeatable beginning," for the obvious reason that any new beginning is permanently excluded from the process of Roman politics. In this context it is not difficult to understand why the inception of an imperial order should generate a comprehensive anxiety and defense of authority, one result of which is the *Aeneid*. Spenser puzzles his critics by grafting himself upon the Virgilian lineage, but his problem is so very like

Virgil's: he too is committed to a conception of an unrepeatable beginning, a sacred source. The difference lies in the greater uncertainty he experiences about the nature of this source. Beginnings multiply themselves wildly in the romance form, which conversely admits a casual disregard for "loose ends." The multiplicity of these beginnings invites dissociation from origins that Spenser points to as his own, especially if those origins are represented as sacred.

The ostensible commitment of *The Faerie Queene* to its biblical, "sacred" pre-text emerges from this context as extremely problematic.[7] The wandering of the narrative farther and farther away from the redaction of the Book of Revelation (which is the "origin" of Book I) can also be construed as an approach (albeit reluctant) to the truer and more dangerous origin of romance. The closure of Book I, unlike the closure of Revelation, which completes the biblical canon, is broken by the continued wandering of Redcrosse Knight, and every closure thereafter is broken more violently than the one before. Spenser desires to ground his text in the origin of the sacred pre-text, but the romance origin must be seen as a powerfully sustained challenge to that aspiration—indeed, as the inevitable displacement of sacred origin. The multiplicity of beginnings in *The Faerie Queene* is one effect of the failure of the sacred origin to move toward a repetition in the later text of its own completion. Every reader of Book VI knows how radically broken Spenser's ending becomes.[8]

What Hannah Arendt calls an "unrepeatable beginning," Edward Said calls an *origin*, and I follow Said here in desynonymizing the two terms.[9] The confusion of the words has served a useful purpose, however, if we are legitimately to conclude that a poetic text desires to support their synonymy. Some such distinction will emerge out of the vicissitudes of Spenser's habitual recourse to origins, whether or not we shade in the historical background. Said distinguishes between a beginning and an origin as, most basically, the difference between an active and a passive relationship in a sequence of terms: "X is the origin of Y" while "the beginning of A leads to B."[10] Why should an author wish to ground his work in the passivity of an origin? This question would be meaningless outside of the context of authority, as Said himself recognizes in a further attempt to distinguish these concepts: "The state of mind that is concerned with origins is, I have said, theological. By contrast, and this is the [historical] shift, beginnings are eminently secular, or gentile, continuing activities."[11]

I am, of course, more than willing to affirm the relation of the sacred/ secular dichotomy to the problem of origins/beginnings, as well as the intrinsic association of sacred, "inspired" origins with the desire to inflate the authority of a text. The historicist argument is something else altogether, and it is much more difficult to verify.

The shift from sacred to secular can be seen to coincide with the supercession of beginnings, but when does this happen? One would like to say: when the secular text no longer exhibits anxiety about its relation to the sacred. At this point the parallel distinctions resist translation into historical terms, and at least one of the conclusions to be drawn from this study is that this resistance in poetic texts is a permanent feature of literary history. Under the covering fiction of inspiration, and its later permutations, the idea of the sacred origin lingers in the secular text. The problem for the poet writing in the ruins of exploded mythologies is not markedly different from that experienced by Spenser, a fact that may now be demonstrated.

The strongest temptation to which the heroes of *The Faerie Queene* are subject is denominated in the medieval system of vices as *accidie,* sloth. The temptation is simply to rest, in its most radical form, to give up. The pervasiveness of this arch-evil impresses the reader as an odd restructuring of the traditional hierarchy of vices. In Canto vii of Book I, Redcrosse drinks from a well whose effects are immediately enervating; he is subsequently seized by Orgoglio, against whom he is now defenceless. We are told in Stanza 4 that the nymph who was "wont to dwell" in this fountain was "out of Dian's favour":

The cause was this: one day when Phoebe fayre
   With all her band was following the chace,
   This Nymph, quite tyr'd with heat of scorching ayre
   Sat downe to rest in middest of the race:
   The goddesse wroth gan fowly her disgrace,
   And bad the waters, which from her did flow,
   Be such as she her selfe was then in place.
   Thenceforth her waters waxed dull and slow,
And all that drunke thereof, did faint and feeble grow.
                    (I.vii.5)

As an allegorical image, the Nymph is intended to objectify a state of moral lassitude in the Knight, corresponding to the fact that Redcrosse has removed his armor, and further emphasized by the editorializing allusion to the pool of Salmacis in Ovid's *Metamorphoses*. The allegory of *The Faerie Queene*, as James Nohrnberg has argued, proceeds by exhaustive analogy, and here the reader is invited to examine what seems to be one example of a complete analogy between two sets of terms.[12] What defeats an examination conducted along these lines, however, is the fact that the two stories, of the Nymph and of the Knight, are not merely adjacent; they intersect causally. In the narrative the fountain is a "source" of Redcrosse's fall to Orgoglio, but morally this makes no sense at all; that is, if we are inclined to see Redcrosse's fall as a moral failure.[13] A conception of purely allegorical causation entails no such problem: the Nymph's failure to participate in the hunt "causes" the fountain's transformation. The first cause in the series, the ultimate "source," is Diana, who would presumably correspond to a divine or providential principle in the allegorical order to which Redcrosse belongs. Spenser's use of "disgrace," cut off from grace, describes the vulnerable condition of the Knight's luxuriation in a pastoral pleasance, and reminds us of the theological analogue; but Spenser does not need to name the analogue for Diana and this is important. The only represented "source" on one side of the analogy is Redcrosse's moral act, the putting off of his armor, which repeats, perhaps, his earlier failure in the House of Pride. The supposed providential source is the allegory itself: the enervating well. Later in the book, when Redcrosse falls into the "Well of Life" during the fight with the Dragon, the intervention of Providence through the source image itself is made more explicit. Here I wish to emphasize the uneven effect of the analogy, intelligible as the intersection of allegorical causation with a problem of representation. The representation of the source is given in the narrative the power of causation as well.

Readers who are schooled in the conventions of allegory usually have no difficulty accepting what Angus Fletcher sees as its "magical causation." The episode of the enfeebling well is an example of the subclass "imitative magic," which "tries to bring real events which the magician wants to control into parallel with symbolic events."[14] The analogy of the Nymph and Redcrosse (with Spenser as the magician-allegorist) is clear, but also perhaps misleading, as all analogies between magic and art disintegrate with further elaboration. The premise of magic is that the world contains no uncaused event. Magic makes available to the allegorist other systems of causation, but no system, by definition, can represent the indeterminacy of a moral act.[15] If the poet does not wish to identify the act itself, which has the traits of a beginning, with a virtual unprecedented origin, then the moment of choice tends to drift out of the range of representation. Redcrosse's sudden decision to rest is given a moral value only to provoke an explanatory fiction of origin ("the cause was this...") that attempts to incorporate the indeterminacy of the act into the system of allegorical causation. The reader is not sure, however, that the story of the Nymph, in *repeating* Redcrosse's action, helps to *explain* it. What I mean to suggest by recomplicating an apparently basic example of an allegorical action is that images of origin in *The Faerie Queene* are imbued with a secondariness that cannot be said to characterize the idea of the true origin. The well or stream as image of origin participates in the causative structure of the poem by immediately becoming secondary, just as in the story of the Nymph the spring is easily associated with the *effect* of Redcrosse's moral lapse but continually resists what seems to be its identification with the cause. The *origin*, like the undetermined act, remains unrepresentable except as something that has already happened, but there is no reason to believe that the poet is unaware that the image of the origin moves by a kind of linguistic inertia into the category of the secondary. That secondariness is exploited in what I have referred to as the economy of origins, the subject I would like to examine in the context of another passage.

In Canto ii of Book II, Guyon and the Palmer encounter three victims of Acrasia's enchantments. Amavia is dying beside the body of her lover, Mordant, who is already dead, and she holds in her lap their baby, who plunges his hands into the blood streaming from its mother's wounds. Amavia tells her story and dies, and Guyon takes the baby to a nearby fountain to wash its hands of blood. But the blood will not wash away, a fact that elicits this explanation from the Palmer:

> But know, that secret vertues are infusd
> In euery fountaine, and in euery lake,
> Which who hath skill them rightly to haue chusd,
> To proofe of passing wonders hath full often vsd.

> Of those some were so from their source indewd
> By great Dame Nature, from whose fruitfull pap
> Their welheads spring, and are with moisture deawd;
> Which feedes each liuing plant with liquid sap,

And filles with flowres faire Floraies painted lap;
But other some by gift of later grace,
Or by good prayers, or by other hap,
Had vertue pourd into their waters bace,
And thenceforth were renowned, and sought from place to place.

                                      (II.ii.5–6)

The situation repeats with greater complexity the episode of the enfeebling well. More interestingly the fountain genealogy delineates in a very displaced idiom the relationship between Guyon, whose name is taken from the river Gihon, and the Palmer, whose purpose is the continued purification of that source.[16] Guyon's problem, as we learn later during his period of separation from the Palmer, is an unacknowledged dependency, related, though not with immediate clarity, to the need for temperate behavior. The Palmer hints that fountain sources are available to the temperate only, those who "hath skill them rightly to have chusd." When we recall that Gihon means "to burst forth," at least part of the Palmer's digression about watery sources comes into focus. Guyon, of course, does not "burst forth" until he is released like a "tempest" (II.xii.83) upon the Bower of Bliss. Until then, his greatest temptation is to revert to a more dangerous fluidity, like Redcrosse at the well, "poured out in looseness on the grassy ground."

Fountains in *The Faerie Queene* are usually reservoirs of energy, sources of power. But true to the secondariness of the image the power ("vertue") comes from elsewhere, from a transcendent source, Dame Nature, whose indescribable otherness, maintained through the end of the *Mutabilitie Cantos*, is one of the marvels of the poem. Her introduction here as the source of sources, from whom "welheads spring," anticipates the theme of generation that more and more overwhelms the poem as it progresses. In this context, however, the proleptic celebration of generative nature highlights the exceptional status of this fountain, which is not an image of fecundity, but of the frozen chastity that follows an attempted rape. The Palmer tells us, after expounding the general subject of water sources, that a Nymph of Diana was pursued by the lusty Dan Faunus (again, we will meet him in the *Mutabilitie Cantos*). She prays to Diana to let her die a maid, and in response to her prayer she is metamorphosed into a stone, "from whose two heads / As from two weeping eyes, fresh streams do flow."

And yet her vertues in her waters byde

For it is chaste and pure, as purest snow
Ne lets her waues with any filth be dyde,
But euer like her selfe vnstained hath beene tryde.
                         (II.ii.9)

The fountain is easily located within the thematics of Book II, since temperance is opposed not only to the kind of lust displayed by Faunus but also to the immovable chastity of the Nymph, a fact which determines the negative virtue of this watery source. Temperance is a form of pure generation, a medium between chaste sterility and sterile self-indulgence. In accordance with the rigorous logic of the Canto, the Bloody Babe is given to Medina, a rather dry personification of the Golden Mean.

At this point the Nymph's fountain seems to be reduced to a negative image of a true source, and the reader may wonder exactly what relation Spenser is trying to establish between the idea of generation and the streams and wells pervading the poem. Where are the streams that flow directly from the "source," Dame Nature? Book II has perhaps already evolved beyond the point where allegorical representations of this order (the "Well of Life") are possible. Generation, as we have already argued, contributes to an economy of origins by establishing a continuity of the source and its effluent, which exchanges its pretension to primary status for a privileged relation to a transcendent and unrepresented source. In the proem to Book VI, this economy is spelled out as a system of interchange:

So from the Ocean all rivers spring
And tribute backe repay as to their king.
                         (VI. Pr. 7)

This ocean is associated with an authority in the present, Elizabeth, and the poet accepts the risk implied by the location of his authorizing origin in a very accessible present. I raise this point perhaps prematurely in order to expose a presupposition underlying much of the concern with origins in *The Faerie Queene*: Is the transcendence of the origin indicated by its pastness? Here we must return to the Palmer's explanation of virtuous fountains in order to recover the temporal aspect of Spenser's argument. The Palmer makes a significant distinction between wells deriving their virtue immediately from Dame Nature, and a second, mediated variety of source:

But other some by gift of later grace,
Or by good prayers, or by other hap,
Had vertue pourd into their waters bace,
And thenceforth were renowned, and sought from place to place.

Guyon and the Palmer live in a world (our world) of *later grace*, clearly distinguishable in this stanza from the virtues flowing out of more primitive sources. "Later grace" is almost redundant, since the word "grace" draws into the context of the argument the recollection of the radical discontinuity that made grace necessary. The hypothesis emerging here is that this world, in its very presentness, contains sources of power that are newly made, whose authority derives from a vertical descent of a higher power. It is this origin that becomes the object of quest ("and sought from place to place"), also the quest of *The Faerie Queene*. Arthur seeks Gloriana, and Spenser "seeks" an apotheosized Elizabeth. These origins may promise nothing more than strength to continue, but because they do not derive from an irrecoverable past, they seem to escape the critique of origins founded upon a resolute doubt at the core of representation. Spenser's acceptance of the secondariness of his water sources is to be equated with his willingness to subsist beneath, as it were, the priority of a transcendent power. The quest for an origin outside of, but cotemporal with, the production of the poem encounters a problem of great significance for literary history: the tendency of the sacred source to degenerate into the secular beginning. The sacred other feeding energy into the poem, whose traces I have described in the image of the source, defines the ideal of "generation." Other tracks might also have been followed, but here I can only suggest that all such paths would lead to the Garden of Venus and Adonis, the ideological crest of the poem, and the most elaborated of Spenser's mythopoetic scenes of generation. It is not my intention to analyze the erotic cores of these central books (such analysis would indefinitely extend my argument) but rather to follow like Alpheus my critique of origin, as it finally emerges fully apparent in the displaced "core" of Book VI. I believe this critique will uncover an alternative, and intractably "secular" origin: the fact of desire.

2. *The Lineaments of Gratified Desire*[17]

Discourse, according to Michel Foucault, is composed of statements, whose formations are various, almost innumerable.[18] One such variant form of statement, the list, will provide us with a means of understanding some currents of significance that run in *The Faerie Queene* well below the level of the sentence. Here is the list: *gens, genus, genius, generation, general, gentile, gentle, gentleman, generous, genealogy, gender, genesis, genital*. Such a list has a *prima facie* relevance in the vastly stratified language of Spenser's epic. The non-English of the poem, like Joyce's non-English, requires of its readers habitual attention to the agglutinative properties of an etymon as important in the Romance languages as *genus*. The cognates in this list develop over a great stretch of time, and for that reason may also be said to comprise a historical argument. For example, the list seems to assert an intrinsic connection between a process of abstraction (the naming of kinds) and the activity of reproduction. The smallest kind may be the clan, or extended family, united by a purely reproductive pattern. Hence the development of "generalizing" as abstraction of apprehended likeness. (Something like this process has been examined in Wittgenstein's analogy of "family resemblances.") A second notion arising from this list is the idea of *gentility*, the *gentleman*, with the corollary *generosity*, a subject that exercises Spenser in Book VI of *The Faerie Queene* and leads him inevitably into the dismantling and reconstruction of genealogical fictions (*vide* the romance of Pastorella). Genealogies are crucial to gentlemen, and in the Renaissance to the tensions heating up the issue of primogeniture. Ideas of origin intersect with this semantic field producing more abstract conceptions of genealogy and genesis, to some of which I have already alluded. At the moment we may allow the word list to recede into the middleground in order to bracket two words that are drawn together by Spenser in the passage I would like next to examine: *genius* and *generation*.

At the entrance to the Bower of Bliss stands a figure called Genius, an effeminate young man who is one of many Acrasian representatives of unproductive lust. He is contrasted with another figure, also a Genius, whose identity is difficult to determine precisely. Spenser identifies this positive figure with the god Agdistes, who is a

> celestial powre, to whom the care
> Of life, and generation of all
> That liues, pertains in charge particulare,
> Who wondrous things concerning our welfare,

And strange phantomes doth let vs oft forsee,
And oft of secret ill bids vs beware:
That is our Selfe, whom though we do not see,
Yet each doth in him selfe it well perceiue to bee.
(II.xii.47)

C. S. Lewis, who puzzled over this stanza in *The Allegory of Love,* was confident that up to the line ending "welfare," Spenser is speaking about the "universal god of generation," a familiar figure in medieval literature. But there is another distinct kind of Genius, which is the "tutelary spirit" or "external soul" of individual men. Spenser seems to be saying that Agdistes is also this Genius, and Lewis finds the composite creature "un-imaginable."[19] The problem is not resolved by the usual recourse to Renaissance syncretism because there remains a logical objection to the confusing of a "universal" demigod with daemons who are defined by the particularity of "individual souls." There must be considerable pressure behind the fusion of the two figures, and a clue to the source of that pressure is provided by the intrusion into this text of yet another allegorical precursor. The "strange phantomes" which Agdistes "doth let vs oft forsee" recall the description of Phantastes in the Castle of Alma; "he could things to come forsee." "Genius" and the correlative "fantasy" are waiting in the wings of Renaissance poetic theory, although Spenser is very careful to subordinate imagination to reason and memory in his anatomy of the mind. The allusion to Phantastes in this passage is attributable, I believe, largely to his elective affinity for the evil *Doppelgänger* of the Good Genius. Villains of imagination in *The Faerie Queene,* of whom the archetype is Archimago (arch-magus and arch-image), often recreate themselves as the *Doppelgänger* of an innocent victim, or produce such figures from their stock of evil spirits. Under the aegis of Agdistes, genius and generation are drawn together as a means of counteracting the power of the double, whose identity is simply desire itself. The problem is once again the Renaissance dilemma of distinguishing sacred and profane love. The Good Genius comes between the converging impulses of desire and imagination, preempting the false reproduction (of shadows, shows) that would result from, as it were, their copulation. The problem of desire enters the poetics of allegory as the possibility of this false image. The language of allegory, however, with its "shadows" and "outward shows," can exactly duplicate an "idle fantasy," and this dangerous similitude needs to be examined now.[20] I offer as context a second word list: *fain, feign, fancy,* and *fantasy*.[21]

The involvement of imagination in desire is confirmed for Spenser by one of those linguistic accidents of which he takes full advantage. *Fain* and *feign*, despite the absence of distinction in Renaissance orthography, are derived from two quite different sources. *Fain* is from Old High German and means "wont, longing, desire." *Feign* is taken from the Latin *fingere*, "to shape or to form," and hence to pretend or to produce a fiction. Spenser puns in a similar fashion on the words *concept* and *conception*. Fancy can of course be used to mean either a desire or love object, or a contraction of fantasy. *Phantoms, phantasms, fantasies,* and *fancies* are then the correlative objects of desire and imagination. Usually Spenser will use one word in the context of the other, in order to suggest a mutual intensification of "affect." For example, Britomart's conversation with Redcrosse about Arthegall in Canto iv of Book III:

> But *Britomart* kept on her former course,
>   Ne euer dofte her armes, but all the way
>   Grew pensiue through that amorous discourse,
>   By which the *Redcrosse* knight did earst display
>   Her louers shape, and cheualrous aray;
>   A thousand thoughts she fashioned in her mind,
>   And in her feigning fancie did pourtray
>   Him such, as fittest she for loue could find,
> Wise, warlike, personable, curteous, and kind.
> (III.iv.5)

Britomart "fashions" in her mind a duplicate (but better) image of Arthegall based on Redcrosse's description, thereby placing at still another remove the object of desire. In this context, we remember that her feelings were first aroused by an image in Merlin's glass. The reader is inclined to the conclusion that whatever system of mutual intensification exists between desire and imagination, the earliest movement of feeling is preceded by a still earlier act of imagination. For many reasons, Spenser remains fearfully ambivalent about this fact. Modern readers have been lectured in the complex self-delusions attending "object choice," to the extent, possibly, that our lack of surprise at the conventional wisdom of Spenser's analysis of desire obstructs a more important insight: a critique of origins (in a more hidden sense, of allegorical origins) is embedded in this language. Coinciding with the allegorist's expressed intention in the letter to Raleigh, Britomart *"fashions a gentleman"* in her mind—"wise, warlike, personable, curteous, kind"—but out of what? Arthegall's failure to correspond to the ideal image makes his portrait vulnerable to ironic reduction, but Britomart cannot know this. Irony is the occupational hazard of allegory, or as its contemporary champions maintain, allegory's true value and distinction.[22] For Spenser the question is whether imagination represents an object or begets it. The betrayal into irony (or the failure of allegorical representation) is in fact a less feared alternative than the prospect of the imagination as beginning, displacing some other and more valued origin.

The power of imagination is therefore reduced by linking it to failed representations, the lesser of two evils. Hence the easy derogation of

> idle thoughts and fantasies
> Devices, dreams, opinions unsound,
> Shewes, visions, soothsayes, and prophecies
> All that fained is, as leasings, tales and lies.
> (II.ix.51)

This is Phantastes, to whom any power of origination is being denied. The digression through the Castle of Alma in Book II provides Spenser with a needed defense against Phantastes the Poet—*his* double. Spenser is thoroughly conventional in tracing his poetry to the more authoritative quarters of Reason, who is in charge of "all artes, all science, all philosophy." Reason is also a censor, a "magistrate," ruling and overruling the false productions of the magus, his unauthorized double. The legal analogue fits into the general scheme of repressed imagination, as Phantastes himself is a typical example of the Renaissance neurotic, the melancholy man. At this point in the poem (but not later) Spenser finds a purer origin in the personification of memory, Eumnestes ("good memory"), who might also be called "true re-presentation." In the proem to Book II, allegory is associated with *anamnesis,* and Canto x elaborately unfolds a version of "antique history" in the chronicles of England and Faery land. These texts are read like scripture; they are prophetic revelations, and they are included *in The Faerie Queene* as a kind of model of what a sacred origin would be.[23] It is as though the narrative cord of the Bible had been unwound into constituent mythical and historical strands. Guyon and Arthur read the stories of the past relevant to themselves, unconscious of the status of the text in which they do this reading. That text must one day be added to the books in Eumnestes' chamber, the same text for *both* books. Spenser cannot, of course, add to the words of the Bible; and yet this is what any sacred text must do, by however remote a process of translation, allegorization, interpretation.

Spenser need not deny the power of imagination to intensify desire, or even its subversive effect upon allegory, but he must resist desire as a source that draws him to the dangerous priority of the "unprecedented" act of imagination. The antecedent of Arthur's dream, which, as the origin of the quest, is the pre-text of the poem itself, risks the truth claims of the allegory in an episode of desire. Arthur wonders "whether dreams delude, or true it were," that is, whether he really was visited by the Faery Queen and not sleeping with an image of his own mind. Some observations on two other episodes of desire—the Bower of Bliss and the Dance of the Graces on Mt. Acidale—will open the question of what gratification might mean in relation to allegorical intentions. Curiously, this end is perceived as an origin: *there was a time in which desire was gratified.* The quest for origins becomes a quest for the gratification of desire. Spenser is eventually disillusioned about the possibilities of anamnesis but his poem continually sets up scenes of possible gratification, or scenes in which such a possibility is explored. From the first of my two examples, Acrasia's Bower, we should not expect any gratification that can be considered authentic within the categories of the poem. But that is not to say that Spenser (as well as Guyon) is not tempted. The following stanza is worth consideration:

Her snowy brest was bare to readie spoyle
  Of hungry eies, which n'ote therewith be fild,
  And yet through langour of her late sweet toyle,
  Few drops, more cleare then Nectar, forth distild,
  That like pure Orient perles adowne it trild,
  And her faire eyes sweet smyling in delight,
  Moystened their fierie beames, with which she thrild
  Fraile harts, yet quenched not; like starry light
Which sparckling on the silent waues, does seeme more bright.
                    (II.xii.78)

Many scenes in *The Faerie Queene,* quoted "out of context," are not very far from pornographic, as critics have almost acknowledged in comments on Spenser's sensuality. The problem here, as with pornography, is precisely the nature of the visual image as a stimulus to desire. C. S. Lewis seized upon what seems to be the exclusively visual nature of the erotic stimulus to conclude that there are in fact no sexual relations at all in the Bower of Bliss, an interesting misreading since we are not told that the lover sleeping in Acrasia's lap has always been so immobile.[24] In the stanza quoted above Acrasia is shedding tears "through langour of her late sweet toyle." This would have to be post-coital *tristesse,* an image of gratified desire. The image *of* gratification places the scene of sexual consummation in a past that the voyeur (Guyon, the reader) has no wish to recover. The fire that quenches not is the desire *of* desire, like the reflection of the starry light that seems *more* bright than the stars themselves. The simile also links the duplication of desire to the idea of representation, or the seductiveness of the mere image. The erotic "fantasy" is desire folding back upon itself, completely emancipated from its object. And this process of duplication or folding back bears a structural similarity, which the poem must deny, to the approved concept of generation, represented in various places as the hermaphrodite, or the snake biting its tail, or the ocean-river interchange. The middle books of *The Faerie Queene* worry this distinction, an under-taking that is analogous to the process of distinguishing the true from the false Florimel.

Allegorical characters are conventionally "seduced" by images, and Spenser only literalizes this metaphor by writing it into a narrative of seduction. Guyon is not finally seduced but the Knight called Verdant is, and it is important to observe what this means in the larger thematic scheme of Book II:

His warlike armes, the idle instruments
  Of sleeping praise, were hong vpon a tree,
  And his brave shield, full of old moniments,
  Was fowly ra'st, that none the signes might see...
                    (II.xii.80)[25]

Verdant is plainly cut off from his especial origins, the implicit argument of the erased "moniments." These are "memorials" of a general nature, or specifically marks on a shield. The legendary "Briton moniments" establish Canto x as the context for determining the relation between memory and desire. The self-activating complex of desire-fantasy comes between the present moment and a past origin, establishing, by virtue of this discontinuity, an aimless and undesirable beginning. This beginning is completely static, like the still postures in the Bower of Bliss; the Knight sleeps, his instruments are idle. Loss of origin is analogous to the blankness of the shield, from which the memory signs are obliterated. This condition of obliteration, the letter erased, is almost the worst evil Spenser can conceive.

The *worst* evil is embodied by the Blatant Beast, who does not so much erase letters as write over them or displace them. He is intended to figure calumny, which supersedes sloth as the most dangerous of vices in Spenser's allegory. I have already suggested that all the monsters in *The Faerie Queene* are prototypes of the Blatant Beast and I want to emphasize here his possible relation to the fantasy by way of introduction to a problem in the interpretation of the Dance of the Graces on Mt. Acidale, the most fully rendered episode of the "lineaments of gratified desire." The Blatant Beast has no overtly erotic signification, but his presence in a book highly charged with sexual themes requires comment. Here is an early adumbration of the Beast in *The Teares of the Muses*:

For the sweet numbers and melodious measures
With which I wont the winged words to tie
And make a tuneful diapase of pleasures
Now being let to run at libertie
By those which have no skill to rule them right
Have now quite lost their natural delight.

Heaps of huge words uphoorded hideously
With horrid sound though having little sense
They thinke to be chief praise of Poetry
And thereby wanting due intelligence
Have mard the face of goodly Poesie
And made a monster of their fantasie...
(547-58)

These stanzas are sung by Polyhymnia, who, as a principle of integration or harmony, is a foreshadowing of the kind of infolded complexity visible in the Dance of the Graces. The poem ends with all of the muses breaking their "learned instruments," a recurrent motif in Spenser's poetry, culminating in the breaking of Colin Clout's bagpipes after Calidore's unwelcome intrusion. The "monster" can be language or even poetry, "let to run at libertie," as though mere words proliferate meaninglessly of themselves unless subject to a perpetual effort of restraint. A certain parallel is established very early in Spenser's career between restraint as a poetic necessity and restraint as a principle of sexual morality. These two themes are usually equated allegorically only where they both fail: in the disastrous collapsing together of desire and fantasy. In Book VI, the two themes belong to different sets of allegorical fictions, which Spenser is very careful to keep apart. The necessity of their distinction arises because he is led in Book VI to consider the possibility of representing the "lineaments of gratified desire" as itself the pure origin he seeks. In other words, he is no longer determined to distinguish the abstract conception of generation from the motivating principle of a desire that could be experientially associated with the will to write. This is a more direct poetic strategy, as the strict recourse to the romance form evidences; romance is the genre of return, of finding the lost origin.[26] It is also a secular form, and I am inclined to believe that at this point Spenser is willing to accept an origin that is secular—the experience of desire—provided that origin can be purified by an uninvoked agency of mediation (let us call it "grace") whose source is unimpeachable. This much of my argument has been implied by Harry Berger, Jr., and other critics, who read Book VI as a book of origins and sources. My second hypothesis, however, departs from the reading of the Mt. Acidale episode now current.

Let me defer for the moment a statement of this hypothesis in order to set down some sentences by two of Spenser's critics, passages intended to epitomize the thematic significance of the Dance of the Graces:

> In the intersection between visible actuality and invisible transcendence, where agape merges with eros, poetry has its life. Spenser's visionary stanzas allow us to see the dance of imagination, the concrete universal emerging from the figure the poem makes.[27]

> Only by turning inward, by self-creation, by tirelessly seeking and wooing and invoking the muses, or eros, or what lies behind them all—only thus do we regain our long-lost heritage. By some process akin to anamnesis we withdraw, we retire, we return to the nursery, we close the circle of beginnings and endings, we come finally to that first Idea, that pure grace which has always moved us...

It is important to take into account the presence of Rosalind as a simple country lass and poor handmaid of Gloriana, if one is to do justice to the realistic basis of Spenser's vision. The triumph of imagination is partly measured by the extent to which it has converted frustration, brute fact, the world of first sight and first nature, into a symbolic intuition of the real. . .[28]

Admirable as Isabel MacCaffrey's and Harry Berger's ecstatic readings of Spenser's famous climax may be, it should be remembered that Spenser could not have meant by "imagination" anything like what these readings imply.[29] Nevertheless both statements go to the heart of the matter, which is the question of origin. Spenser does seem to locate in this episode an erotic origin of the poetic text, and this origin does also allow for the subsumption of the image of desire into a transcendent source. If there is any "triumph," however, it is in the poem's movement *against* imagination, and this is where formulations like those quoted above are misleading. Berger argues (and his analysis is substantially reaffirmed by MacCaffrey) that Spenser achieves his triumph by bracketing, as it were, the activity of imagination, without losing sight of the possible and imminent impingement of the "real" world. This acknowledgment of the real context permits a free flight of imagining and even the touching of the imaginary image to the real (figured as the country lass, Rosalind). The idealized representation is a victory won at the cost of an ultimate defeat, since the immediate vision is dissolved by Calidore, the Blatant Beast returns, and then the poem itself disintegrates at the ungentle touch of this reality.

And yet the persuasiveness of this particular interpretation is dependent upon a mutual exclusivity of imagination and reality that is completely foreign to Spenser's poetic. Imagination is *not* equivalent to the activity of making poems and poetic self-consciousness cannot be assumed in this poet to mean reflection on the opposition or supposed reconciliation of the imagined and the real (the functional opposition is between the fantastic and the *true*). A triumph of imagination can be conceived by Spenser only as a reduction, a loss of authority, the poem as a mere "heap of words." I cannot find any passage in the poem where imagination is given a positive meaning, nor does the historical background sketched in chapter 1 provide us with a contemporary consensus for interpreting imagination as anything but the usurper of textual authority, the intruder into the sequence of representation. The fantasy has much more to do with the "real" in Berger's phrase (or MacCaffrey's "visible actuality") since that world is riddled with delusion. Calidore brings with him a tendency to be seduced by the mere image, and surprisingly he does not unlearn this mistake in his encounter with the Graces. He begins in the state of infolded desire ("he himselfe his eyes envued") and even Colin's sage discourse is said to feed his "greedy fancy," possibly because he still has one eye on the "place, whose pleasures rare / With such regard his senses ravished." We recall his attention was similarly divided in an earlier episode between Meliboe's sermon and Pastorella's beauty. The "dance of imagination" that MacCaffrey sees, or Berger's "triumph of imagination," begs the question of exactly what is being "represented" in this passage, and what relation this representation bears to the allegorical image.

The object of representation is precisely what precedes the fiction and strictly speaking does not *need* representation. Spenser gambles on the absolute priority of desire in order to exclude the autonomous self-generation of the image and place the activity of the poet under the authority of a transcendent agency. In short, he stages a scene of pure inspiration, excluding entirely from this scene its consequence: the poem. We do not hear what Colin Clout sings, only that he is singing. His experience is visionary, not imagining but pure *seeing*, and not subject to the temporal displacements of representation. The singing and the seeing of his beloved are simultaneous: "Thy loue is present there with thee in place" (VI.x.16). Colin Clout is addressed as the other by the poet at this point (like Coleridge's daemonic Kubla poet, who also sings and sees at once, he is most "other" precisely at the moment of vision). And we, the poet, the reader, the voyeur Calidore, must remain outside of that coincidence of time and place within the charmed circle of the dancing graces.[30] Colin experiences pure presence in its temporal and spatial manifestations but to the reader that presence is already *there* and not here. The gratification of desire is represented deliberately at this remove because it is sheer priority. We may feel that we are the excluded other because we are "outside," but it is Colin who is truly other, and Rosalind, and Gloriana. The dance of the Graces on Mt. Acidale is a moment of "inside-out," an expression that might be offered for the topography of inspiration, if such a thing could be.

Is this the origin of Spenser's allegorical image? The reader must certainly suspect that he has never read any poem written by Colin Clout in a state of rapture, "in the midst" of an epiphany. The poem we read begins with *the experience of an imagined loss,* not the loss of any gratification really experienced, but the loss of the "lineaments of gratified desire." The origin is preserved as a pure "idea of origin" and as such is removed from the temporal sequence of poetic composition. Spenser stages the scene of his inspiration, knowing he was never inspired. The poem therefore begins with any Calidore-like transgression, which is to say, anywhere, because *The Faerie Queene* is the record of perpetual *erring.* The poet has a vision of a vision—he sees himself inspired—but the experience he needs to recover is the loss itself, the moment at which the sanctity of the poetic origin could still be upheld not because the content of a vision is remembered but because a feeling of loss is remembered, the feeling of the vanished god, or the violated sacred place.

To admit the need for loss, for the experience of longing rather than the experience of vision, is to propose a fact about the nature of poetry that the sacred poet would not be inclined to accept. The transgression of Calidore leaves open the possibility that the graces may never return, which does not mean that Spenser loses faith in his inspiration but that he may never again be able to reexperience its loss:

For being gone, none can them bring in place,
But whom they of themselves list so to grace
Right sorry I (said then sir Calidore)
That my ill fortune did them hence displace.
                                        (VI.x.20)

The final displacement of the sacred place delivers the poem over to the world, the secular, and the ultimate effect of this event is the breakdown of the narrative (the freedom of the Blatant Beast) and the dismay of the poet. The modern reader may find the pathos of this loss truly moving, but that pathos might be too easily tempered by such theories as that of Northrop Frye, whose notion of displacement I mention here in order to dissociate it from the kind of event taking place in Spenser's poem.[31] It is true that the great ambition of allegory, as its etymology indicates, is to bring sacred mysteries into the marketplace, to make the "displacement" of the sacred a triumph. For the critic who locates the value of secular literature in its displacements of the sacred, an allegorical conception of poetic meaning will inevitably be pulled toward the center of critical theory, as has certainly happened in Frye's *Anatomy*. The decay and final collapse of this ideal in *The Faerie Queene* should not be glossed over, nor need it be offered as evidence that the poem fails. The last movement of *The Faerie Queene* completes its critique of origins by giving up the truth claims of allegory as a veil behind which lies a putative sacred origin. The text that emerges from this critique is the secular text, and the question that immediately presents itself concerns the authority of these human words. What authority can such a text have if it is created in the continual absence of a speaking God?

CHAPTER THREE

The Ground of Authority:
The *Mutabilitie Cantos*

Insofar as the past has been transmitted as tradition, it possesses authority; insofar as authority presents itself historically it becomes tradition. Walter Benjamin knew that the break in tradition and the loss of authority which occurred in his lifetime were irreparable, and he concluded that he had to discover new ways of dealing with the past. In this he became a master when he discovered that the transmissibility of the past had been replaced by its citability and that in place of its authority there had arisen a strange power to settle down, piecemeal, in the present and to deprive it of "peace of mind," the mindless peace of complacency.
    Hannah Arendt, "Walter Benjamin: 1892–1940," Introduction to *Illuminations*

1. *The Loss of Authority*

The achievement of *The Faerie Queene* with respect to its quest for a sacred and "authorizing" origin was to make possible a different mode of allegory in which the concepts of authority and origin can be analyzed as distinct. The intrinsic bond between them has been dissolved, or perhaps one might say that in the allegorical equation the sign of equality has been tipped over to stand vertically as a barrier. In the *Mutabilitie Cantos* the figures for authority and origin (Jove and Dame Nature) become vulnerable to the interposition of the usurper Mutabilitie (that is, she seeks literally to "come between" them). From the very beginning of the *Cantos* the special relationship between Jove and the source of his authority is put into question. Mutabilitie is the figure for disjunction itself, the opposite of "constancy" in Spenser's terms, although Mutabilitie too is paradoxically disunited from her signification in the *peripeteia* of Canto vii. She is ultimately absorbed into the authoritative rhetoric of continuity, but not before these terms have undergone considerable redefinition. More espe-cially, and I point here to the projected conclusion of this argument, the "constancy" nominally defended in the *Mutabilitie Cantos* is redefined as a quality of the secular order, while the greater discontinuity, between the sacred and the secular, is allowed to stand, untouched and even deepened.

Mutability is a perennial concern of Spenser's poetry, and yet it has been possible to discuss another of his habitual interests, the relation of authority to origin, without pausing to acknowledge the destructive energies of this harshly conceived image of time. The sudden entrance of this figure upon the center stage of Spenserian allegory is not an effect without a cause, and in fact the thematization, or allegorization, of mutability can be seen as the logical extension of the critique of sacred origins. This causation is un-folded in another, but still relevant, context by Hannah Arendt:

> Authority, resting on a foundation in the past as its unshaken cornerstone, gave the world the permanence and durability which human beings need precisely because they are mortals—the most unstable and futile beings we know of. Its loss is tantamount to the loss of the groundwork of the world, which indeed since then has begun to shift, to change and transform itself with ever-increas-ing rapidity from one shape into another, as though we were living and struggling with a Protean universe where everything at any moment can become almost anything else.[1]

The quotation refers specifically to events of our own century, but nothing in this passage would have seemed alien to Spenser. The true literary lineage of Mutabilitie begins with Proteus, who is one of those figures for whom Renaissance poets have intensely ambivalent feelings.[2] The event that was supposed to have occurred during the earlier part of the twentieth century, according to Arendt, was the "loss of authority," pre-sented as another "fall" because "since then" things have been sadly differ-ent. The world has been given over to ungovernable and perhaps even unintelligible change. It may be impossible to write history without re-course to lapsarian fictions, but I am concerned less with what "really happened" than with the fact that human beings tend to see the original Fall as an event repeated in the immediate past. We always *remember* a time before the Fall. The *Mutabilitie Cantos* obviously trade in such fictions—Mutabilitie (as one of the Titans) is vaguely associated with the original Edenic catastrophe (vi.5-6), which is then repeated, with reference to

Spenser's recent experience, as the story of Arlo Hill. The immediate past covertly described in this story seems to involve events in Ireland, which were certainly violent enough to generate some of the pessimism darkening Spenser's later work. But the *poet's* immediate past is Book VI of *The Faerie Queene*, and it is that compositional event which precipitates a "loss of authority" and intensifies the anxiety attached to the perception of mutability. The "groundwork of the world" shifts if authority in the world cannot be linked to an origin that is sacred, transcendent. An analogous subversion takes place at the level of representation, which is curiously mocked in the *Cantos*:

And by her side [Cynthia's], there ran her Page, that hight
Vesper, whom we the evening starr intend.
                    (VII. vi.9)

This coy reduction of figural language (Cynthia, Jove, Mercury, and the whole cast of "characters" are not immune) poses a serious question about what Spenser himself "intends" by such tonally ambiguous allegory. The problem of justifying or defending the secular order generalizes the more specific question of the secular text, and I want to insist here upon the continuing analogy of these terms in the *Mutabilitie Cantos*. When the poet reemerges in the epiloguizing stanzas of Canto viii, a judgment has been delivered upon poetry as well.

Many of Spenser's critics have remarked upon the unusually legalistic quality of Mutabilitie's claim to an extended rule over the heavens, and notwithstanding the episode of push and shove with Cynthia, the conduct of her case is very orderly. One wonders, until Nature clears this up, what difference it would make if she were to succeed, since the argument that she already controls even the motions of the translunary agents is *prima facie* defensible. The heavenly bodies are as subject to change as the mutually transformative elements, which are called the "groundwork. . .of all the world" (vii.25). Mutabilitie seems to be asking only that she be acknowledged by name for her power in fact. The distinction corresponds to one that political historians might wish to make between authority and power, that is, the investing of authority has more to do with the consensual recognition of a title than with actual displays of force. The point is later made that Jove possesses sufficient power to retaliate against Mutabilitie's attempted usurpation, but that such a response would be inappropriate:

But ah! if Gods should strive with flesh yfere,
Then shortly should the progeny of man
Be rooted out, if Jove should do still what he can.
(VII.vi.31)

A contest of thunderbolts does not occur precisely because Jove's *author-ity* is being challenged, and that is for Spenser a legal question. The moment reenacts a more primordial crisis of human social evolution, when the law intervenes in a conflict that would probably have ended not with winners and losers but with wholesale destruction. The anthropological pertinence of Spenser's allegory supports the contention that at some basic level the *Mutabilitie Cantos* conduct an analysis of authority, the object being to justify the rule of Jupiter. What we do not know at the moment is what he represents, and why this analysis should put so much pressure on the *boundary* between heaven and earth. In fact, the real difference between the heavenly and earthly realms is minimized in the *Cantos*; they seem to have a figural status only, and that is a point worth emphasizing. If the boundary between earth and heaven is so arbitrary, what, precisely, is being divided from what?

Mutabilitie bases her claim to move across this threshold on the priority of her lineage to Jove's, an argument from origins that should arouse suspicion after the experience of *The Faerie Queene's* critique:

"I am a daughter, by the mothers side,
Of her that is Grand-mother magnifide
Of all the Gods, great Earth, great Chaos child:
But by the fathers (be it not envide)
I greater am in bloud (whereon I build)
Then all the Gods, though wrongfully from heaven exiled.

"For Titan (as ye all acknowledge must)
Was Saturnes elder brother by birth-right:
Both, sonnes of Uranus: but by unjust
And guilefull meanes, through Corybantes slight,
The younger thrust the elder from his right:
Since which, thou Jove, injuriously hast held
The Heavens rule from Titans sonnes by might;
And them to hellish dungeons downe hast feld;
Witnesse ye Heavens the truth of all that I have teld."
(VII.vi.26-27)

These lines must have had a most extraordinary effect upon contemporary readers familiar with the tangles of genealogy. It is difficult to overestimate the importance of genealogy, accurate, fudged, or totally fabricated, to anyone with "pretensions" in Renaissance England—including, of course, the dubious House of Tudor.[3] In the mythological context of the *Cantos*, Jove has no argument by which to dispute the accuracy of Mutabilitie's account, and if priority of origin *were* the true ground of authority, he would have no choice but to step down. The fact that he does not subverts the cherished doctrine of primogeniture, but, more importantly, severs the defense of authority from all appeals to temporal priority, at least at this point in the poem. Jove's rebuttal is worth examining in this light:

> "But thee faire Titans child, I rather weene,
>   Through some vaine errour or inducement light,
>   To see that mortall eyes have never seene;
>   Or through ensample of thy sisters might,
>   Bellona; whose great glory thou doost spight,
>   Since thou has seene her dreadfull power belowe,
>   Mongst wretched men (dismaide with her affright)
>   To bandie Crownes, and Kingdomes to bestowe:
> And sure thy worth, no lesse then heres doth seem to showe.

> "But wote thou this, thou hardy Titanesse,
>   That not the worth of any living wight
>   May challenge ought in Heavens interesse;
>   Much lesse the Title of old Titans Right:
>   For, we by Conquest of our soveraine might,
>   And by eternall doome of Fates decree,
>   Have wonne the Empire of the Heavens bright...
>   (VII. vi.32-33)

Jove's bloody rise to power needs little more than a passing reference ("conquest") after Mutabilitie's lurid rehearsal, and to the argument of the *fait accompli*, Jove can only add a very vague but important invocation of Fate's "eternall" decree. The argument from an origin in time turns out to be something of a scandal, but the doom of Fate is outside time. Jove makes a halting gesture toward grounding his authority in some ontologically other mode of existence. These lines introduce the possibility of two realms that really are different, and if that is so, then the division between heaven and earth, the lunar threshold, may be a figure for that more important and mysterious division. The nature of Mutabilitie's crime as a transgression—the immediate threat is to Cynthia, the lunar boundary—is dimly perceived by Jove in the first line of the passage quoted, where her "vaine errour" is described as a desire to "see that mortal eyes have never seene." The further attribution of envy as a motive defines the limits of Jove's insight, since it is doubtful, given what we have just read, that Mutabilitie simply wants more power. But neither is it anywhere indicated that she wants to see something she has never seen before, and the incongruity of this line dislodges it from its context. The act of transgression can be represented as a visionary experience, and in fact precipitates the epiphany of Dame Nature. The remainder of the *Cantos* is concerned in one fashion or another with visionary experiences, and at the moment I am content to indicate the apparent incongruity of this idea in the context of the larger allegorical examination of usurped authority.

2. *The Curse of Babel*

In the following paragraphs I would like to step back from my text a little distance in order to appropriate a set of terms contained in an essay by Owen Barfield. The essay is called "Imagination and Inspiration," and in addition to its obvious relevance to the more historical language of this study, its reflections upon the idea of the "threshold" will provide a useful conceptual context.[4] I have already pointed to the mediational function of imagination in Renaissance thought, and consequently the inherent "betweenness" of its status in psychological theory. I share with Barfield a concern for rehistoricizing the concept while denying to it a privileged status as a faculty, synchronically conceived. Barfield emphasizes that the "essential, the distinguishing feature of imagination, as such, is that the whole concept of it is founded on the assumed intransigence of that threshold between mind and matter," an idea for which the Cartesianism of the seventeenth century provides the evidential basis. The image in the mind is said to copy a material sensation (later, in fact, this will become a definition of ideas) but never to move back across the threshold upon which sensations impinge. The "assumed intransigence" burdened Descartes with a "mind-body" problem, for which he provided some shifty solutions. The problem may already have been implicit in Renaissance perspective, with its three-dimensional "extension" and hypothetical "point" of view. This much said, we may leave imagination and Cartesianism out of the picture for the present and consider the question of what "intransigence" attaches to the idea of the threshold.

Barfield's very anti-Cartesian assumption (shared to some extent by Spenser as a *pre*-Cartesian) is that the world can be divided into ontologically different areas and that the barriers between them are permeable. Nevertheless, most crossing movements, or attempted crossings, are not successful, and these failures are of two kinds. In the first case:

> If. . . we endeavor to speak, or even to think, on the further side in ideas formed only on this side, in categories of thought and modes of speech, which are almost by definition only applicable to this side, then an unhappy consequence seems to follow. I venture to nickname this unhappy consequence "the curse of Babel" because the Tower of Babel may be seen as the symbol of an endeavor to penetrate a threshold—the threshold between earth and heaven—by using materials exclusively manufactured on the hither side of it.

The "opposite error"—and it is a mark of Barfield's spiritualism that he calls it an error—is named the "curse of Zacharias. . . who, you will recall, was stricken dumb on coming out of the Temple—that is, on recrossing the threshold."[5] The threshold to which these two stories refer is the one that Spenser seems to evade in his allegory: the division between natural and supernatural (remembering that the heaven/earth distinction is drawn entirely within the pagan system, which, as a whole, is opposed to the Christian-transcendent, and non-localized realm of Dame Nature). Barfield wants to restore this division and its permeability, a strategy that need not be endorsed here except insofar as it has provided us with a means of perceiving the threshold in historical motion. The immutability of the translunar world, for example, was already doubtful in Spenser's time, and hence Mutabilitie's challenge reflects a modern anxiety. The line between heaven and earth retains a shaky figural status, and the subversion of this threshold threatens every threshold with reduction to a merely linguistic barrier. The result is a condition of semantic flux; you cannot step through the same door twice. Mythology is a vast warehouse of threshold figures, but no one of these figures can really stand for what the Christian believes to lie beyond that threshold. Spenser's commitment to redactions of pagan myth creates an ultimate obstruction to the visionary impulse, as the episode of Faunus and Diana, to which we now turn, evinces.

Some points of intersection with the enclosing allegory are immediately evident: Faunus' desire to see Diana naked associates him, somewhat in the manner of a Shakespearean subplot, with Mutabilitie's act of aggression against Diana in her lunar aspect, and this story is projected out of Jove's allusion to voyeurism as a motive. Faunus corrupts the Nymph Molanna (parodying the serpent's temptations of Eve) in order that "he close might view / That never any saw save onely one." The "one" referred to in this line is Actaeon, whose story provides the model for Spenser's free variation. The presence of Ovid's redaction here, as a determining pre-text, is undeniable—the reader senses that the problem of the *Metamorphoses* has drawn Spenser into a very extensive engagement with Ovid[6]—but the various myths feeding into the narrative line of the *Cantos* are surprisingly confused and contradictory. The subject has been studied by Richard Ringler, in an article whose useful hypothesis I will quote here. Ringler's purpose is "to show how Spenser in the Faunus episode rejects protean change by establishing a highly Ovidian atmosphere, conflating three stories of metamorphosis, and then denying three times that metamorphosis occurs."[7]

I will set aside some of Ringler's details and examples in order to consider mainly the nature of the reference to Actaeon and Diana. Until the mention of this myth, the reader is reasonably certain that Ovid's *Metamorphoses* has given Spenser the structure of the Faunus story, but the full reference complicates the genealogy:

The simple maid did yield to him anone;
  And eft him placed where he close might view
That never any saw, save onely one;
Who, for his hire to so foole-hardy dew,
Was of his hounds devoured in Hunters hew.
             (VII.vi.45)

This text departs from Ovid in two important respects: Spenser's appropriation of a moral from Natalis Comes (Actaeon's foolhardiness in contradistinction to his innocence in Ovid), and the fact that in Spenser's version, Actaeon is killed dressed in hunter's clothing, not metamorphosed into a stag. Faunus is not transformed either, but he is covered in deerskins, as though in *fake* metamorphosis. Ringler says that Spenser rejects metamorphosis and this point is well taken. The parodic allusion can be turned against the pagan scheme, thereby puncturing the mythological text and allowing for the appearance of Christian themes through the rents, as it were, in the redaction of myth. I want to insist upon Spenser's adherence to versions of classical mythos, the "story," because there are a number of interesting uses being made of allusion to the *form* of pagan myth. There is a sense in which the obvious revision, or obvious *faking*, of the pagan mythos is being made to carry a large burden of meaning.

The context of the *Metamorphoses* as a poem establishing continuity in the midst of flux conditions responses to even those texts where the specific *version* of the Ovidian story is rejected. Let us hypothesize, then, that the *Cantos* allude not simply to Actaeon, or Arethusa, but also to a mode of Ovidian writing that I will call secularized mythology. Ovid's anthology of god stories does not aspire to the authority of a sacred text, despite the misreading of medieval Christianizers, who conjectured that at least some of the Holy Spirit's revelation had been left over for classical authors. The Bible exerted a gravitational attraction upon analogous texts like the *Metamorphoses,* whose meanings were developed allegorically as a translation of the primary signs in the sacred text. The history of Ovid's poem is a relevant consideration here, although only as a general background to the question of what Spenser means by engaging the tone and metamorphic impulse of the *Metamorphoses* so closely while deviating from its usual method of closure. The later "sanctification" of Ovid (*Ovide moralisé*) seems to us now so contrary to the spirit of the work, which accepts the burden of an awesome religious tradition, and deliberately lightens that burden by serving up the old myths largely divested of their numinous aura. The loss of the power inhering in the sacred text is recompensed in the humanizing of the tales themselves, and the metamorphoses, formerly signatures of divine interventions, are now closer to figures for human responses to the fact of mutability, or the uncontrollable contingency of circumstances. As has been argued in recent scholarship, metamorphosis can easily be taken too seriously in Ovid, when the poem in fact displays a multifarious use of its figurative devices, usually in the service of a sophisticated psychology.[8] Anthropomorphism as a *literary* device is self-consciously secular.

Spenser would of course consider metamorphosis a serious (if mistaken) proposition about the relation of the divine to the human, but it is also likely that his reading of Ovid penetrated through the layers of medieval and Renaissance allegory to the worldly intent of Ovidian redaction. If this is true, then Spenser has a very good reason to declare that Ovid is not the model for his story but only another variant version, even an incorrect one (that is, Actaeon was *not* metamorphosed). Ringler believes that Spenser took the allegorical content of his reading of the Actaeon myth from Statius, who presents Actaeon in the Faunus-like act of creeping forth "from his unholy spying-place to profane, O Delia, thy chaste fountains."[9] The "profanation" becomes the reason for Actaeon's punishment as it does Faunus', and the parallel extends to the structure of the entire episode: Arlo Hill was once a sacred place, and as a consequence of its violation, it is now profane. The divergence from Ovid amounts to a contradiction. The Actaeon of the *Metamorphoses* does not profane any sacred place, and the Goddess Diana responds to his accidental intrusion with a severity that elicits a measure of disapproval:

> Rumor in ambiguo est; aliis violentior aequo
> visa dea est, alii laudant dignamque severa
> virginitate vocant: pars invenit utraque causas.
> (III.253-55)

> Common talk wavered this way and that: to some
> the goddess seemed more cruel than was just; others
> called her act worthy of her austere virginity; both
> sides found good reasons for their judgment. (Loeb translation)

If Diana suffers a violation, the seriousness of that crime is greatly diminished by the irony of the narrative. In the confrontation between divine and human values, the rational-human displaces the arbitrary-divine, whatever the outcome of the story, and this is the usual effect of Ovid's "secular mythology." Spenser's story of "profanation" incorporates the secularizing movement of its Ovidian pre-text but points to an opposing value judgment. We may read Spenser's Faunus story as itself a reading of the *Metamorphoses*: From Spenser's point of view, it is as though Ovid profaned the stories of the gods by intruding upon his sacred sources like the foolish Actaeon, or the still more foolish Faunus. Spenser wishes to avoid a similar violation, an intention that forces him to convey his meaning by further redactions of pagan myth rather than by direct treatment of Christian texts. This type of redaction is a necessary limitation for Spenser, who could not, as Milton later will, rewrite the sacred text by means of interpolation.

For Spenser, the gods do not take leave of this world so lightly; the Diana of his *Cantos* is more just than violent, and her Astraea-like departure is a serious loss, a figuring of a more disturbing absence. The violence that provokes the flight of the goddess occurs in the stanza recording Faunus' response to his "vision" of the naked Diana:

> There Faunus saw that pleased much his eye,
>   And made his hart to tickle in his brest,
>   That for great joy of some-what he did spy,
>   He could him not containe in silent rest;
>   But breaking forth in laughter, loud profest
>   His foolish thought. A foolish Faune indeed,
>   That couldst not hold thy selfe so hidden blest,
>   But wouldest needs thine owne conceit areed.
> Babblers unworthy been of so divine a meed.
>   (VII. vi.46)

There are many curious things about this stanza, not the least of which is the incongruous tone. The increasingly comic tone of Canto vi deserves some attention here, because it threatens to overwhelm the burden of loss implied by a straightforward reading of the narrative. At this point we are also uncertain about the gravity of Faunus' crime, but we can give it a familiar tag: Faunus is guilty of "laughing in church." The nature of this impropriety is obscure, to say the least. Our willingness to condemn is softened by an instinctive urge to sympathize, perhaps because the exclusion of so basically human a response is disturbing. The gods really do diminish us to enlarge themselves, and it may well be that the boundary of the sacred place is meant to defend against the hunger of the gods for the sacrifice of our human pleasures. This uneasiness may also contribute to the magnification of Faunus' crime in the stanza quoted. The "silent rest" is too unmistakably a Sabbath demeanor, and the entire stanza heavily underscores the epiphanic nature of the experience, spoiled though it may be.

The language of religious experience, the "hidden blessedness," the "divine meed," vexes the question of incongruity, and one wonders how even the possibility of religious experience can be sustained in a scene that degenerates into comic voyeurism, especially as the "some-what" that

Faunus sees is surely the genitalia of the goddess. The image itself is part of an elaborate iconography (a Spenserian precedent would be the *mons veneris* of the Garden of Adonis), the intent of which is to link the idea of a secret, sacred place to the part of the body which is always covered. (The word "some-what" is also a "covering.") It is possible that Spenser is at least trying here to incorporate into a developing argument about the very nature of sacred experience the literary pose he perceives to be most antithetical to that aspiration. The *Fowre Hymnes* enact a similar transformation of the most human into the most humanly divine, and the play of dialectical changes upon themes of vision and blindness in those poems is an instructive gloss upon the more complex strategy of the *Mutabilitie Cantos*. I would argue that the failure of this strategy generates the incongruity of tone that pervades the episode, as vision falls back into mere voyeurism.

Faunus' crime might be described as a voyeuristic rape, or an attempted transgression of a threshold whose true significance, misconceived by him, is religious. In the last line he is called a *babbler*, a word that has attracted to itself, though the etymology is false, the curse of Babel. Spenser may not have known that the word *Babel* actually transliterates the Semitic *babi-li*, which means "gate of God," though the confusion of these two meanings is particularly fortuitous. Laughter, as a kind of failed verbalizing, can be a hysterical response to an overload of sensation, such as one might expect to experience at the threshold. It has a much closer relation to its opposite, silence, than might at first be supposed. The eventuality of being stricken "dumb" or "speechless" by an intense experience is equally likely, and yet we feel it is also more appropriate. Faunus ought to have remained silent, suffering what Barfield calls the "curse of Zacharias." The *Cantos* propose no third alternative to the terms of this dilemma. The remainder of this analysis will be conducted under the rubric of the response Faunus failed to make.

3. *Silence and Rest*

With the introduction of "rest" as a motif that will be developed into the decrescendo coda of the *Mutabilitie Cantos*, the apparently incongruous meanings determining the plot and subplot of the poem can be envisioned as a whole. Schematically they would be as follows, with the threshold represented by a simple mark of both division and relation:

    nakedness——veil, dress
    silence——language
    rest——motion

The term "motion" generalizes the problem of mutability according to the
formula given in the ultimate stanza: "For all that moveth doth in change
delight." The authority of allegory might be defended as the strength of
the relation between one side and the other, but what the *Cantos* allegorically represent is the "intransigence" of the threshold. Mutabilitie touches
language and the "veil of allegory" with the *restlessness* of her aspiration.
Having said this, I would withdraw the schematization, or suggest that all
of the terms on the right side can be collapsed into the mark of division-
relation. They constitute the threshold itself, or the possibility of meaning,
and this is the significant revelation toward which the *Cantos* are moving.
The "dark conceit" of allegory finds itself in competition with silence as
two incompatible gestures toward a reality of ultimate value. The degeneration of motion into mutation, language into inarticulate laughter, and
the veil or garment into the impenetrable barrier, blocking movement in
both directions, compels the retreat of allegory (or its movement into self-
critical irony), and raises the uncomfortable possibility that the "veiling"
of truth is a darkening of already lucid manifestations of the divine in the
world. The idea was not unknown to the more radical wing of English
Protestantism, and their intense mistrust of tropes and rhetorical devices is
useful to recall here. Spenser does not completely ally himself with the
linguistic radicalism of some of his contemporaries, yet an acknowledgment of their "pure" feelings perhaps accounts for the valedictory tone of
the *Cantos*. This poem gives up its aspiration to vision in the very completion of its summary movement—Mutabilitie's calendar of changes—but
only as a last poetic gambit. A sense of what might be achieved in the
compendious repetition of poetic subject matter *as* subject matter can be
seen in the passage describing Dame Nature's garment, where the allegorical image is foregrouded as the veil itself. No attempt is made to suggest
in any detail what lies behind the veil, and this strategy produces what I
will call a "bright conceit":

    Whether she man or woman inly were,
    That could not any creature well descry:
    For, with a veile that wimpled every where,
Her head and face was hid, that mote to none appeare.

That some doe say was so by skill devized,
  To hide the terror of her uncouth hew,
  From mortall eyes that should be sore agrized;
  For that her face did like a Lion shew,
  That eye of wight could not indure to view:
  But others tell that it so beautious was,
  And round about such beames of splendor threw,
  That it the Sunne a thousand times did pass,
Ne could be seene, but like an image in a glass.

That well may seemen true: for, well I weene
  That this same day, when she on Arlo sat,
  Her garment was so bright and wondrous sheene,
  That my fraile wit cannot devize to what
  It to compare, nor finde like stuffe to that,
  As those three sacred Saints, though else most wise,
  Yet on mount Thabor quite their wits forgat,
  When they their glorious Lord in strange disguise
Transfigured sawe; his garments so did daze their eyes.
                        (VII.vii.5-7)

Dame Nature's features are not "subject" to description at all, only the effect of those features upon viewers if the veil were to be removed. Here is the classic justification of allegory concluding in a typical claim for representational status: "Ne could be seene but like an image in a glass." The allegorical image is a partial transparency or a reflecting surface—both metaphors are common. But is that what we see in the following stanzas? The foregrounding of the veil poses a more difficult problem of representation, much like the linguistic conundrum of giving the "meaning of meaning." In this instance the figure for figuration cannot itself become the subject of further expansion and hence we have reached a ground:

... my fraile wit cannot devize to what
It to compare, nor find like stuffe to that...

Being itself the "like stuffe" of predication, the veil becomes a bright conceit, illuminating nothing but itself, as though both interior and exterior disappeared in the brilliance of pure surface.

Stanza 7 "compares" this veil to the garment of Christ at the Transfiguration, but of course there is no difference between these two garments and therefore no comparison. Figuration is itself transfigured. The Apostles did not see "their glorious Lord" in the nakedness of his divinity. They saw a surface, whose otherness ("strange *disguise*") brooked no penetration by human vision. As they were descending Mt. Tabor, they were told by Christ to "tell the vision to no man, until the Son of Man is risen." The Transfiguration, like the Resurrection it prefigures (and we can hear the evangelist harmonizing the two events in the latter clause of Jesus' injunction) appears to be a major point of mythological impact upon the historical narrative of the Gospel, and therefore just the right analogy for the entrance of Dame Nature into Spenser's more displaced redaction of an original epiphany. Obviously the Apostles would no more have been able to remain silent about the event on Mt. Tabor than they were about the empty tomb, but is there not a sense in which their speech began immediately to betray the vision, whatever it was, they were so privileged or doomed to experience? That betrayal forms no part of the intention of religious discourse; nor is it the intention of allegory to lie. Spenser must pay tribute here to the better way, to silence itself, and this must be the meaning of that allegorical erasure, which is his bright conceit. Visionary experiences have perhaps always been interpreted as experiences of the divine, and not, as Spenser more interestingly intuits, of the threshold. The text on the Transfiguration quite explicitly demarcates an upper boundary of the expressible in art, as though a finger had been drawn across the sublunary sphere of language.

The ambiguous identity of Dame Nature, our uncertainty about the *allos* she is intended to figure, can be adduced here as further evidence of a strategic indirection. Nature is an avatar of the Sabbath God, and she adjudges the petty infighting of the pagan deities, but she belongs neither to the pagan nor to the Christian hierarchy. She is rather the historical interface. Her immediate disappearance behind the veil makes us wonder about what her presence really means, since our perception of her apart from the veil is always indirect, even when, presumably, her subjects are said to look at her face. If this illusion of her presence is intensified as a result of the foregrounding of the surface itself, then the value of the poem as surface, the ground of its authority, is precisely this foregrounding. The presentation of the veil modulates easily in the following stanza into the interplay of texts, the continuity of textual reference, as folds or layers in the veil of Dame Nature:

So hard it is for any living wight,
  All her array and vestiments to tell,
  That old Dan Geffrey (in whose gentle spright
  The pure wel head of Poesie did dwell)
  In his *Foules parley* durst not with it mel,
  But it transferd to Alane, who he thought
  Had in his Plaint of kindes described it well:
  Which who will read set forth so as it ought,
Go seek he out that Alane where he may be sought.

                    (VII.vii.9)

There are two arguments I would like to make about this passage, one having to do with the "true" textual history of Dame Nature, the other defining the authority of the text which diverges from the true history.

1. An account of the iconographic history of Dame Nature is given in Alice Miskimin's *The Renaissance Chaucer*, and I am drawing upon the details of her work in the following sentences. Miskimin's book has the advantage of recognizing the literary historical importance of this passage, as well as its crucial meaning in the *Mutabilitie Cantos*. The seemingly deferential pose of Stanza 9, she argues, "unobtrusively conceals the originality of its richness, far more ornate and complex than its predecessors."[10] Miskimin assimilates this fact to the larger argument that Spenser's art asserts an autonomy over the domains of nature and art incompatible with the medieval pose of deference he seems to be imitating in Stanza 9. The use of the inexpressibility topos to enhance while partially concealing such ambitions is clever, and points to the genuinely "modern" character of Spenser's poetry, but in this text, most especially in this passage, one wonders whether the topos is not being taken seriously as defining a limitation. The distinction between nature with a small "n" and Spenser's Dame Nature, who is *outside* of her domain, adds a complex irony to the names standing here as both poetic "subjects" and personified "subjects" of a transcendent ruler. Why should the topos of inexpressibility become attached to Dame Nature, whose very name would seem to assure the continuity of language as representation of things-in-the-world? In the traditional texts, Nature is more closely associated with the idea of *anima mundi*, a pantheistic deity whose transcendence is only partial. This does not seem to be the case in Spenser's poem, and I would therefore resist the

conclusion that the quantity of words concerning Dame Nature adds up to a description *of* her.

A second detail will clarify this problem: In most medieval depictions of the Goddess Nature, her gown is represented as torn. This gown is usually embroidered with allegorical images and indeed it is a perfect emblem of itself: the allegorical text. In *De Planctu Naturae*, it is the poet who is responsible for tearing the veil. Miskimin reminds us that Chaucer omitted this detail, also Spenser, and that in the interim between Alanus and Spenser the symbols on the gown have disappeared.[11] The Renaissance poet would not be inclined to follow Alanus in his typically medieval derogation of poetry and in fact Boccaccio simply inverts the story given in his sources by having the *enemies* of poetry rip her gown; and, "as puffed up as if they knew the whole subject of divinity, they rush forth from the sacred house, setting such mischief affoot among ignorant people as only the wise can calculate."[12]

In Boccaccio's view, as I discussed in chapter 1, the poem can transcend commentary to become a kind of sacred text. The fact that neither Chaucer nor Spenser present Nature's veil as torn points forward to an increase in the authority of the poetic text, but the fact that Spenser also links himself to the medieval topos of modesty tugs the argument in the opposite direction. The violation of the threshold, a pretense to the authority of revelation, is certainly rejected, and Spenser indicates just this in acknowledging Chaucer as his chosen precursor (that is, he is more like Chaucer in declining to describe the veil than like Alanus). The foregrounding of the surface itself announces the emergence of that text we have come to know as "literature," an event that is always occurring, but whose nature is here most sharply defined: Literature emerges in an effort to distinguish itself from the sacred text, from the word of God, without giving up a *scriptural* authority.

We begin to understand, finally, what is at stake in the defense of Jove, because whatever authority Spenser acquires for himself in the act of citation, that authority is simply another expression of what Jove represents. Nature's authority is beyond dispute or defense but some authority at a lower or intermediate level is being defended, and that authority can be associated with what remains of words and text, what remains after the ambiguous doom of transcendent Nature: "Let things continue to be as they have been."

2. My second argument, which follows necessarily from the first, begins with a recollection of Dame Nature's mention in Book II of *The Faerie Queene*. The passage is already familiar to us:

Of those [springs] some were so from their source indewed
  By great Dame Nature, from whose fruitfull pap
  Their welheads spring...
(II.ii.6)

The mystique of origins, now regarded as an exploded mythology, yields up metaphors in the service of an intertextual history:

That old Dan Geffrey (in whose gentle spright
The pure wel head of Poesie did dwell...

The transference of the metaphor, already begun in *The Faerie Queene*, is like the delegation of authority. The transcendent origin will now recede with Dame Nature, "whither no man wist," and in its place will be found Nature, not the deity, but the world itself. In retrospect, it seems clear that the narrative of the *Mutabilitie Cantos* has been structured by Spenser's ambivalent approach toward a moment of apocalypse, the final content and meaning of "revelation." The deferral of this apocalypse restores to poetry its only *materia poetica*: time. The *Cantos* discover at this point their illegitimate confusion of time and mutability, perhaps the most startling forgetting in the poem, a forgetting of Spenser's own beginning in *The Shepheardes Calender*. In the pageant of changes making up the bulk of Canto vii, it is not so much mutation as time that is represented, and Nature's verdict declares that within time there is continuity; or rather, within continuity, like the unmoving face of the clock, there is the motion of time.[13] Mutabilitie forgets the fact of continuity, in this larger sense, just as Jove forgets the discontinuity that established his lordship.

    The poem projects out of these two figures two models of tradition and change, one of which, in order to maintain the authority of tradition, forgets the violence of change; the other of which forgets the fact of continuity in its vision of history as a discontinuous series of violent moments. Mutabilitie is the poet of the latter view, and she does produce a beautiful poem on temporal change; discontinuity is her song: death, chance, and time. But she forgets that the seasons return. That Spenser incorporates and does not reject the Mutabilitie poet within him is surely the reason why Dame Nature does not punish Mutabilitie for her attempted transgression. The arbitration of Nature corrects the mutual misunderstanding of Jove and Mutabilitie by asserting a more authoritative rhetoric of continuity, which does not forget the fact of violence, but absorbs this violence (even the wolves and thieves who inherit Arlo Hill) by deferring the apocalypse (the return of Dame Nature) that would end the violence forever.

The rhetoric of continuity established by the citation of literary *auctors* (already, it is worth recalling, an archaic gesture) subsumes divergence from tradition, even permits such divergence, without incurring the anxiety of the "text without authority." Spenser knows very well that his distortions are essential to his meaning; yet he no longer sees this as a boast of autonomy. It has even been suggested, a discontinuity indeed, that he never read *De Planctu Naturae* (though this seems unlikely). The quest for ultimate origins ("Go seeke he out that Alane where he may be sought") is amusingly frustrated in a reference that is deliberately vague; Alane shares the uncertainty of his location with those transcendent sources, as difficult to invoke as he is to find. And yet the uncertainty, just because it is not lamented, can be read another way. What matters to Spenser here is less the authority of Alane than of literature itself. It is that authority (continuity) to which Spenser defers, and which authorizes even his most extravagant divergences and distortions.

Now this position would seem curiously modern were it not for the fact that we can enclose the entire rhetoric of continuity within a larger structural discontinuity, implicit throughout this argument and explicit in the epiloguizing stanzas of Canto viii. These lines perform for *The Faerie Queene* the same function as Ovid's epilogue to his book of changes. There Ovid finds a life in the text for the name of the poet; the *nomen* survives even the death of the *numen*, a triumph we feel strongly in the poet's defiance of Jove:

Iamque opus exegi, quod nec Iovis ira nec ignis
nec peterit ferrum nec edax abolere vetustas.
cum volet, illa dies, quae nil nisi corporis huius
ius habet, incerti spatium mihi finiat aevi;

parte tamen meliore mei super alta perennis
astra ferar, nomenque erit indelebile nostrum
quaque patet domitis Romana potentia terris,
ore legar populi, perque omnia saecula fama,
sequid habent veri vatum praesagia, vivam.
(XV.871–79)

And now my work is done, which neither the wrath of Jove, nor fire, nor sword, not the gnawing tooth of time shall ever be able to undo. When it will, let that day come which has no power save over this mortal frame, and end the span of my uncertain years. Still in my better part I shall have an undying name. Wherever Rome's power extends over the conquered world, I shall have mention on men's lips, and, if the prophecies of bards have any truth, through all the ages shall I live in fame. (Loeb translation)

The expression "through all the ages" is given by Ovid as the word from which we derive our "secular": *per omnia saecula...* This may be no more than an accident, and yet I think it one of the more singular occurrences in the history of language. Why, after all, should our very Christian notion of the worldly, everything opposed to the sacred, be conveyed by a word meaning simply a "period of time"? We might oppose time to eternity in much of our pious utterance, but we habitually forget that time is hidden in our word for the not sacred. If the poet cannot escape the temporality of his medium, there cannot be sacred poetry. The *Mutabilitie Cantos* move inexorably to the enforcing of this dichotomy, redeeming time only insofar as it works toward its ultimate undoing. The "dilation of being" referred to by Nature can only be seen on the hither side of the sacred as a condition of entropy, a slowing down of the restless movement of things to the "time" when "all shall rest eternally":

When I bethinke me on that speech whyleare,
  Of Mutability, and well it way:
  Me seemes, that though she all unworthy were
  Of the Heav'ns Rule; yet very sooth to say,
  In all things else she beares the greatest sway.
  Which makes me loath this state of life so tickle,
  And love of things so vaine to cast away;
  Whose flowring pride, so fading and so fickle,
Short Time shall soon cut down with his consuming sickle.

Then gin I thinke on that which Nature sayd,
  Of that same time when no more Change shall be,
  But stedfast rest of all things firmely stayd
  Upon the pillours of Eternity,
  That is contrayr to Mutabilitie:
  For, all that moveth, doth in Change delight:
  But thence-forth all shall rest eternally
  With Him that is the God of Sabbaoth hight:
O that great Sabbaoth God, graunt me that Sabaoths sight.
                                        (VII.viii.1-2)

Weighed against the "pillars of eternity" a rhetoric of textual continuity seems a small victory. But it is the only ground of authority on this side of the impassable boundary of the sacred, the same ground, perhaps, that Nature "still viewed" before she spoke. Until or unless a voice on the other side speaks again, the human word remains its own authority, built up out of past voices that declare their continuity with the present merely by continuing to speak. These words, or the works constituted by them, become canonical in the very process of acknowledgment, as Spenser acknowledges Chaucer, who acknowledges Alanus de Insulis. The survival, the *vivam* of the text, is declared by the revelation of the veil as "bright conceit"—but nothing more. Spenser is very close here to a Hebraic view of the secular order, a good exposition of which is given by the anthropologist, Henri Frankfort, in discussing a text from the Old Testament. He remarks about the Song of Hannah in 1 Samuel 2:

> Notice that the last verses state explicitly that God created the existing social order; but, quite characteristically this order did not derive any sacredness, any value, from its divine origin. The sacredness and value remain attributes of God alone, and the violent changes of fortune observed in social life are but signs of God's omnipotence.[14]

I believe we are to understand Nature's affirmation of the Jovian hierarchy in the same light. Jove as authority, or Spenser as author, must seek a human ground in the continuity of the human word. Jove is related to the earliest rulers of the heavens as Spenser is to Alanus de Insulis: an inheritor of power in spite of violence, usurpation, and discontinuity.

I have called Mutabilitie a poet, but her mistake is really that she does not know she is a poet. She reads the calendar of changes too literally as her creation; and she has written herself so completely into the text that she cannot conceive of any other order: "For heaven and earth I both alike do deeme." The pagan gods are guardians at the gate, protecting the inviolability of the sacred threshold against the refusal of Mutabilitie even to see that threshold. The element of temporality which is the true subject of poetry can be understood only within such conceptual bounds, or *at* the threshold, we might say. Anything other than the vastly inclusive calendar is outside, sacred and unrepresentable.

Outside too is the rest promised by the poet's undiminished visionary longing, a longing to be free of the play of images. This desire is balanced equally against the "delight" in change and motion, the "secular." The concluding stance, though it seems to return to an almost medieval pluralism, a weariness with both the freedom and bondage of the human word, wins its authenticity through the agon of a very modern aspiration. Milton, to whom the remainder of this book is devoted, challenges the intransigence of the threshold with the zeal of a prophet, *Moses Anglicus* as he styled himself. He begins, or defines his beginning, with the name of Spenser, repeating in that gesture the Spenserian deference to Chaucer and Alanus. We may want to see, as the story of Milton's very complex lineage unfolds, a momentous discontinuity in that embrace.

CHAPTER FOUR

"Some Superior Power": Spenser and Shakespeare in Milton's *Comus*

The Stars with deep amaze
Stand fixt in stedfast gaze,
  Bending one way their precious influence,
And will not take their flight,
For all the morning light...

Milton, "On the Morning of Christ's Nativity"

1. *The Voice of Comus*

Among the many poems of Milton not intended to be read or produced as drama, a large number manifest a submerged but easily detectable dramatic structure. Voices succeed or interrupt one another in a pattern for which "Lycidas" might be taken as the model: the reader does not quite know where to close the quotation marks. The poem as a "succession of voices" suggests an analogy to literary history, which, if it can be said to have an intelligible structure, might be understood as poets talking and listening to one another. The power of Milton's voice is confirmed by the number of poets who have listened to him, and by the fact that he so often gravitates toward the center of literary histories; but the source of that power has much to do with Milton's own ear, "touched" by the poets who talk to him. If the *Maske at Ludlow* is a drama in the obvious sense (and even, we must assume, a successful production), it is also a dialogue whose speakers are not the children and friends of a noble family, but poets of the English Renaissance. I propose to consider here that more interior drama.

As Milton's annotators have exhaustively evidenced, *Comus* is particularly rich in poetic voices, both those that we call "Miltonic" and a crowd of other presences whose identity is established by allusion. I begin with the voice of Comus himself, where the masque pauses to consider the fluid relation of sounds and meanings. The dancing of Comus and his rout, we remember, is interrupted by the entrance of the Lady, and Comus hears in the sound of her footsteps a meaning that defines by antithesis the salient quality of his own language:

Break off, break off, I feel the different pace
Of some chaste footing near about this ground.
                    (145-46)

Different because the Lady is not dancing, but *chaste* for reasons that only Comus, as yet, can tell us. The lady calls the noises she has heard a "tumult of loud Mirth," and indeed *mirth* is the most interesting and significant term one might bring into association with the speech that introduces Comus' anti-masque. Reading through the invocatory octosyllabics with which Comus begins this speech, we are reminded of that other poem written under the aegis of mirth, less daemonic certainly, but the true antecedent of the enchanter's "allegro" verses:

Meanwhile welcome Joy and Feast
Midnight shout and revelry,
Tipsy dance and jollity.
Braid your Locks with rosy Twine
Droppings odors, dropping Wine.
Rigor now is gone to bed,
And Advice with scrupulous head,
Strict Age, and sour Severity,
With their grave Saws in slumber lie.
                    (102-10)

Comus' exordium edges the negative shades of meaning in "L'Allegro" a little further into darkness. Conversely the Attendant Spirit descends from the "daemons" of "Il Penseroso" to become in the *Maske* the "unseen Genius of the Wood." The *l'allegro* voice is heard most strongly in the last couplet of Comus' speech, where it is precisely and unmistakably recollected:

Come, knit hands and beat the ground
In a light fantastic round.

(*Comus*, 143-44)

Come, and trip it as ye go
On the light fantastic toe.

("L'Allegro," 34-35)

Our habitual, if often slightly trivializing metaphor for the way in which allusion works—echo—has to be taken seriously in Milton's poetry, both in relation to texts by other poets, and earlier Miltonic texts. What are we to make of such a close relation between Comus' words and the language of "L'Allegro"?

We might begin by putting a little pressure on the word "fantastic" as it is used in "L'Allegro" and *Comus*. As a characterization of dancing, the word is not more than appropriate, but as a conventionally "literary" word, it conveys specific tonal information. The association of fancy (desire) and fantasy (imagination), as we have seen, provided Spenser with a fundamental motif in *The Faerie Queene*: the mental self-delusion that so frequently leads his heroes astray, projected allegorically in Book I as "error," or more ambiguously as Phantastes in Book II. Milton of course inherits other, not so heavily loaded meanings of "fantastic," but his inclination in *Comus* is to take the word more in its Spenserian sense. Its appearance in the masque is less innocent than its identical predecessor, as the context of besieged chastity engages the context of "unreproved pleasures free." The latter phrase gives us the proper context for reading such passages as the Hymeneal celebration in "L'Allegro":

There let *Hymen* oft appear
In Saffron robe, with Taper clear,
And pomp, and feast, and revelry,
With mask, and antique Pageantry—
Such sights as youthful Poets dream
On Summer eves by haunted stream.

(125-30)

The masque is the very genre in which we would least expect the triumph of chastity, and the later Miltonic exercise (the "mask of chastity") chastens the genre itself—the very form in which youthful poets are apt to excel. Similarly, Comus' "fantastic round" (described as "antic" in the stage directions of the Bridgewater manuscript)[1] darkens the taper-lit processions of "antique pageantry," as though antiquity itself had lost all dignity in a regression to a lawless primitivism.

From the later perspective of the Ludlow *Maske*, this mode of poetry, which may be loosely characterized as *fantastic* or *allegro*, can also be associated with literary figures, as in the following lines from "L'Allegro":

Then to the well-tred stage anon,
If Jonson's learned Sock be on,
Or Sweetest Shakespeare, fancy's child,
Warble his native Wood-notes wild.
(131-34)

"Fancy's child" (itself an echo of *Love's Labor's Lost* I.i.171) concentrates a cluster of meanings about a number of poets whose names function metonymically in "L'Allegro," and possibly in all of Milton's writings. More than many poets, Milton tends to assign a unified significance to poetic careers; his prose comments, particularly in the very artful autobiographical digressions, confirm his habitual reading of the poetic character as a kind of poem. The association of Shakespeare with fancy, which occurs in the earlier epitaph, "On Shakespeare," counteracts the overwhelming effect of Shakespearean language by placing him within orders of thinking and being (the fantastic and the natural) that stand in opposition to the more controlled exercise of human reason.[2] Nature stands in need of a reasoned reformation (as much as human traditions), a reformation that is at least partly undertaken in "Il Penseroso," where natural scenes are *invested* ("civil-suited morn") with a more rational significance. The civilizing of nature, one might add, functions as a model for the deifying of man, since the very possibility of attaining to the "prophetic strain" that is the end and essence of the *penseroso* mode involves the silencing of the natural man, which is simultaneously the listening of the poet for a higher voice.

If Comus may be said to recollect the language of "L'Allegro," against which can be ranged the *penseroso* glimmerings in the speech of the Lady, her brothers, and the daemon, the Lady herself completes a dichotomous rereading of both earlier poems:

> A thousand fantasies
> Begin to throng into my memory,
> Of calling shapes and beck'ning shadows dire,
> And airy tongues that syllable men's names
> On Sands and Shores and desert Wildernesses.
> (205-9)

The Lady's memory is very densely packed; she recollects either the Circe myth, or the myth of the Sirens, in anticipation of the trial she is about to undergo, but she also remembers Shakespeare, whose presence, at least one critic has noticed, is particularly strong in this passage, again as a representative of "fantasies" that imply the gratification of desire.[3]

Now we may also recall the opening of "Il Penseroso," which describes apotropaically a state of mind analogous to, though less negative, than that which the Lady is trying to suppress:

> Hence vain deluding joys,
>   The brood of folly without father bred,
> How little you bested,
>   Or fill the fixed mind with all your toys;
> Dwell in some idle brain,
>   And fancies fond with gaudy shapes possess...

Comus' crew of "gaudy shapes" literalize this possession. The Lady defends herself against the magician's power by a moral entrenchment; she has a "fixed mind," though this fixity is mocked by the predicament in which Comus places her. At this point we might pause to consider whether a reading of Milton's "L'Allegro" and "Il Penseroso" from the retrospective stance of *Comus* does not violate what seems in the earlier poems to be an evolving stance, rather than an exclusive choice. The Lady, one suspects, would have chosen with *il penseroso*, and therefore "reads" that text with a greater bias than Milton's readers are enjoined to bring to his companion poems. This bias is another way of looking at echoes as indicative of the Lady's more urgent need to choose. Her wandering is more dangerous than the peripatetic lingering of her Miltonic predecessors.

In "Il Penseroso," Milton places himself in a poetic-philosophical line that includes Plato, the Greek tragedians, Chaucer of the unfinished *Squire's Tale*, and unnamed bards who sing "in sage and solemn" tunes

Of Tourneys and of Trophies hung,
Of Forests, and enchantments drear,
Where more is meant than meets the ear.
                    (118-20)

The principal allusion here, as Warton noted long ago, is to Spenser, whose version of Chaucer's *Squire's Tale* Milton recollected in phrasing the lines on that subject in "Il Penseroso."[4] "Sage and solemn," of course, looks forward to the "sage and serious" Spenser of *Areopagitica*, as well as to the "sage and serious" doctrine of virginity in *Comus*. The two recapitulated histories, then, conclude with summary references to Shakespeare in "L'Allegro" and Spenser in "Il Penseroso," a fact that I am adducing as a preliminary piece of intertextual evidence, testimony to the richness and complexity of Comus' voice as an echo of a sound that originates with Shakespeare.[5] The *Maske*, in its continuous allusions to a literary past already partially organized in "L'Allegro" and "Il Penseroso" further develops an implicit dichotomy between two types of poetic aspiration that can be represented, artificially but not inaccurately, by Shakespeare and Spenser.

2. *"Spirits of another sort"*

To the foregoing argument, some empirical observations may be added. John Carey, in his edition of *Comus*, notes the large number of Shakespearean echoes (thirty-two), and indeed, most critics would agree with him that Shakespeare is Milton's "stylistic master" throughout the *Maske*. "Surprisingly Spenser contributes only one or two phrases, but his effect on the vocabulary is considerable."[6] We tend to read the narrative as Spenserian allegory (so Woodhouse reads it), especially as the theme of chastity or temperance, so predominant in *The Faerie Queene,* is treated in largely negative, ironic fashion by Shakespeare.[7] The question of genre, which has provoked such a volume of controversy about the success or failure of the *Maske*, further divides arguments about "sources" into mutually exclusive alternatives. Most of the masques suggested as sources are surely less important for themselves than for the conventions they make available to Milton; though, to be sure, an exhaustive reading of *Comus* would have to take these works into account. I have necessarily simplified the historical genesis of Milton's work, hoping to avoid both the heavily doctrinal emphasis of allegorical readings and the possible trivialization of a purely generic reading. Milton's engagement with his predecessors is as reliable a synecdoche for the meaning of *Comus* as one might desire; which is to say that the density of its allusions is an impressive fact. In this sense too, Milton preempts whatever impulse toward reductiveness might lurk in "source hunting," as he has already "led us back" to these sources.

If one were to conclude anything at all from the numerical evidence of verbal echoes, then certainly Shakespeare and not Spenser would figure as the major influence upon Milton's verse. In fact, Angus Fletcher has concluded just this, though his argument is much more creditable than the usual source hunting that fuels debates in literary history. The major revisionary statement made by Fletcher in *The Transcendental Masque* must be quoted here, both for its dialectical elegance and for the purpose of introducing my own defense and subversion of the traditional view:

> Although much has been made in literary histories of the link between Spenser and Milton, we need to insist on the relative unimportance of this link. Milton was not unduly perturbed, surely, by the example of the *Faerie Queene*. Milton perceived the problem of being Milton: it was that he came after Shakespeare. As the most self-conscious sort of genius, he found himself, willy-nilly, post-Shakespearean. It was an impossible prospect, which he met by burying his meanings, interring them in the signs and syntax. He could not afford the Shakespearean openness, even if he had been able to imagine it. His epoch prohibited such "freedom of invention and presentation"...[8]

In revising Fletcher's revision of conventional literary history, I would insist upon the *relative* importance of the link between Spenser and Milton. Milton certainly obscured his own early and deep involvement with Shakespearean drama when he remarked to Dryden that Spenser was his "original," but his representation was not entirely false. We do not yet fully understand the complexity of this triangular relationship because the links between the three poets are both intertextual (the matter of echo) and contextual (large areas of shared concern). The associative chain of Comus-fancy-"L'Allegro"-Shakespeare, which adumbrates one side of the triangle, advances the idea of imagination as a context, an idea that engages both poets, and leads the later poet to seek out relevant texts among his predecessors (or remember such texts). Verbal echoes are often meaningless to us because we have no context within which to understand what appears to be an arbitrary recollection. Angus Fletcher has already commented very interestingly upon allusion in *Comus*; indeed, he juxtaposes contexts more radically than is necessary to defend the hypothesis I am proposing. The principle behind his analyses can be endorsed, however, as it is expressed in his discussion of the word "viewless" in *Comus* and *Measure for Measure*: "My own view is that the apparent disproportion of contexts, between *Comus* and *Measure for Measure*, fixes the deeper meaning of their being drawn together."[9]

Another example: The reader senses that when the Attendant Spirit echoes Ariel ("There I suck the liquid air/All amidst the Gardens fair," 980–81) the recollection is not irrelevant to the meaning of Milton's lines. Such allusions look like examples of cryptomnesia; we need to supply a *tertium quid* before we can begin to make intelligible the involvement of the pre-text in the later act of composition. That the meaning of the borrowing is not immediately apparent only confirms its importance as allusion, that is, a memory and not a reference.[10] Direct reference does not require that we lay stress upon the temporality of texts; mere comparison of Ariel and the daemon places the two figures side by side—they are no longer a "succession of voices." In Milton's text Ariel is a ghostly presence, a *past* voice. As I will argue shortly, Milton is interested in defining for himself the nature of a daemonic agent as a mediator of the supernatural, and hence his daemon is a transvaluation of Shakespeare's very "concept" of Ariel. Ariel lives "where the bee sucks," far below the ethereal realm from which the Attendant Spirit descends, and this fact implies both Milton's greater dependence upon and higher claims for daemonic agents in art.[11]

Comus, I believe, is most deeply engaged with the Shakespearean text that is itself a poem of and about imagination: *A Midsummer Night's Dream*. To a slightly lesser extent, Milton is also rewriting the Shakespearean parable of the artist in and outside of the world: *The Tempest*. Verbal echoes necessarily possess an evidentiary value in this argument, but our general sense of affinity between the Shakespearean and the Miltonic texts derives from the more difficult and perhaps inevitably vague conviction of a context, a communication as it were, in a fluid medium between texts. I propose here three ideas to serve as contexts for a mutual interpretation of Milton's *Comus* and its Renaissance pre-texts. They are briefly stated here before being treated at length individually:

1) Daemonic agents, or the nature of mediation
2) The relationship of desire to imagination
3) Metamorphosis and transfiguration, or the effectuality of art.

The first category points to the presence of non-human characters in both the play and the masque, specifically as these figures are responsible for the complications of the plot. *The Tempest* contributes its Ariel and Caliban to the literary heritage of the Attendant Spirit and Comus, and it occasions as well a more circumspect recollection of Prospero. Milton's magus is necessarily evil, a darkened version of Oberon or Puck, rather than a *human* magus, like Prospero. Shakespeare seems always to exempt his daemonic agents from the heavy burden of moral choice, a human burden, where Milton's daemonic figures polarize the universe into conflicting forces of good and evil. The daemonic medium is more plastic than the representation of human beings and lends itself to revisionary definitions of the human. Spirits, to borrow Oberon's phrase, are "of another sort"; they are whatever you need them to be.

Daemonic agents mediate spatially between levels of reality and temporally between phases of history. The fairies of *A Midsummer Night's Dream* take us back to a pagan or folklore past—which, despite the Greek mythology, is primarily English. Comus mediates *forward*: he testifies to the persistence of "paganism" in an English society that is in the process of becoming more fully Christian. Spatially, Shakespeare's fairies carry us into the world of art or imagination, which lies above or outside of our mundane world (i.e., to the wood outside of Athens). Milton's daemon, whose origin seems at first to be the sphere of fixed stars, mediates between the earth and a somewhat ambiguous supernature (more of this later). If one accepts the intrinsic connection between daemonic agents and mediation, then the necessity of these figures in works of art is immediately evident. Insofar as the artist lives within what seems to be a hierarchical universe, he tends to rely upon the daemonic to represent the interaction between levels of reality. In this context one understands the drive of "modern" art to dispense with daemonic agents, or to collapse the hierarchy of levels in what Stevens would call a "poem of the earth."

Both Shakespeare and Milton project myths of modernism in the process of exploring the daemonic. Shakespeare's myth can be associated with the "unaccommodated man" of *King Lear*, though we see this man almost always undergoing an ironic regression. When Lear calls "Poor Tom" by this phrase, we know that never was a man more accommodated than Edgar in the disguise of nakedness. Whatever vision Lear wins for himself at the end of the play, from this vision the audience is suddenly and pathetically excluded. The daemonic returns in the later plays, not to be relinquished until the pen goes down with the wand "deeper than e'r plummet sounded."

The homologous myth of Protestantism, which we may call "unaccommodated God," is no less modern and presents us with no less difficult an aspiration. Here the artist must identify with his daemonic agents, as Milton does to a remarkable extent in *Paradise Lost*. The Attendant Spirit is a lesser Raphael as Comus is a lesser Satan, and together they dramatize the up and down movement of human existence—the falling away from, and rising to, a vision of God. Again, however, accommodations impose themselves as our human aspiring can be viewed alternatively as a divine descent, a translation of the divine into human terms. This ambiguity of perspective is preserved in the cautious closing lines of *Comus*, where virtue permits us to follow the daemon in his ascent, *or* ("Or if virtue feeble were") open ourselves to the descendental accommodations of divinity.

The second category, the relation of desire to imagination, will allow us to make even more specific connections between the contextual and the intertextual. Shakespeare, one scarcely needs to observe, invariably associates poetic production with procreation, a conventional trope that Milton resisted. Chastity is the alternative trope, borrowed from Spenser, by which Milton wishes to represent the essence of the poetical character, his own psychological constitution substituting in his prose for a description of poetic structure. The poet "ought himself to be a true poem." Shakespeare's marriage comedies usually explore the wish-fulfilling world of imagination, but the themes of chastity and imagination engage each other as contesting figures most especially in *A Midsummer Night's Dream*. If this seems dubious, we need to remember that the action of the play begins with the prospect of a punitive virginity. The familial laws of Athens prevent the natural coupling that is made possible only by the elaborate detour through the wood. Milton, we feel, is responding to another kind of sympathy, not Shakespeare's but Diana's:

> The moon, methinks, looks with a wat'ry eye
> And when she weeps, weeps every little flower
>   Lamenting some enforcèd chastity.
>   (III.i.183–85)

The Lady makes her transit through the wood so that this very chastity may be tried against the power of an enchanter to "enforce" her virture.

Nevertheless, Milton finds in *A Midsummer Night's Dream* much more than an antithetical poetic. The moon in the above quotation establishes a symbolic hegemony over the entire play, but its association with love and poetry is very problematic. Theseus says that "the lunatic, the lover, and the poet/Are of imagination all compact," hinting at the covert association of the moon (Luna) with the entire complex of meaning suggested by Titania's words. That this particular complex is the symbolic substratum of the play is strongly attested both by its consistency and by its early introduction. In his complaint against Lysander in the second scene of Act I, Egeus says:

Thou hast by *moonlight* at her window sung
With *feigning* voice, *verses* of feigning love
And stolen the impression of her *fantasy*.
(I.ii.30–32, italics mine)

But the moon is a surprisingly inconsistent symbol; elsewhere it is allied to the chaste Diana of mythology. Theseus reminds Hermia that if she does not marry Demetrius, she will be "chanting," before too long, "faint hymns to the cold, fruitless moon."

Oberon's story of how Cupid's arrow strikes the flower called "love-in-idleness," missing the "imperial votress" (a possible allusion to the virgin queen) imposes the same conflict upon the imagery:

But I might see young Cupid's fiery shaft
Quenched in the chaste beams of the wat'ry moon,
And the imperial vot'ress passed on,
In maiden meditation, fancy-free.
Yet marked I where the bolt of Cupid fell.
It fell upon a little western flower...
(II.i.161–66)

Oberon uses the bleeding pansy to engineer his plot against Titania, streaking her eyes with the juice that makes her "full of hateful fantasies." Milton's antithetical counterpart, haemony, derives from a different literary tradition and functions *against* illusion-making power. The relation of haemony to moly suggests Milton's revisionary stance toward his classical sources; his acceptance of archaizing plot devices such as magical flowers is by no means easy. Moly defends against the Circe that *is* classical literature, and haemony is turned against the power of a more immediate voice. The intensity of Milton's resistance is measured by the very incongruity of the Lady's *allusive* situation. She cannot, as does Odysseus, master her predicament by sleeping with her captor.

Shakespeare's poesis is characterized by the omnivorous incorporation of conventional images, whose meanings, even when inconsistent, can be systematized within the expansive structure of the drama. The image of the moon involves chastity as a catalytic agency in the enterprise of an art serving "procreative" ends—much as a celibate priest weds two lovers. The virgin moon only begins to shine when the daylight world becomes obstructive of these ends. The nonreproducing fairies, unreal creatures of imagination, bless the multiple marriages and disappear into their own world, having *amended* (Puck's word) a defect in Athenian society by means of healing fictions.[12]

Shakespearean art confronts the reality of desire, and the concomitant necessity of expression, by limiting the claims of art. Milton never underestimates desire, though its representation in *Comus* in terms of "beck'ning shadows" implies an altogether different conception of the place of desire. This means finally a return to *The Faerie Queene*, Spenser's brooding epic on the self-delusions of the mind. Miltonic limitation contends with the possibly reductive notion of art as a projection of desire by overvaluing limitation itself, a strategy familiar to Miltonists as his idealization of Spenserian temperance (not, we should emphasize, the "chastity" of *The Faerie Queene*, Book III). The anxiety underlying this intertextual engagement concerns the effectuality of art, ultimately the authority of authorship. This anxiety is countered in two alternative but similarly magical modes of self-representation that I have identified as metamorphosis and transfiguration. Artists represent themselves as magicians in the act of imitating the transformative powers of their archetypes, a return to origins that promises new resources of power, art restored to the efficacy of the priest-shaman's binding word. Metamorphosis can be expressed in rhetorical terms as transfiguration, or passing beyond figures. Poetic power or authority would not be simply a figure for real, literal power, but the thing itself. The reader will note that transfiguring as a *rhetorical* concept is self-contradictory—the contradiction is meaningful as an expression of the poetic ego's tremendous longing. Milton's magical chastity, espoused in the

Apology for Smectymnuus, seeks to inform the poetic text with a power *already possessed* by its creator. Can the text attain the power of an ego? Modern readers are not disposed to answer this question definitively (at least not in these terms), although Milton's words on the text as "the precious life-blood of a master spirit" may come back to haunt us.

Shakespeare's less intense aspiration, on the other hand, seems to have no less powerful an appeal—his dramatic ego is presented in movement away from his archetype, always in the act of breaking his wand. The poet therefore gains this authority by becoming one of us, by turning back upon his fictions, as though he were also the audience, the interpreter. Hippolyta's comment upon the story of the lovers argues for the authority of Shakespearean language without violating the reality principle that seems to devalue the truth content of art:

But all the story of the night told over,
And all their minds transfigured so together,
More witnesseth than fancy's images
And grows to something of a constancy...
                            (V.i.23–26)

The lovers *are* transfigured, whatever one may think about the truth of "fancy's images." Puck hints at much the same idea in his epilogue, a context that we need to remember when the play's masque-like coda is echoed by the Attendant Spirit.

Shakespeare's early version of transfiguration is reworked with much greater complexity in *The Tempest*, but I must pass over those "sea changes" to comment upon a problem more specifically related to *Comus*. The metamorphoses of *A Midsummer Night's Dream* are playful, like Bottom's "translation" into an ass, and the mock dramatization of the Pyramus and Thisbe story. The largely comic borrowings from Ovid (also "translations") have no tonal correspondence in Milton's own magic transformations. The power of Comus is regressive only, and when he and his bestial ex-humans threaten the Lady with an "Ovidian" metamorphosis, we are suddenly aware that his primitivism is also a kind of obsolescence:

Nay Lady, sit; if I but wave this wand,
Your nerves are all chained up in Alabaster

And you a statue; or as Daphne was,
Root-bound, that fled Apollo.

(659–62)

Comus suffers from a literary obsolescence that signals his belatedness in a world being enlightened by the Christian faith. The allusion to Apollo is charmingly inappropriate, since it reminds the reader that metamorphosis was as arbitrary as the will of the gods in the pagan world. Yet the tempter retains some power over the Lady, as Shakespeare and Ovid continue to linger in Milton's revisionary poem.

Against the moral lapse and poetic regression evinced by Comus' art Milton advances his own startlingly magical transfiguration. The speaker is the Elder Brother:

So dear to Heav'n in saintly Chastity,
That when a soul is found sincerely so,
A thousand liveried Angels lackey her,
Driving far off each thing of sin and guilt,
And in clear dream and solemn vision
Tell her of things that no gross ear can hear,
Till oft converse with heav'nly habitants
Begin to cast a beam on th' outward shape,
The unpolluted temple of the mind,
And turns it by degrees to the soul's essence,
Till all be made immortal: but when lust
By unchast looks, loose gestures, and foul talk,
But most by lewd and lavish act of sin,
Lets in defilement to the inward parts,
The soul grows clotted by contagion,
Imbodies and imbrutes, till she quite lose
The divine property of her first being.

(444–60)

The Neoplatonic commonplaces perhaps matter less than the poetic issues being tried (in the strong sense of *trial*) in philosophical language. When we bring a pre-text from *A Midsummer Night's Dream* into association with this passage, the nature of Milton's transvaluation of commonplaces is illuminated. Titania says to Bottom:

And I will purge thy mortal grossness so
That then thou shalt like an airy spirit go.
                              (III.i.145–47)

Although Bottom may be lucky to get his own head back, no personage in
the play actually moves permanently up or down in the ladder of being;
transfiguration takes place on another plane, without recourse to literal
metamorphosis. Milton pushes his idea of transformation much further,
implying a real change in the nature of man. Outside of the pagan scheme
of metamorphosis only the exaltation and incarnation of Christ afford
analogous examples of changes in essence, but much as Milton needs some
such conception to legitimize the transfigurative claims of his art, the
theological analogue is hedged about with difficulties.[13] Theological ideas
are present in the passage from *Comus*, less explicit than the Platonism, yet
the word "incarnation" is cautiously avoided. Instead Milton uses two
words, "imbodies" and "imbrutes" (one of which is a neologism), in order
to place the idea of incarnation into a negative context.[14] The aspiration
expressed in the poem is inexactly analogous to the theological scheme,
and this discrepancy is a matter of concern.

Incarnation, it must be acknowledged now, has an analogical relation in
the Renaissance to imagination, which Shakespeare had already noted
himself in describing the fantasy as "bodying forth the forms of things
unknown." Here is a less ambiguous text from Pico della Mirandola: "If,
yielding to the senses, phantasy shall decline to apply itself to the business
of virtue, so great is its power that it afflicts the body and beclouds the
mind, and finally brings it about that man divests himself of humanity, and
takes on bestiality."[15] To prove a point, we may wave our own interpreter's
wand over the last phrase and produce the theological formula for incarnation: "…and God divests himself of divinity, and takes on humanity."
Milton is understandably uneasy with the startling dual meanings of
incarnation, and even his most extended treatment of the subject, the
"Nativity Ode," continuously elides the historical moment of Christ's
descent by moving back and forth between creation and apocalypse.

"The Passion" is an even more telling example of the uneasiness Milton
experiences in approaching the human Jesus. This is not to attribute yet
another heterodoxy to his thought, but rather to argue his response to

incarnation as complicated by that discrepancy between his poetic and his received theology (and this discrepancy reflects once again the perennial Western labor of merging Platonic and Christian theology). Milton's ideal of spiritual transformation, which he continues to espouse through the agency of Raphael in *Paradise Lost* (V.469-503) is here too extreme to draw into its company of analogues the obvious Christian precedent, the Transfiguration, or the later Pauline extension of this possibility to every follower of Christ: "But we all, with open face beholding as in a glass the glory of the Lord, are changed (*metamorphöomai*) into the same image from glory to glory, even as by the Spirit of the Lord" (2 Cor. 3.18). The strange revision of the Pauline triad (faith, hope, chastity) is the only recognition of that absent theological analogue. The Transfiguration remains as distanced from Milton's scene of spiritualization as the Incarnation remains from his scenes of descent to "this dim spot." Milton's poetic is anti-incarnative, and chastity, as a revision of both the Pauline virtues and the Shakespearean fancy, moves beyond "charity" to reverse the great incarnative act initiated by that charity. So man, eventually, becomes god.

3. *Disenchantment and the Stars*

The younger brother characterizes the "divine philosophy" he has just heard his sibling espouse as "charming," reminding us that chastity functions as a counteractive magic in the *Maske*. The tempter himself describes the Lady's song as "enchanting" and makes an interesting comparison to his mother, Circe. If we wonder why the Lady's magic is not sufficient to free her from Comus' bondage, perhaps we ought to subject chastity itself to a more rigorously disenchanting interpretation. From the point of view of what Paul Ricoeur calls a "hermeneutic of suspicion" the concept of chastity as a transfigurative strategy is particularly vulnerable to rhetorical reduction: what, after all, does moving "beyond figures" mean? What ground does Milton have to distinguish his transformations into spirit from those old pagan metamorphoses? I think it possible to demonstrate that *Comus* contains its own severe critique, and as a motto for the elucidation of this critique I offer this very sensible statement of the younger brother's:

...Beauty, like the fair Hesperean Tree
Laden with blooming gold, had need the guard

Of dragon watch with unenchanted eye.
                    (393-95)

The critic is rather like the uncouth dragon: he guards a mystery by
remaining himself unenchantable. The elder brother, who is fond of mys-
tifying his subject, discourses on chastity as a "hidden strength" which is
obscurely related to the strength one seeks from heaven. When the younger
brother raises this question ("the strength of heav'n"?) he is answered, "I
mean that too." The moment does not escape awkwardness:

I mean that too, but yet a hidden strength
Which, if heaven gave it, may be term'd her own.
                    (418-19)

This paradox (contradiction?) is at the troubled center of Protestantism
and of Milton's poetic longing as well. I must continue to question its
validity. Autonomy is an overdetermined concept in the masque, as it is in
Milton's prose. The problem of the Lady's continued dependence (her
inability to "stand" alone) will eventually take on the burden of the poet's
large and partially concealed struggle to justify his authority in relation to
prior "*auctors*," as well as to a voice that is discontinuity itself—the breaking
of the divine voice into the human text. Neither does Milton stand alone.

The presence of higher powers in the masque (the Attendant Spirit) tells
us from the very beginning that chastity is not enough. A hermeneutic of
disenchantment can be constructed out of the masque's repeated references
to another higher power, the stars, which are both aboriginal signs and
agencies of supernatural influence. The action of *Comus* takes place on a
starless night; the stars are an important absence pointing to hidden presences. Darkness draws attention to the lack of direct providential guidance,
a condition about which both the Lady and the elder brother complain, the
latter most interestingly in this passage:

Unmuffle ye faint stars, and thou fair Moon
That wont'st to love the traveller's benison,
Stoop thy pale visage through an amber cloud,
And disinherit *Chaos*, that reigns here
In double night of darkness and of shades:
Or if your influence be quite damn'd up

With black usurping mists, some gentle taper,
Though a rush Candle from the wicker hole
Of some clay habitation, visit us
With thy long levell'd rule of streaming light,
And thou shalt be our star of *Arcady*
Or *Tyrian* Cynosure.

(331–42)

The star of Arcady, in the constellation Ursa Major, and the Tyrian cynosure (Ursa Minor, whose tip is the polestar) are associated in Ovid's *Metamorphoses* (II.409–541) with the story of the rape of Callisto.[16] In the old metamorphic scheme mortals could become immortal by "stellification," but no such archaic transformation is impending for the Lady. The elder brother's insistence upon the magical defenses of chastity leads him to propose an internalization of transcendent agencies. Chastity is its own source, with "sacred rayes," and Virtue

could see to do what virtue would
By her own radiant light, though sun and moon
Were in the flat sea sunk.

(373–75)

Figuration, a turn to tropes, substitutes for metamorphosis, and though we should expect some such substitution to pervade the imagery of the *Maske*, some of the implications are disturbing. The Attendant Spirit, we know, comes from the stellatum, "swift as the Sparkle of a glancing Star," but here the daemon's relation to stars has more than the force of a simile. A few lines later Comus make a counterclaim that blurs our sense of consistency in the meaning of stars (like Mutabilitie's "heaven and earth I both alike do deeme"):

We that are of purer fire
Imitate the starry choir
Who in their nightly watchful Spheres
Lead in swift round the Months and Years.

(111–14)

The stars as signs are too meaningful, and this overload complicates the transition from stars as agents to stars as metaphors. Comus is as entitled as the Attendant Spirit to draw analogies between his activity and the motion of the stars, so long as we have not decided what the stars are signs *of*. The puzzle is only deepened with the reference to Venus in line 124 ("Venus now wakes"); to what order does she belong?

William Empson recognized some years ago the persistent ambiguity of stars in Milton's work; the poet seems to be writing in a gray area somewhere between what we would call semiology and its parodic original, astrology.[17] The difficulty of eliciting a determinate meaning from the stars in *Comus* points to a curious intersection of history and rhetoric. The complete transformation of aboriginal signs into figures of speech is not yet possible, although the pressure behind such a displacement into trope is strongly felt. In *Paradise Lost* the stars are associated with angels, usually the *fallen* angels, a fact which tends both to implicate astrology as a regressive pagan system and to highlight the significance of Christianity as a historical enlightenment.

In *Comus* Milton poses for himself the problem of finding an adequate substitution for whatever agency the stars represent without making explicit reference to Christian doctrine. The Lady first introduces the idea of such a substitution in her recourse to sound or voice in the absence of light. In the *Maske*'s most important song, she implores Echo to tell her where her brothers are:

> Tell me but where,
> Sweet Queen of Parley, Daughter of the Sphere,
> So mayst thou be translated to the skies
> And give resounding grace to all Heav'ns harmonies.
> (240–43)

"Resounding" promises the return of Providential aid (grace) without demanding precise identification of this grace or asserting the Lady's extreme and discontinuous self-reliance. The repetition of something like stellification ("translated to the skies") further hints at a sublimation that is quite literally "subliminal," a transformation of the "starry threshold" into a resonant membrane. Possibly the Lady does not understand the full significance of her song, because she receives no answer from Echo. She carries within herself a new theologico-poetic principle, which she calls "chastity," or more severely, "virginity," but she is powerless as yet to prove its effectuality.[18]

In her debate with Comus, the Lady speaks of the "sun-clad power of chastity," and associates this power with her own voice, recollecting at the same time the effectuality of Orphic poetry. In the contest of raw power, however, Comus is still winning. Comus argues his intrinsic relation to the night world of stars, and he prevails in this world until the sun rises on the new dispensation in which he will be only a memory, a literary allusion.[19] In the meanwhile he defends his usefulness by appealing to the "waste fertility" of pagan nature against the Lady's conception of a temperance that functions doubly as a precept of human behavior and a law of nature. "Accuse not nature," Raphael later says to Adam, although in that passage, as in this, the argument is at cross-purposes. Nature in the *Maske* is the spatial analogue for a historical divide, on either side of which the meanings of words are different. Comus possesses a primitive wisdom closer than the Lady knows to a buried meaning of temperance, from *tempus*, time or season. Everything in its season, Comus says, and this is *my* season. And the mind itself has its seasons, one of the more interesting conclusions of this argument:

> If all the world
> Should in a pet of temperance feed on Pulse,
> Drink the clear stream, and nothing wear but Frieze...
> . . . .
> The Sea o'erfraught would swell, and th'unsought diamonds
> Would so bestud with Stars, that they below
> Would grow inur'd to light, and come at last
> To gaze upon the Sun with shameless brows.
> (720-36)

This is to threaten a return of the repressed, or what Carey glosses as "hell-dwelling spirits, demons and monsters of classical mythology,"[20] all creatures of the night world, the season of the stars. The historical discontinuity is therefore repeated within the mind itself, which may not be able to achieve a complete enlightenment. More especially threatening to the poetic ego is the figure of the stars themselves, which shine in the *Deep*, the earth. The trope of diamonds-as-stars moves to invert the direction of astral influence. These stars are images of negative influence, emanating from the topographical area of repression and hinting at the equally dangerous possibility of a temporal regression.

Comus' speech presents another darkened version of the *allegro* land-scape, with its "faery Mab" and "Lubber Fiend," derived appropriately from Shakespeare, and not from the more decorous world of Spenserian romance. (The entire passage is the most Shakespearean of the many pastiches in the *Maske*.) The moral counter-theme is almost overwhelmed, however, by the arch-theme of plenitude, and though Nature may not really exhibit the "waste fertility" Comus attributes to it, the attractiveness of that "spawn innumerable" is undiminished even by the Lady's Orphic invocation. The relation that I have argued between the voice of Comus and Shakespearean language is not new,[21] but I do wish to meditate a little longer on the fate of this voice. The argument of Comus' speech is precisely embodied in its style, a display of metaphoric extravagance and furious coupling of ideas and images. Milton's refusal to distinguish moral and stylistic judgments permits him to adopt a unified stance in relation to the tradition from which he is freeing his poetry. Consider, for example, Comus' restatement of the *carpe diem* theme, which implies the identity of Elizabethan style with its characteristic libertine trope:

If you let slip time, like a neglected rose,
It withers on the stalk with languished head.
                    (744–45)

The Elizabethan "sources" are legion of course—the sense of urgency and ripeness are conspicuous qualities of the age—but the pre-text from *A Midsummer Night's Dream* is the most proper intertextual locus for the debate between chastity and plenitude as alternative poetic principles:

But earthlier happy is the rose distilled
Than that which, withering on the virgin thorn
Grows, lives, and dies in single blessedness.
                    (I.i.76–79)

The "dear Wit and gay Rhetoric" of an age, and of that age's leading poet, are scarcely distinguishable from the "waste fertility" of Comus' nature. When the Lady threatens his "magic structures" with the disintegrating power of her own voice ("shatter'd into heaps o'er thy false head"), we hear behind her words an earlier dissolution, of "cloud-capped tow'rs" and "gorgeous palaces." Shakespeare's (or Prospero's) dismissal of daemonic agencies in the Hymeneal masque of *The Tempest* is suddenly seen anew, as Milton's allusion exerts a powerfully revisionary force. The inaugurative act of Miltonic voice banishes strong spirits—the magicians themselves, the invokers of the daemons. The Shakespearean "tempest," also a *tempus* or season, is over.

Discontinuities, even those achieved by the most covert of allusions, are inherently dangerous. That renunciation can become a form of repression is Comus' greatest insight. Although the threatened return does not occur, the stars do return at the end of the *Maske* ("the stars grow high"). These are not the star-like creatures of the deep, but neither are they quite the stars to which the Attendant Spirit refers in his very first words. The moment at which we are now poised is very like the predawn stasis of the "Nativity Ode," when the stars are reluctant to withdraw before the rising sun. That dawn (a simultaneous setting of the pagan gods) may not ever reach completion in Milton's poetry, although one might want to argue that *Paradise Regained*, as a poem of radical discontinuities, approaches that full enlightenment. *Comus* evades the threatened return of the cacodaemonic and wins for itself a qualified enlightenment by enacting a more genial fiction of returns, to which we now address ourselves.

The *Maske* turns and returns in the transition from the Lady's speech to the tempter's recognition that "she fables not."

She fables not, I feel that I do fear
Her words set off by some superior power...
(800-1)

The Lady's words anticipate the full epiphany of the "superior power," but the poet evidently feels that he is not yet ready to channel that power into his verse. The Lady declines to speak in the voice of the higher power, and the epiphany remains incomplete.

This withdrawal from the moment of divine descent into human voice prepares for the authoritative return to another pure, but still human, origin—Spenser. He enters the poem first allusively, with the appearance of the two brothers; they smash the enchanter's cup, repeating in that action Guyon's rough treatment of "Genius" before the Bower of Bliss. The allusion has the effect of associating Guyon, and his purifying quest, with Spenser himself; he too had declared the purity of his origin—in Chaucer, the "pure well of English undefil'd." The completion of this triad establishes a line of English poetry determinedly independent from the secular triumphs of the Elizabethan age.[22] The canonical moment prepares for a more open acknowledgment of Milton's "original," as Spenser is interposed between Milton and the persistent *memory* of Shakespeare. Spenser becomes the source of the counteractive magic, "reversing" the continued and attractive temptation to regress into the Shakespearean plenitude. Stilling his own urgently hierophantic voice, Milton allows Spenser to speak through him in the mediated persona of Meliboeus, the "soothest shepherd that ere pip't on plains." The story of Sabrina is perhaps the least Miltonic resolution one might have expected, but the startling influx of eudaemonic deities into the Spirit's invocation (including even the dangerous Sirens!) is the best testimony we have to the success of Milton's self-limitation, as Spenser, Ovid, and classical mythology rush in to fill the space occupied by the Shakespearean plenitude. Natural space, visually "thronged" in Comus' speech, becomes verbal space, the space of allusion and echo. The repetition of "Listen and save," concisely recapitulating the plot of the *Maske,* means also "To listen is to be saved." The Lady is now appropriately silent.

Returns, like allusions, are inexact repetitions that announce a "progress of poesy." Sabrina's "quick immortal change," which revises Spenser's account of the Sabrina story in *The Faerie Queene,* anticipates the more powerful transformation of Edward King into the "genius of the shore" even as it looks back to a poetic mode that is aboriginal. Within this eschatological scheme, the association of Spenser with the concepts of chastity and virginity serves as the literary link to an earlier source of power—and this origin is both early and *now.* The restoration of continuity prevents both the loss of authority imposed upon Shakespeare's text and the discontinuity represented by the Lady's self-reliance. The setting of *Comus* therefore remains consistently pre-Christian ("night sits monarch yet in the mid-sky") and it is that world to which Sabrina and the daemon return.

The idea of metamorphosis is reintroduced into the poem with Spenser as a consciously archaizing figure that resists rhetorical reduction. Sabrina's "immortal change" substitutes for the idea of the "transfigurative," of which we have no example in the poem, only a declaration of its possibility. The figure is bounded by the repressed on one side (sexuality) and by the inexpressible on the other (the "superior power"); only the figure in the middle has voice, though as yet it has no name. I should like to call it a *pre-figure*, and to recollect that Milton's early poetry is much informed by motifs of the prefigurative, the annunciative. We can take as a motto for the sublimity of this stance, the line Wordsworth liked so well, from *Paradise Lost*: "He onward came, far off his coming shone." In such a line we hear the excitation of standing on the threshold before the advent of the "superior power." The attraction of this deferral is very great, and contends impressively with the rather different sublimity of Christ's arrival and triumph over the rebellious angels. *Comus* can be said to linger with this moment of anticipation.

Prefiguration is related to a matter of anxiety as well as pleasure in Milton's early career, his concern with the danger of *prematurity*, of a precociousness that might possibly spend itself before the great work is accomplished. The lingering of "paganism" in his work, even in those poems (like the "Nativity Ode") that seem impatient to herald an apocalypse, is a necessary and self-imposed restraint, a continuous purgation and deferral. The Spirit's epilogue, which has both puzzled critics and reassured them that Milton was not so fixated, after all, on the subject of chastity, might be read more profitably as a statement on the limits of the present, of the incomplete epiphany as a powerful stance for the young poet to adopt. Shakespeare returns in these lines (the Spirit echoes both Ariel and Puck) but these ghosts subject the *Maske's* conclusion to a very gentle haunting.

Equally significant are the internal allusions, second readings of the *Maske* itself. The Gardens of Hesperus (equated with the Elysian Fields, and perhaps with the stars)[23] are recollected, but not the "unenchanted dragon." He is no longer necessary if chastity is recognized as one of the *Maske's* preliminary (before the threshold) figures. Lines 996–1010, which were added sometime after the acting version of *Comus* was completed, further clarify the structure of the *Maske* by inexact repetitions. The story of Venus and Adonis, so important to the Spenserian understanding of sexuality, is in its Shakespearean version the story of a failed seduction, like the one we have just read. Milton declines to adopt the story as his model, and demotes Venus from her stellar position to the intermediary paradise the Spirit describes (incidentally locating the Spirit himself in a middle realm, both spatially and temporally). In the place of Venus, and in the *place of her story*, another substitution is written:

... and on the ground
Sadly sits the Assyrian Queen;
But far above in spangled sheen
Celestial Cupid her fam'd son advanct,
Holds his dear Psyche sweet entranct
After her wandering labors long,
Till free consent the Gods among
Make her his eternal bride...

(1001–8)

Lastly the return of the stars, and an assertion of Miltonic power to make new stars. Cupid and Psyche are like new stars in that they take the place of the morning-evening star, Venus, and in her position they both retain the memory of the pagan world that we live again with the coming of every night, and herald the dawn that disperses the old stellar deities. If the diurnal system in its endless repetition seems a contradictory figure for the heralding of enlightenment, that is just the point. Cupid and Psyche are limitary figures; they adjust the poet to the limitations of his prematurity, which is perhaps why Milton has them give birth to "Youth and Joy." Prefigurative figures are part of an extensive analogy between the poet and the poem: as a youthful poet, Milton is a prefiguration of his own future greatness.

One final note on the subject of allusion: From the retrospective stance of the Spirit's epilogue, Comus looks very much like Cupid's shabby original, a "fam'd son" himself, as Psyche is perhaps the Lady, "sweet entranct" after her wandering labors. Continuities extend from these lines through both the *Maske* and its antecedents—the epilogue is also a "secondary revision" of Shakespeare's dream thought, a still more antithetical origin. The "spangled sheen" of line 1003, my last and perhaps most illustrative example, echoes Puck, who uses these words to describe the quarrel of Oberon and Titania:

And now they never meet in grove or green
By fountain clear or spangled starlight sheen
But they do square...

(II.i.28–30)

Shakespeare's play is written to figure the healing of the divisions it represents, and Spenser too shows his figures "waxing well" of their wounds. Milton reinterprets the marriage resolution, the healing union, as the continuous deferral of any final poetic stance; the epilogue is a kind of anti-Shakespearean marriage comedy, and the marriage of Cupid and Psyche sounds less a note of finality than of indeterminate beginnings, of *newness*. The new myth is invented in the made darkness of an occlusion—Shakespeare's starlight ("spangled starlight sheen") disappears in Milton's contracted line, which gives us a *metonymy* for starlight, a different trope for this different starlight. As new stars, Cupid and Psyche derive from no single text, but they are a manifold echo of everything in literature they are meant to transcend. The "daughter of the sphere"—Echo herself—gives them the literary space in which they shine, reflecting the old stars and echoing the old voices. Echo, as the Lady promised in her song, is "translated to the skies." In Lawes' version of the songs, he had written "transplanted," a word consistent with the Lady's meaning; but we feel that Milton's choice is more profound. The sense of movement, of aspiration, is fused with the act of verbal revision, which is indeed "translation." The word resonates with Milton's most intense poetic longing.

CHAPTER FIVE

The Visible Saint: Miltonic Authority

... strength alone though of the muses born
Is like a fallen angel...

Keats, "Sleep and Poetry"

The shadow of the object fell upon the ego.

Freud, "Mourning and Melancholia"

1. *"The vindication of a private name"*

If Milton defers to the authority of Spenser in the concluding movement
of *Comus*, his gesture of deference is enacted without recourse to the *name*
of Spenser, an omission that can be construed as itself a more complex
form of deference. The substitution of Meliboeus for Spenser points to the
trope of metonymy, whose complicity in Milton's conception of authority
(as well as in much of our utterance on the subject) needs to be noted here
as a preliminary grounding of the following argument in the domain of
rhetoric.[1] Figures of authority are seldom addressed by name but rather by
metonymic substitutions: "Your grace, highness, holiness." Less monar-
chical governing bodies are no less characterized by the prevalence of this
figure. Democratic institutions tend to substitute function for proper name
just as the older monarchies relied upon the supposedly innate (but associated) qualities of those in power, a "nobility." It is not immediately clear
why a relation by contiguity should dominate the rhetorical invocation of
authority, although rhetoricians inevitably draw attention to this relation
in their textbook examples (as in "a crown for the King" or "the White

House for the President"). One might like to consider (or dream of) power as truly inner, self-possessed, but the power of one man over any number of people almost never reduces to the quantity of individual strength. Power, even if it is the naked force of an obedient military, stands in a contiguous relation to its users (authority)—in fact, merely *stands* when it is most successful. My ultimate concern is with this relation, or disrelation, between power and authority, very much at the center of *Paradise Lost*, but my way through to that concern will be the problem of naming, both the strategy by which a name is invested with authority, and the metonymic substitutions used to enhance the authority of that name.

The name, of course, is John Milton, whose reputation in his own lifetime awaited the slow formation of an identity between name and achievement. The lack of reputation is a problem for the young writer, but oddly less acute for the poet than for the pamphleteer. The inauguration of the poetic career is simultaneously halting and ambitious, dispersed over a large number of years and attended with anxiety about the future realization of a projected epic poem. And yet the greater anxiety for the younger writer concerns his contemporary reputation, since the complete awakening to the problem of authority takes place not in the prospective but in the *retrospective* texts, the autobiographical digressions in the prose pamphlets. The intervening career of political polemicist raises much more immediately the question of the writer's authority, especially as the aim of persuasion risks the name of the polemicist in the possible failure of this aim.[2] Although polemicists can protect themselves against this eventuality by publishing anonymously, the argument headed by a reputable name inevitably embarks upon its task of persuasion with the significant advantage of acknowledged authority. Milton's awareness of this dilemma is expressed in a text that is itself pervasively concerned with the name of John Milton, although this name is nowhere mentioned. The pamphlet was published anonymously, but in fact, the identity of the author was easily discovered. Here is one paragraph from the pamphlet now known, somewhat inaccurately, as *An Apology for Smectymnuus*:

> I could not to my thinking honor a good cause more from the heart, then by defending it earnestly as oft as I could judge it to behoove me, notwithstanding any false name that could be invented to wrong, or undervalue an honest meaning. Wherein although I have not doubted to single forth more then once, such of them as were thought the chiefe and most nominated opposers on the

other side, whom no man else undertooke: if I have done well either to be confident of the truth, whose force is best seene against the ablest resistance, or to be jealous and tender of the hurt that might be done among the weaker by the intrapping autority of great names titl'd to false opinions, or that it be lawfull to attribute somewhat to guifts of Gods imparting, which I boast not, but thankfully acknowledge, and feare also lest at my certaine account they be reckon'd to me many rather then few, or if lastly it be but justice not to defraud of due esteeme the wearisome labours and studious watchings, wherein I have spent and tir'd out almost a whole youth, I shall not distrust to be acquitted of presumption. Knowing that if heretofore all ages have receav'd with favour and good acceptance the earliest industry of him that hath beene hopefull, it were but hard measure now, if the freedome of any timely spirit should be opprest meerely by the big and blunted fame of his elder adversary; and that his sufficiency must be now sentenc't, not by pondering the reason he shews, but by calculating the yeares he brings.[3]

The extremely oblique line of argument, although it characterizes much of Milton's prose, is here so utterly attenuated by the suspension of the period that we may well wonder what logic sustains these sentences as grammatical "units." The absence of an easily discernible logic, even "subject," has an interesting and idiosyncratic effect peculiar to this type of sentence and therefore revealing as Milton's habitual choice. The sentence advances like a wave thrown up by an object moving just beneath the surface of the water. This under-subject, really a "motivation," is Milton's unhappy consciousness of being unable to speak his own name, which feeling produces at the surface of the sentence the worried attack upon the "intrapping autority of great names," mingled or interspersed with relevant information about the "timely spirit" who has genius and ambition, but no reputation. At this point in Milton's career (1642), his name would be a worthless counter in the polemical game, and his best defense is an attack upon the illegitimate attribution of authority to mere reputation, a good strategy from one point of view but counterbalanced nevertheless by his desire for this very authority.

But the notion of "defense" directs us back to the occasion of this pamphlet and the reasons for my own disinclination to emphasize yet these historical circumstances. The *Apology* is explicitly *pro vita sua*: Milton had been libeled by the writer of a previous pamphlet (probably the son of Bishop Hall), and yet the controversy did not begin with either of these figures. The originating pamphlet was written by Bishop Hall himself in defense of episcopacy, and it provoked a response from five Presbyterian clergymen who wrote under the acronym *Smectymnuus*. The acronym is already an example of wordplay, an indication of the potential for controversy to develop into an elaborate game of figures. Milton's apology is not for Smectymnuus but for himself, specifically for the rhetorical stance of writing *as though* he were the equal in reputation of his opponents. The *Apology* is virtually exhausted by this self-defense, adding little to the antiprelatical arguments of its more cautious predecessor, *The Reason of Church Government*, and for that reason succeeding less well. The success or failure is of no immediate concern to us, but the self-defense by means of tropes is interesting in itself, and justifies, I would hope, the bracketing of ideology. Fundamentally, I am interested in understanding how Milton creates a sense of authority *prior* to any actual achievement as a writer.

The writer of the *Apology* has without question a warrant to speak of himself in response to the personal attack of a published pamphlet; but whether this warrant ought to be utilized is doubtful, since any response at all implies the possibility of taking too seriously the usual invective of controversial polemic. Hence Milton wonders whether, and even concedes that, "the best apology against false accusers is silence and sufferance." His very obscurity argues for the advantage of this response:

> Albeit that in doing this I shall be sensible of two things which to me will be nothing pleasant; the one is, that not unlikely I shall be thought too much a party in mine owne cause, and therein to see least; the other, that I shall be put unwillingly to molest the publick view with the vindication of a private name; as if it were worth the while that the people should care whether such a one were thus, or thus. (1:870)

Silence is an admirably ideal rejoinder, but who will call attention to this eloquence? Milton's suppression of his own name is as much silence as his text will allow, and it is indeed the unspoken pretext of the entire utterance. He must now find a way to defend himself without speaking this name, an intention which will necessarily throw him back upon figures of speech; these are truly the walls behind which resides the otherwise defenseless name:

> But when I discern'd his intent was not so much to smite at me, as through me to render odious the truth which I had written, and to staine with ignominy

that Evangelick doctrine which opposes the tradition of Prelaty, I conceav'd
my selfe to be now not as mine own person, but as a member incorporate into
that truth whereof I was perswaded, and whereof I had declar'd openly to be a
partaker. (1:871)

The "conceiving" is almost as elaborate or fanciful as what the age would
call a *conceit*; the figure here is a synecdoche, by which Milton becomes a
part of the whole truth he defends. To defend himself is not exactly the
same as defending truth, but the trope permits the argument to move
forward by means of this substitution. Milton is now able to repeat, even
to solicit, the worst accusations of his antagonist, since all such libels
rebound upon the libeler; they strike against the book itself, the "plain
authority of scriptures," which cannot be stained with *ignominy*, the bad
name. Although the synecdochic ploy is successful in its immediate end of
permitting a defense of the unspoken name, the trope looks too much like
rhetorical legerdemain to sustain the argument for long. Synecdoche also
entails an interesting and possibly subversive ambiguity in the direction of
the relationship between part and whole, as well as in the sense of "partak-
ing," either "taking part in" or "taking part of." The problem is in the
nature of representation itself, because Milton is claiming nothing less than
to "represent" truth. Synecdoche cannot complete a defense of either the
name or the truth of the anti-prelatical stance, but it does establish the need
for a self-portrait, which is what the *Apology* then provides.

Much like its predecessor in *The Reason of Church Government*, that self-
portrait is overextended, more detailed than is called for by the occasion of
specific charges. In the earlier pamphlet the motive behind this excessive
production is also identifiable as Milton's desire to invest his character with
authority, although the means of self-aggrandizement is quite literally
"preposterous." The young writer trades upon his authority as a future
great poet ("I might perhaps leave something so written to aftertimes as
they should not willingly let it die"), almost as though his present authority
were derived as a consequence of his signing a contract to become great. I
wish to recall this contract with his auditors in moving on to the next
tropological strategy, because Milton himself recurs to this contractual
obligation as a means of precipitating a powerful metaphor: "And long it
was not after, when I was confirm'd in this opinion, that he who would not
be frustrate of his hope to write well hereafter in laudable things, ought
him selfe to be a true Poem, that is a composition, and patterne of the best

and honourablest things"(1:890). The famous metaphor achieves its effect by a further reduction, of the poet to the poem, which is also an act of internalization. Milton introduces this line of argument with the expressed intention of displacing his defense from external appearance to "inmost thoughts": "So if my name and outward demeanor be not evident enough to defend me, I must make trial if the discovery of my inmost thoughts can." The "contract" to produce the epic poem (itself an *externalization*) demands in the present the conscious reformation of the poet's character; this "inside" must correspond to, as well as produce, the future "outside." This implicit correspondence is the source of the metaphor's power, which almost allows us to forget that the great poem is not yet written.

The metaphor carries the argument forward only very briefly, however, perhaps as a consequence of the greater violence of the reduction. The involvement of the trope in the contract formulated in *The Reason of Church Government* is a weakness as well as a strength, and the movement inward to the act of self-recognition is much easier than the return, the reemergence of the ego as poet. Milton looks inside of himself and in that deepest and most central place he regards the poet. But to prove that he is a poet is in fact a greater task than any defense of moral character.

At this point the *Apology* arrives at a double crisis: The author has asserted an identity without offering a sufficient evidential basis (this could only be a *poetic* achievement), while the charge of promiscuity is about to be taken up, a very sensitive subject which Milton had already, in *Comus*, associated with the problematics of poetic authority:

> So that even those books which to many others have bin the fuell of wantonnesse and loose living, I cannot thinke how unlesse by divine indulgence prov'd to me so many incitements as you have heard, to the love and stedfast observation of that vertue which abhorres the society of Bordellos. Thus from the Laureat fraternity of Poets, riper yeares, and the ceaselesse round of study and reading led me to the shady spaces of philosophy, but chiefly to the divine volumes of Plato, and his equal Xenophon. Where if I should tell ye what I learnt, of chastity and love, I meane that which is truly so, whose charming cup is only vertue which she bears in her hand to those who are worthy. The rest are cheated with a thick intoxicating potion which a certaine Sorceresse the abuser of loves name carries about; and how the first and chiefest office of love, begins and ends in the soule, producing those happy twins of her divine generation knowledge and vertue, with such abstracted sublimities as these... (1:891)

Milton's antagonist had the misfortune to attack where Milton's defense would very likely be most strong, which is to say that chastity is already a defensive posture. The Lady of *A Maske* has taught us the resistant strength of this virtue, and her indignant voice returns here to chide an accuser who does not possess the charm of his precursor, Comus. Indeed, this voice is forced to create a more charming accuser, the "certain sorceress" who is "the abuser of love's name." She is clearly a poetic daughter of Comus, just as he was earlier *her* mythological son. The interchangeability of the names (Comus and Circe) is as interesting as the fact that they are both suppressed. They are both illegitimate metonymies for "love's name," whose eloquent absence here corresponds to the omission of Milton's own name. The *Apology* evolves at this moment its strongest defense, metonymy, even as it narrows still more the focus of this defense. The paradoxical strength of this reductive phase is even more remarkably evident in the following pages, which are given over to a defense of the "tart rhetoric" in Milton's earlier pamphlet, *Animadversions*.

Our understanding of the tropological structure of Milton's essay should allow us to predict the outcome of this particular defense, since the problem of linguistic decorum nicely intersects the area of concern about poetic identity. Milton must be able to emerge from this attack *stronger* in his chosen identity, but again without yielding to the desire to offer his name as authoritative in itself. The existence of biblical models for the "tart rhetoric" of *Animadversions* yields up a stock of names whose utterances can be likewise "substituted" for the text being defended. The most authoritative name is, of course, Christ's, and yet Milton stops short of emphasizing the analogy of his own language to Christ's, preferring instead to take over from this name one of its metonymic associations, *Zeal*. According to the fable he constructs for this occasion, the qualities that were unified in the figure of Christ were divided among his followers; to Milton himself descends Zeal. Deference to authority by name permits the prior author to transfer authority to the later, but never can this relationship be established as one of equality. The later author must present himself as less than the earlier, a fact which complicates Milton's use of this trope and perhaps is ultimately responsible for the shifting of metonymy into allusion. We would distinguish allusion from quotation by its obliqueness, and by the absence of the prior author's name. For the moment, I will defer this line of argument in order to set before us the text that is the climax of Milton's *Apology*:

For in times of opposition when either against new heresies arising, or old corruptions to be reform'd this coole unpassionate mildness of positive wisdome is not anough to damp and astonish the proud resistance of carnall, and false Doctors, then (that I may have leave to soare a while as the Poets use) then Zeale whose substance is ethereal, arming in compleat diamond ascends his fiery Chariot drawn with two blazing Meteors figur'd like beasts, but of a higher breed then any the Zodiack yields, resembling two of those four which *Ezechiel* and *S. John* saw, the one visag'd like a Lion to expresse power, high autority and indignation, the other of count'nance like a man to cast derision and scorne upon perverse and fraudulent seducers; with these the invincible warriour Zeale shaking loosely the slack reins drives over the heads of Scarlet Prelats, and such as are insolent to maintaine traditions, brusing their stiffe necks under his flaming wheels. (1:900)

As a metonymy for "John Milton," Zeal is the most authoritative trope in the *Apology* and the final vindication of the private name. The word *Zeal* emerges from a suspended and suspenseful parenthesis, as though we had encountered this blazing figure much to our surprise while turning a corner. The effect is quite like that of an enjambed line, where the first word of the new line unexpectedly continues the grammatical logic of the preceding line while suddenly heating up the emotional temperature. We also have leave, Milton tells us, to consider this transition as a formal shift from prose to poetry. The voice we hear is the voice of a poet, even though he is speaking about the polemicist's breach of decorum. The eruption of the poetic voice, in this and other "purple patches" of Milton's prose, has the validating function of establishing authority on grounds other than established reputation. The mantle of Ezekiel and St. John enfolds the nameless poet, and images from those texts express "power and high authority," an influx from nowhere it seems, but in fact the result of a succession of increasingly effective tropes. That Milton should distinguish here between "power" and "authority" is worth noting, because the reductive strategy of metonymy need not have led us *this far*. The final phrases of the passage are hyperbolic, suggesting the complicity of metonymy and hyperbole, or the occasional necessity of authority to prove itself in the release of power. Harold Bloom associates metonymy with the Pauline doctrine of *kenosis*, the self-emptying of Christ (in Paul's words, Christ "made himself of no reputation." Phil. 2.6–8).[4] Kenneth Burke's linking of metonymy to reduction implies more abstractly what this Pauline association reveals about the structure of the trope.[5] The reduction to Zeal, a single and single-minded motivation, is a phase preparatory to the self-aggrandizement of the ego, like the shrinking of a star before its explosion as a nova. The wholesale destruction concluding Milton's paragraph has the quality of a wish-fulfillment fantasy: the utter humiliation of one's enemies. Its propriety here is determined contextually by the limitation of Zeal to mere agency.

The extent of this limitation is immediately an issue for Milton, possibly because the hyperbole has partially undone, or reversed, the direction of the metonymy. In the next paragraph, a return to the citation of authority signals a further defense, this time a defense of the very excess we have just read:

> Thus did the true Prophets of old combat with the false; thus did Christ himselfe the fountaine of meekness found acrimony anough to be still galling and vexing the Prelaticall Pharisees. But ye will say these had immediat warrant from God to be thus bitter, and I say, so much the plainlier is it prov'd, that there may be a sanctifi'd bitternesse against the enemies of truth. Yet that ye may not think inspiration only the warrant thereof, but that it is as any other vertue, of morall and generall observation, the example of *Luther* may stand for all: whom God made choice of before others to be of highest eminence and power in reforming the Church; who not of revelation, but of judgement writ so vehemently against the chiefe defenders of old untruths in the Romish Church. (1:900-1)

Milton is careful to associate himself with Luther in *not* claiming to be inspired. To have made such a claim at this moment would have shifted the discussion onto an entirely different plane, for then there would have been no need to establish a defense of character. God chooses whom he will, or in Milton's words, he "sends out his seraphim with the hallowed fire of his altar, to touch and purify the lips of whom he pleases" (1:821). Milton will eventually lay claim to this inspiration, whose authority is absolute and *literal*. Inspiration has no figurative status in Milton's discourse; it is defined by no substitutions. It is the ultimate defense of authority in that it needs no defense.

We find it difficult to conceive of authority except in terms of signs and symbols, linguistic displacements or tropes, as though authority *were* this mediation. Two important problems are touched on here, important to both the poet and the Protestant polemicist. Authority without mediation is a Protestant dream, a desire fraught with nightmarish possibility. Milton's ecstatic fantasy (of ascending the biblical chariot under the name of Zeal) is the Prelate's nightmare. It may be that we preserve our humanity in the willingness to distinguish between power and authority, even to deny the priority of power on moral grounds. This is as much as to say that we remain human by granting priority (fictively) to the figurative rather than the literal. Milton can be seen to move toward a reversal of this gesture, or a restoration of the literal origin, in the one last passage I would like to quote from the *Apology*. Having denied to himself the prophetic inspiration, he grants to England the prophetic role, proposing the not uncommon notion that God has covenanted with the English people. The terms of the covenant are curiously stated: "if the will and the endeavor shall be theirs, the performance and the perfecting shall be his" (1:928). The "his" in this sentence refers to God, a surprising reversal of the usual relation between will (God's) and service (ours). God, Milton says, is the "immediate performer of their [the Reformationists] desires." The distinction between power and authority, temporal and semantic, is effaced in the merging of these two wills. In the psychology of inspiration the primary will can become confused with the will of the agent, with results that look very much like self-delusion. The priority of human will to divine agency restores power as well as authority to the human agent, but the sentence places this dangerous priority in the context of a conditional clause, which is already half a fiction. Milton is not yet ready to speak for and as a "superior power."

The second question raised by this text, already implicit in my argument, concerns the problem of poetic origins, the sources of poetic power. Power allies itself to the literal and the original, but there seems to be no way of achieving this alliance in poetry except by the most blinded representations. Few poets, least of all Milton, accept the loss of power enjoined by the absence of the literal, or as we may now say, of a literal origin. But neither is it necessary to consign the dream of such power to the realm of delusion. Milton's belief in his literal inspiration, the subject of my remaining researches, is a vastly complex and ultimate defense, distinguished by as much light as darkness.

2. *Satanic a priori*

I am preceded in these researches by William Kerrigan, whose study, *The Prophetic Milton*, is perhaps the finest recent book on this subject. I have accepted throughout this chapter his thesis concerning the literal inspiration of *Paradise Lost*, and his conclusion will therefore be incorporated as a premise of my argument. The advantage of this procedure—of not having to reargue his case—entails the disadvantage of establishing the following pages in a relation to a study whose success or failure is wholly relevant to my own. My disagreement with Kerrigan on some particulars does not vitiate the thesis of his work, as will be clear shortly. Two questions concerning method, however, are of more immediate urgency and require comment.

First, one scarcely needs to emphasize that if Milton believed himself to be literally inspired, this belief, in its very blatant intentionality, must at some point raise an *interpretive* difficulty. I have already put some pressure on the sense of "literal" in this book, recognizing in advance the problems generated by that word. The literalizing of figures is common in *Paradise Lost*, and authorizes this probing into the process of literalization.

Second, the problem of intention raises an even more vexed question of evidence. Milton tells us he is inspired in his poem. If the critic is to regard all such utterances as purely figurative self-representations, the burden of proof would be upon him to demonstrate that all utterances within a poem are *intentionally* figurative. The bracketing of poetic statement in this manner sounds more sophisticated than it is; the notion of the literal is not so easily discarded. The "I" writing the poem is regarded from the bracketed perspective as a *persona*; so Anne Ferry, in *Milton's Epic Voice*, regards the "blind bard" as though Milton were not in fact blind, and as though he did not believe himself to be a bard. Milton's habitual stance, both in his poetry and in his prose, is to present himself as he is, or believes himself to be. The intention to represent oneself in this way, whether or not it is successful, must mean something. The "I" of the poem, as Kerrigan argues, always refers to John Milton, and this identity of self and representation (again, we do not decide the possibility of this identity) is bound to Milton's conception of his authority as a poet. He does not merely present himself as an inspired poet, with a knowing and ironic wink at his less credulous readers. He does not admit any distance between himself and the poet in the poem, and we can sense in the refusal to admit this distance a hunger for the literal, for the nonfigurative ground of the poetic act.

Although I am not prepared to rehearse here the evidence and arguments of Kerrigan's work, I do wish to emphasize with him the renewed historical importance of inspiration. Kerrigan reminds us of how truly alive the notion of prophecy is in the seventeenth century; some of that testimony is given in chapter 1 of this study. We have already noted, however, that Calvin argued with great force against "special revelation," as did all the major reformers except those we would now locate at the radical fringe. Milton himself did not necessarily attribute his early work (with the possible and problematic exception of the "Nativity Ode") to divine inspiration, nor does he perceive the existence of prophets as a necessary phenomenon of Reformation. And yet he does claim for his major poetic text this very mode of mediation (even "dictation" as he says in the invocation to Book IX). Historians such as Christopher Hill have a good *prima facie* case for associating Milton with the radicals, and I would follow Hill on points of doctrine (really, heresy), only stopping short of blurring the distinction between the poetic text and the "word" revealed to the radical reformer.[6] Neither Kerrigan nor Hill would allow us to make this distinction, which is fundamentally generic. The theological content of Milton's *De Doctrina Christiana*, for example, while it does not differ significantly from what can be detected in *Paradise Lost*, is supported by no claim to prophetic inspiration:

> For assuredly I do not urge or enforce anything upon my own authority. On the contrary, I advise every reader, and set him an example by doing the same myself, to withhold his consent from those opinions about which he does not feel fully convinced, until the evidence of the Bible convinces him and induces his reason to assent and to believe... Most authors who have dealt with this subject at the greatest length in the past have been in the habit of filling their pages almost entirely with expositions of their own ideas. They have relegated to the margin, with brief reference to chapter and verse, the scriptural text upon which all that they teach is utterly dependent. I, on the other hand, have striven to cram my pages even to overflowing, with quotations drawn from all parts of the Bible and to leave as little space as possible for my own words, even when they arise from the putting together of actual scriptural texts. (6:121-22)

The rhetorical stance of the Epistle to *De Doctrina*, from which this quotation is drawn, is metonymic in the sense that it establishes the authority of Milton's text by putting passages *together*, arguing by contiguity. The authority of Milton's name is authorized by the displacement of his *words*, and a consequent replacement of his name.[7] The *De Doctrina*, whatever it may actually have achieved, does not pretend to go beyond scripture in any way. The relation of *Paradise Lost* to scripture is much more complex, since the epic argues by expansion and condensation rather than textual repetition. Its hermeneutic principles are concealed behind its rhetoric.

All of Kerrigan's historical evidence for the resurgence of prophecy will not help us to make the final movement toward an understanding of why Milton should wish to see himself as Mosaically inspired. There is simply no necessity in such an act, unless this poem were indeed to be considered a new sacred text. Such a pretension would have to contend with the closure of the Bible, a text to be opened again only by an act of monumental hubris. Kerrigan accepts this hubris without judgment: "The epic is offered as another Testament. Writing with the prophetic inspiration higher than 'those Hebrews of old,' Milton assumes divine authority for every word, every event in *Paradise Lost* that does not appear in Scripture."[8]

Rather than follow Kerrigan to his sublime, if problematic conclusion, I would like to consider the question from another point of view. If (granting the inspirationalist premise) God chooses Milton to create a new scripture, why must this scripture take the form of an epic poem? Are not the expectations created by the genre in conflict with the intentions of a sacred text? I am inclined to read the intersection of epic invocation with biblical inspiration as, in its origin, an ambivalence of identity. The ego of the poet–prophet cannot easily leap over or erase this hyphenation; for Milton this is a question of primary identity. The prophets may have been good poets but Milton is first of all a poet. This ambivalence repeats the textual incompatibility of sacred and secular, already a matter of urgency in the Renaissance, because the thing we call "literature" is coming into being, a nameless proliferation of texts which are *not sacred*. Let us hypothesize, then, that Milton wins for himself the identity of prophet in the renunciation of the not sacred, rather than the intention to produce a sacred text. The act of renunciation ultimately renounces figuration itself, and the moment of inspiration is a moment of literal influx, between but not within, the movement of tropes. The structure of this moment will be analyzed (following Milton's own procedure in *Paradise Lost*) first as it fails, and then as it succeeds. The failed prophet in *Paradise Lost* is called Satan, and he is, as our hypothesis predicts, a successful poet.

I am less concerned with the "problem of Satan," which I deliberately

evade here, than with Satan's problem: the "begetting" of Christ. That
Milton should identify the beginning of cosmic history with the exaltation
of Christ is eccentric theologically,[9] but for Satan this "strange point and
new" is traumatic, unacceptable on grounds he himself does not certainly
apprehend. The fortunate coincidence of the figurative "begetting" with
the sudden revelation of the Messiah's literal priority, his participation in
the "begetting" of the angels, elicits from the (formerly pious) Lucifer one
of the more interesting speculations in the poem:

> That we were form'd then say'st thou? and the work
> Of secondary hands, by task transferr'd
> From Father to his Son? strange point and new!
> Doctrine which we would know whence learnt: who saw
> When this creation was? remember'st thou
> Thy making, while the Maker gave thee being?
> We know no time when we were not as now;
> Know none before us, self-begot, self-rais'd
> By our own quick'ning power...
>   (V.853-61)

One might remark of such a speech that it is designed for its already
receptive auditors, and yet this eruption represents too powerful and universal a wish to dismiss as mere rhetoric. We have no evidence that Satan
had formulated such a theory prior to Christ's exaltation, or that the subject
of origins had any meaning in heaven before this moment. The diminishing of Satan's authority, real or imagined, provokes this inquiry into
origins. The desire to be self-begotten (as Freud expresses it, to be the
father of oneself) is fundamental, contradictory, and entails repressive
consequences.[10] The band of Ethereal Sons gathers in the north to plot an
originative patricide much like the band of sons in *Totem and Taboo*. The
sexual-erotic motive is absent from the catastrophe of *Paradise Lost*, but not
the emphasis upon the primacy of the father, for which Milton had the
warrant of both the Bible and traditional theology, even the rudiments of
anthropology: "In the beginning this authority seems to have been placed,
as all both civil and religious rites once were, only in each father of the
family." This is Milton, not Freud, in *The Reason of Church Government*
(1:836). Some implications of a theological nature are disturbing. Milton's
story, we need to remember, exhibits the total complicity of the familial

analogy in the events of universal history. The contextual pressure of this denatured analogy is everywhere tremendous, as "The Father" and "The Son" are not merely metonymic signs. The authority of the Father inheres in his *being* the Father, before, as it were, we recognize any other attributes of deity.

In the passage quoted Satan happens to be speaking to a good son, Abdiel, who is somehow mysteriously aware of information no longer available to Satan. Satan seems genuinely not to know that he was created by the Son, a failure to which the ambiguous use of the name "Son" contributes. Abdiel's telepathic knowledge would be called revelation on Earth, which is perhaps why he is so strongly identified with the prophetic tradition; he is the type of the biblical prophet. Milton too is identifying with the good son, but darker links with the bad son are not difficult to find, and have recently been subject to much interpretation.[11] Satan becomes a revolutionary in the act of rejecting a revelation, the pure word of God that all the angels are privileged to experience. The failure to receive the word is compensated by recourse to a fantasy of origins, the desire to be self-begotten. Here at last we can establish a continuity with that other usurper of origins, imagination, because out of the silence of failed inspiration the Satanic imagination is born.

What Satan imagines is of course unimaginable, but this is only to say that imagination aspires beyond sensory perception and finally beyond itself. Here is Milton rhetorically imitating this aspiring:

Satan exalted sat, by merit rais'd
To that bad eminence; and from despair
Thus high uplifted beyond hope, aspires
Beyond thus high, insatiate to pursue
Vain War with Heav'n, and by success untaught
His proud imaginations thus display'd.
                    (II.5-10)

The representation is saturated with an unusual irony, precisely the distance between self and representation Milton cannot allow in the invocational mode. And yet the rhetoric does some of the work of invocation, generating movement out of itself, as Satan is forced to do, by a process of repetition rather than conjugation. Syntactically, Satanic aspiration is the result of the chiasmus which reverses the order of presentation while substituting "aspires" for "hope": "high . . . beyond . . . hope; aspires . . . beyond . . . high." The nominalist in every reader would argue that the words in the second half of the chiasmus lose meaning but they also generate strength, evidently out of nowhere. This generation *ex nihilo* Milton associates with imagination, which enters with Satan into the poem.[12] The draining away of meaning in the words of the sentence allows one to imagine the impossible, the one mental activity sustaining Satan in the project he knows will ultimately fail.

The consistency of the Satanic context of imagination is testified elsewhere in the poem, particularly in the sequence recording Eve's dream:

Assaying by his devilish art to reach
The Organs of her Fancy, and with them forge
Illusions as he list, Phantasms and Dreams,
Or if, inspiring venom, he might taint
Th'animal spirits that from pure blood arise
Like gentle breaths from Rivers pure, thence raise
At least distemper'd, discontented thoughts,
Vain hopes, vain aims, inordinate desires
Blown up with high conceits ingend'ring pride.
                    (IV.801-9)

The "conceits" have priority here, "ingend'ring Pride," and not the other way around. Milton is contending with the very problem Spenser uncertainly resolved in his discourse of "Fancy." The language of inspiration, commingling with the psychological terms, further complicates an already difficult moment, providing us with morally incompatible bases for a conception of imagination as a kind of internalized inspiration: the injection of venom, and the "gentle breaths from Rivers pure." The lines are also sadly proleptic. Satan will arise from a pure River as a less pure mist, to "inspire" a snake, whose rhetorical venom will gain "too easy entrance" into Eve's heart. The false inspiration collapses immediately into imagination, as though one were the demystified version of the other. Subsequent fantasies then build upon the initial error, as Adam later says: "But apt the Mind or Fancy is to rove / Unchekt, and of her roving is no end" (VIII.188-89).

Within the dream itself, imagination seems to preside entirely over the "dream-work," reacting not only upon the raw material of Eve's experience but upon the language of the poem ("fair it [the tree] seemed, / Fairer to my Fancy than by day"). The argument of the angel in the dream, that Heaven is "by merit" Eve's, surely means less to her than to the reader who has already read the ironic presentation of exalted Satan, "by merit rais'd." The image of Eve as a goddess, flying over the "Earth outstretcht immense" now inhabits her mind where no such image existed before. The conceit is a necessary basis for the "ingend'ring" of pride. Adam calls this matter an "addition strange," though the phrase on any other lips would be disingenuous. He further conjectures that "evil into the mind of God or man / May come and go, so unapproved, and leave / No spot or blame behind." The hypothesis is necessary if the reader is to absolve Eve of guilt at this point, and, indeed, we are not told that in the dream Eve eats the fruit. The elision itself absolves of guilt. Following the moral scheme of the poem, we do not read an act into this empty space, reserving that space for the will alone. Adam sees this point of origin (of the as yet uncommitted original sin), but worries over an even more prior source: "nor can I like / This uncouth dream, of evil sprung I fear: / Yet evil whence?" His long statement on imagination ought to be read with some lingering doubt about the relation of fancy to the Satanic presence:

> But know that in the Soul
> Are many lesser Faculties that serve
> Reason as chief; among these Fancy next
> Her office holds; of all external things,
> Which the five watchful Senses represent,
> She forms Imaginations, Aery shapes,
> Which Reason joining or disjoining, frames
> All what we affirm or what deny, and call
> Our knowledge or opinion; then retires
> Into her private Cell when Nature rests.
> Oft in her absence mimic Fancy wakes
> To imitate her; but misjoining shapes,
> Wild work produces oft, and most in dreams,
> Ill matching words and deeds long past or late.
>   (V.100-13)

The psychology here is so utterly conventional that one may want to call it regressive. It is difficult to believe that these notions were not already obsolete, given the much more suggestive discussions of imagination available to Milton in many texts, from Sidney to Bacon and Hobbes. But that is just the point: there is a striking narrative distance between the Satanic "inspiration" of Eve and Adam's psychological explanation of this event. The distance works to conceal a more interesting and subterranean confusion. Satanic *imitation*, like imagination, is tediously parodic, misjoining the shapes of the heavenly paradigm, as Fancy misjoins the shapes of earthly perception. Could Eve have had such a dream without the presence of Satan at her ear? The question has the heuristic value of allowing us to consider Satan and imagination as interchangeable signs; Milton hints at the substitutability of the terms only in the most covert fashion. When we meet the phrase "wild work" again (the only other use of the phrase), the context is war in heaven:

War wearied hath performed what war can do,
And to disorder'd rage let loose the reins,
With Mountains as with Weapons arm'd, which makes
Wild work in Heav'n, and dangerous to the main.
                    (VI.695–98)

The war has the same quality of fantastic substitution (mountains for weapons) as the dream, and suffers the same reduction to the category of the unreal. It is literally undone by the Messiah, who puts the mountains back into their places. The unreality of the war in heaven is also involved with poetic, specifically epic, conventions, another dangerous context, and one which Milton consistently qualifies with his revisionary contempt. Fictions can be degraded to dreams, but what is really degraded is the movement of imagination against pure mimesis. When Adam dreams, he sees only what his eyes would see if they were open. His dream is a perfect mimesis by a completely cooperative faculty of imagination, the only example in the poem of such harmony. The narrative distance, then, between the Satanic inspiring of Eve and the reductive psychology of imagination marks a more significant distance: between Milton's poetics and the concept of imagination.

If Milton is more aware of this concept than he desires to indicate, he is also aware of a dream behind Eve's dream, the literary *locus classicus* of the relation between imagination and poetry:

The poet's eye in a fine frenzy rolling
Doth glance from heaven to earth, from earth to heaven,
And as imagination bodies forth
The form of things unknown, the poet's pen
Turns them to shapes and gives to aery nothing
A local habitation and a name.

(A Midsummer Night's Dream V.vi.7–12)

It takes a presence no less than Satan's to displace this text from what would otherwise have been a conspicuous position in Milton's poetics. Milton's poetic successors seem not to remember his obvious antagonism toward the imagination; literary history records only the splendid collision of Satan with a specifically literary historical concept. The figure of Satan animates the idea of self-begetting already implicit in the language of imagination. Henceforth imagination is associated particularly with Milton, often with Satan, since no poet can create a more impossible fiction than Satan is already living through.[13] And yet the imagination is repressed in Milton, not simply because of its inherent proclivity to misshape, as the Protestant theologians were well aware, but also because the grandeur of the Satanic character has the effect of elevating associated qualities, such as intellectual curiosity. Milton's poetic instincts were curiously right and wrong; the repression of imagination is a significant failure, a failure ultimately to evict the Shakespearean pre-text from the domain of literary history.

We only begin to understand what this means when we remember that Milton's "aery shapes" faintly echoes Theseus' line, "Turns them to shapes and gives to aery nothing," omitting, as I noted in chapter 1, the word *nothing*. Theseus describes a truly daemonic poet in this passage, who looks less like any figure we need identify with Shakespeare than like *il penseroso*:

Dissolve me into ecstasies
And bring all heaven before mine eyes...

(165–66)

This poet, we know, *is* Milton. By the time *Paradise Lost* is being written, however, the mature author denies both the *furor poeticus* (frenzy) and the *ex nihilo* (the airy nothing). Kerrigan argues that the biblical model of a placid inspiration has displaced the classical Greek mania in Milton's poetics,[14] but the preference for *creatio ex se* is more obscurely related to his notions of poetic composition. The analogy of creation is an inestimably important intersection of the two poetics. For Milton the idea is even more than an analogy; *Paradise Lost* begins with the invocation of a muse whose authority derives from its presence at the moment of creation:

> Thou from the first
> Wast present, and with mighty wings outspread
> Dove-like satst brooding on the vast Abyss...

In *De Doctrina* Milton argues at length against *creatio ex nihilo*; his abyss is not empty but full, even when the lexical choices imply the opposite ("void") (6:299ff.). God creates *ex se*, drawing out of himself the forms to be imposed upon an already teeming universe. This matter too must ultimately be *ex se*, as Milton further argues, evading with this source/terminus some of the problems intruding into *Paradise Lost* with classical notions of chaos. To what extent is Milton relating his activity as a poet to the divine model of creation? One would like to be able to demarcate a boundary here, but that is not possible because of the difficult psychological structure of identification. If indeed Milton is trying to repress imagination as origin (as Spenser before him resisted its originary power), not all of the actions of the poetic ego, as an agency of repression, will be equally visible. Rather than slide too easily into analytic terms, let me present, as an analogy, the problem as it is worked out in Freudian texts on the genesis of authority. I propose by this means to accomplish two things: first, to sophisticate somewhat the language of identification, which has been very loosely and confusingly applied to the dealings of the Miltonic ego; and second, to establish that the problem of authority in Milton's epic does express itself through the dynamics of identification.

Genealogically, the formation of an internal authority coincides with the setting up of an "ego ideal" within the psyche, and this is a consequence of the dissipation of the Oedipus complex.[15] Some of this genealogy is of course not relevant, as the family romance of *Paradise Lost* is defective;

there is no mother deity and therefore no sexual tension arising from competing object choices. This defect, which is in itself interesting, does not remove Milton's plot from the vicissitudes of identification. On the contrary, the multiplication of sons reestablishes conflict at another level, as the conflict between the Messiah and Satan. We sense, without much reflection at all, the participation of the poet in this conflict, and therefore the presence of a differentiation homologous to that which Freud posited as taking place within the instinctual substrate.

From this point on, I shall borrow Paul Ricoeur's formulation of the problem, because it will eventually lead us to a central difficulty in the analytical understanding of authority. Freud wishes, Ricoeur says, to make the "economic process of the distribution of cathexis correspond to the historic process of the introjection of authority."[16] The problem, as it emerges in *The Ego and the Id*, is that "from the historical point of view the superego is inherited from parental authority, but from the economic point of view it derives its energies from the id."[17] This problem occurs because Freud wants to construe the ego ideal as a differentiation of the id, and therefore attach it to the economics of desire. Desire precedes identification, which is founded upon its frustration, a fact which Freud analyzed fully in the paper on "Mourning and Melancholia."[18] The melancholic has lost the love object, whose attributes become incorporated (introjected) as an ideal which permits libido to be redirected to the ego (Freud's "secondary narcissism"), even as the ego ideal turns a highly critical eye upon this very ego. The ambivalence of feeling toward the love object, therefore, is repeated within the psyche itself, and taints the genesis of authority with the love–hate nature of its origin ("object choice has regressed to identification"). Ricoeur does not finally accept this construction, and in a later chapter of his analysis argues that it should be possible to conceive of introjection as non-regressive,[19] a possibility that we must explore if we are to escape a thoroughly Satanic reading of *Paradise Lost*.

Because we know, of course, who suffers the loss in the opening cataclysm of cosmic history. Our difficulty in conceiving of Satan's prior stance toward the Father is precisely why the problem of origins is so crucial to the war in heaven, and incidentally why there should have arisen a Satanic reading of the poem. The angel Gabriel remarks in his confrontation with Satan:

who more than thou
Once fawn'd, and cring'd, and servilely ador'd
Heav'n's awful Monarch?

Words to which we usually respond, could this be Satan? Whatever else happened at the moment of the Messiah's exaltation, the loss of God as Lucifer's object choice is immediate and irrevocable. The pattern of Satanic behavior then follows the genesis of melancholia, as Satan begins to imitate God, to become what he has lost, to introject. Critics who deny the strength of the Satanic reading forget how powerful this love-hate really is, that this *ambivalence* is the source of the Satanic negative energy. Gabriel's further comment should give us pause in our meditation on authority:

who more than thou
Once fawn'd, and cring'd, and servilely ador'd
Heav'n's awful Monarch? wherefore but in hope
To dispossess him, and thyself to reign?
                                    (IV.959-61)

This is a rather dark view of identification, and one to which, we hope, Milton did not subscribe. Here is Freud again on the originary ambivalence of authority, from *The Ego and the Id*:

> The super-ego is, however, not simply a residue of the earliest object-choices of the id; it also represents an energetic reaction-formation against those choices. Its relation to the ego is not exhausted by the precept: "You ought to be like this (like your father)." It also comprises the prohibition: "You may not be like this (like your father)—that is, you may not do all that he does; some things are his prerogative."
>   (p.24)

Where Freud posits as "prerogative" the possession of the Mother, the defective romance of *Paradise Lost* points to the seemingly arbitrary elevation of the Son, which eventuates in the act analogous to the repression of the Oedipus complex: the repression of the Son's name by Satan. After the revolt in heaven, his name is *never* spoken by his sibling and adversary, except (and this exception proves the rule) in a single metonymy:

O thou that with surpassing Glory crown'd,
Look'st from thy sole Dominion like the God
Of this new World; at whose sight all the Stars
Hide thir diminisht heads; to thee I call,
But with no friendly voice, and add thy name
O Sun, to tell thee how I hate thy beams
That bring to my remembrance from what state
I fell, how glorious once above thy Sphere...
                                    (IV.32-39)

The displacement of feeling upon the innocent object follows the pattern
of a projection, the inverse of introjection, but a closely related defense.[20]
The association of angels with stars, particularly the fallen angels (a metonymic convention in *Paradise Lost*), the recollection of their "diminisht
heads," the granting of dominion over this world to the "Sun"—all of these
utterances can be traced to the repressed subscript of an address to the
Messiah. The metonymies of sun and stars evolve historically into pagan
religion, which Milton interprets according to his enlightened hermeneutic as the renaming of the devils, or the false naming of God. The sun to
pagan worshipers is not a name but a god itself. In this sense Milton's
conception of paganism can be allied to Freud's notion of regression, as
well as to the projections Freud believes to be the basis of primitive
religion.

The long soliloquy to which these lines form an introduction reveal
more about Satan the melancholic than we can hope to recover from the
rhetorical brilliance of the public speaker, and for the reason that the
repression is here closest to the surface. The nominal subject of Satan's
meditation is the debt of gratitude he once felt toward his creator, but
which he construes in retrospect, much as if he were his own analyst, to
have been a delusory burden. The internal analyst, however, participates in
the present self-delusion of the speaker because he does not succeed in
forcing his patient to recognize the *son* in the *sun*. Instead, Satan remythol-
ogizes his fall as an attempt to quit "in a moment... the debt immense of
endless gratitude," as though his ambition derived from an *excess of love*.
The desire to be, as well as have, the Father, is frustrated in the begetting of
the Messiah, whose presence is once again denied and concealed behind a
dynamics of desire:

... whom hadst thou then or what to accuse,
But Heav'n's free love dealt equally to all?
(IV.67–68)

Heaven's free love cannot really be dealt equally to all since all are not equal. The Messiah's superiority by "merit" and "birthright" is a fact as well as a decree. If this is so, then we can lift a final layer of self-delusion from this speech, and say that even more deeply repressed (a "lower deep") is a desire to be the Son, or, in the place of the Son, to recover at least that much of a mutuality of love. Identification occurs with the hated object and contributes in large measure to the self-hatred that pervades the soliloquy.

Where the partners are unequal, there cannot be equal love, and from this truth authority is deduced. That the parent cannot love or be loved sufficiently insures the future introjection, which in turn establishes authority. We recognize as authorities only those with whom we have already identified—or so Freud, who could not conceive of authority apart from the internally answering chord of secondary narcissism. But this authority is predicated upon loss and alienation, really upon the solipsistic self-containment of the psyche, which cannot possess *anything* external to itself. Ricoeur's reservation is necessary here, because it is based upon the perception that "In Freudian theory the external fact par excellence is authority."[21] We need to consider the possibility of introjection without the cataclysmic initiating loss if we are not to yield the poem entirely to a Satanic-Freudian view of authority.

The model of identification implied by the fictional motifs of analytic language cannot, without difficulty, be generalized to illuminate the Miltonic ego. When we say that the poet identifies with his creations we intend something of a different order of meaning from the psychogenesis of authority; and, indeed, the limitations of the analytic analogy are intrinsic. Nevertheless we recognize the value of these paradigms. The Satanic experience of defeat before the unalterable otherness of authority carries with it a pathos which is the burden of the human condition, and is related by a complex series of consequences to the emergence of the literary historical Satan as a figure of sublimity. Satan reifies a possibility within Protantism itself, which in its extreme forms widened the gulf between God and man and knocked away the bridges across that abyss. The poet owes much of the sublimity of his self-representation to the congruence of

Satanic and epic aspirations, since he too wings that abyss, a point that is now generally acknowledged.[22] The possible failure of these aspirations would plunge the poet into the very fall already suffered by Lucifer, a fall into Satanic identity. But this does not happen, and the mechanism of introjection does not tell us why.

In the psychological language familiar to Milton, inspiration remains distinct from imagination, not subject to a Hobbesian reduction. At the same time, however, we wonder how the poet can possibly establish his authority without identification. There is almost an ethical divide confronting us at this point, because we still have the option of crediting to Satan *all* of the energy in the poem, acknowledging Freud's problematic belief that the ego ideal derives its energies from the id. This would mean, from a literary historical stance, the imagination as origin (a fictive rather than a literal origin), and from the psychological, pure internality, the *absence* of external authority. Readings of Milton have tended to divide along these lines, which happen also to correspond to the different ways in which poets and scholars have responded to the Satanic energy. This energy, which the Romantics inevitably call "imagination," is more or less Satanic in every major poet after Milton. It should be possible, then, to take seriously a Blakean reading of the Miltonic ego without lending to that reading any more hermeneutic credit than we have already given to the language of psychoanalysis.

Two final comments, one about Satan, the other about the good son, and we shall be able to return to the ground of tropological analysis. Readers of *Paradise Lost* have always found it difficult, if not impossible, to imagine the Lucifer who preceded Satan. The earlier incarnation is not so unimaginable, I would like to believe, but the moment of transition, of origin, remains as evanescent and inexplicable as the moment of creation itself. The two origins share at least their mystery in common, and for that reason, I would like to return to Satan's meditation on his "self-begetting" and remystify that discredited notion:

>   who saw
> When this creation was? remembrest thou
> Thy making, while the Maker gave thee being?
> We know no time when we were not as now,
> Know none before, self-begot, self-rais'd ...

If we allow this text to drift slightly into the ironic, the words become suddenly and undeniably true. The already fallen angels no longer know the time when they were not, as now, *fallen*. They might remember their former happiness, but they are no longer who they were; their identities are immutably altered, and the continuity with a former identity is lost. Lucifer becomes Satan, and in the gap between these two identities is the origin that Satan seeks. He does indeed create himself *as Satan*, self-authored, self-begotten. Sin does not create him; he is prior to sin, it is his own creation. What Satan can claim as his ultimate achievement is the making of discontinuity, points in time where something completely new can be born of itself, without cause, without dependent relation to any past. This is the *creatio ex nihilo* to which Milton objected so deeply in *De Doctrina*, preferring instead the assurance of continuity in the idea of *creatio ex se*.

We have already acknowledged the *poetic* desirability of this *ex nihilo* creation, and, in order to redress the balance, it is necessary to stand outside the poem, with the Milton who is more than a poet, and place the entire Satanic story in its true genre, *tragedy*: "If thou beest he; But O how fall'n . . ." The loss of identity plunges the self into a condition of mental vertigo, like the fall through chaos. I want to point to another curiously similar loss of identity in the poem, by way of transition to the more complex "identification" of John Milton. One of Milton's critics has observed that whenever the Messiah leaves the confines of Heaven, he is no longer called by any name signifying sonship, but rather simply "God."[23] He cannot be God, of course, but it is as though, outside of Heaven, the distinction between identities were allowed to lapse. This confusion of names must be understood as strategic, and yet something more is intended than a fiction. Let us call it a "fiction of the literal," admitting the primacy of the fiction, while seeking to specify the element of the literal. Provisionally, this element can be construed as *power*, which in the cosmos of *Paradise Lost* is infinitely transferable; that is, it does not suffer a change in transference such as necessarily describes the movement *into* language, the "transferring" of literal to figurative. So God to the Son:

> Into thee such Virtue and Grace
> Immense I have transfus'd, that all may know
> In Heav'n and Hell thy Power above compare. . .
> (VI.703–5)

This power, even in the execution of a "task transferred," is the *same* power in the Son as in the Father, unaltered by movement away from its origin, and therefore expressive of the same authority. Some such model governs the text I will now consider, the invocation to Book III.

3. *Secondary Hands*

The alternative available to us now, that Milton identifies with Christ, is only too tempting because it so easily resolves the dilemma of the Satanic reading.[24] The relationship between the Messiah and the Father can be considered paradigmatic, but not of Milton's relation to Christ. To identify with the Son would mean something of a different nature than the Messiah's identification *with the Father*. This question intrudes upon our line of inquiry because all along we have been suppressing the consequences for the poetic ego of identification with Satan, assuming only (what seems indisputable) that Satan is a good poet. Satan does not write the poem of *Paradise Lost*, but—and this question follows from the inspirationalist premise—does Christ? The more "literal" our notion of inspiration happens to be, the more the imitation of Christ is going to look like a thoroughgoing identification. Distance from the Father is not circumvented but *maintained* in the merging of the poetic ego with the Messiah, and I suspect that Milton desired this distance, a *dividing* of God as he expressed the concept in his poem *Ad Patrem*.[25] At the same time, when one looks for all the covert overlappings in the description of poet and Son, such as exist between Satan and the narrator, these intersections seem to be much more general than specific, more a matter of shared intention than of parallel linguistic expressions. If Milton identifies himself as a poet with Christ, that process emerges as very problematic, because Milton too is forced to suppress the name of his muse, as Satan could not speak the name of Christ. Metonymy becomes the necessary trope of invocation, reminding us of the unsettling fact that the names of the gods are aboriginally conceived to be substitutions for one unspoken "original" name. It is as though this name were "literal" and all the others displacements or figures.[26] The name of the muse, however, becomes literal in *not being spoken*; the poet speaks in tropes but the *prophet* restores the literal name by not speaking it, by calling our attention to the very displacements of language. The duality or ambivalence of Miltonic identity underlies what would otherwise be this puzzling obsession with naming in the poem. Nowhere is the problem more acute than in the opening lines of the most critical of Milton's invocations:

Hail holy Light, offspring of Heav'n first-born,
Or of th'Eternal Coeternal beam
May I express thee unblam'd? since God is Light,
And never but in unapproached light
Dwelt from Eternity, dwelt then in thee,
Bright effluence of bright essence increate.
Or hear'st thou rather pure Ethereal stream,
Whose Fountain who shall tell?
                              (III.1-8)

I would like somewhat peremptorily to pass over the lineage of light symbolism, which has been documented fully by scholars interested in the many concepts crowding the only too inclusive realm of reference encompassed by light. The assumption behind such inquiry is that light is invoked as a figurative expression, and the assumption, while it can be sustained through the passage quoted above, begins to decay by the twenty-first line of the invocation:

                    thee I revisit safe,
And feel thy sovran vital lamp; but thou
Revisit'st not these eyes, that roll in vain
To find thy piercing ray, and find no dawn;
So thick a drop serene hath quencht thir Orbs,
Or dim suffusion veil'd.

The crux also represents the first crossing in an invocation whose structure is crossing itself: chiasmus. What appears to be crossed here is the boundary between the figurative and the literal. This lament for the poet's blindness implies that all along the light being addressed was simply the physical phenomenon itself. There are several reasons for construing this contradiction as a temporally determined revision rather than a simple synchronic dichotomy, not the least of which is that the invocation is concerned with re-seeing. The iterated "revisit" carries its Latinate sense of "to go to see again." And since the thing seen (or now not seen) is light itself, the way back to a rereading of the opening lines, of the sign which is "light," is opened up in the act of verbal revision. Light is that by which things are seen, but it also has an active power, as though blindness represented light's self-willed absence ("thou revisit'st not"). An error, a wandering away from the truer sense of light, must be located at some point in these lines, since this error is responsible for the impasse of "thee I revisit'st... but thou revisit'st not."

The inadequacy here is partially one of critical terminology; the figurative light we would like to identify with the thing invoked is mistaken for a metaphor, even for a moment by the poet himself ("since God is Light"). All figures are not metaphors, although at this time of invocational (also vocational) crisis, the poet might desire the easier trope. The Richardsons, in what is still one of the better commentaries on the poem, understood the necessity of metonymy in the context of invocation: "the ancients were very Cautious by what Names, and in what Manner they Addressed their Deities, in Imitation of Whom Milton is so in this Hymn to Light."[27]

I have already assumed that the unnamed name is Christ, not without some weariness with the volume of criticism contending the contrary.[28] External evidence is infinitely debatable, since Milton was no respecter of traditions, and I would like to recollect here only two internal pieces of information. First, we know that Satan is going to parody this invocation in his address to the Sun in Book IV; our understanding of both passages is immeasurably deepened by the recognition of how extensive this parody is. Second, the language of direct address to the Son is wholly consistent with the language of invocation. Here are the angels singing a *laudate* to the Messiah:

Thee next they sang of all Creation first,
Begotten Son, Divine Similitude,
In whose conspicuous count'nance, without cloud
Made visible, th'Almighty Father shines,
Whom else no Creature can behold; on thee
Impresst th'effulgence of his Glory abides,
Transfus'd on thee his ample Spirit rests.
Hee Heav'n of Heavens and all the Powers therein
By thee created...
                                        (III.383–91)

Both Christ and the muse of the invocation are defined by an ontological secondariness, one an effluence, the other an effulgence. Both are involved by transference of power in the act of creation; they are interchangeable signs of secondariness, just as Satan and imagination were interchangeable signs for false priority. Readers who conjecture that Milton's muse is the Holy Spirit misconceive the structural relations governing the transference of power in the epic. It should be possible to argue now that this muse cannot be the Holy Spirit, indeed, cannot be anyone but Christ, because the epic itself is a "task transferred," the work of "secondary hands." If we need to seek evidence for the negative side of this position outside of the epic, we need go no farther than *De Doctrina*, on the denial of creative agency to the Spirit:

> Sometimes it [Spirit] means the power and virtue of the Father, especially that divine breath which created and nourishes every thing. In the latter sense many interpreters, both ancient and modern, understand that passage in Gen. 1. 2.: that we should interpret the word as a reference to the Son, through whom, we are constantly told, the Father created all things. (6:282)

My only reservation involves the relation of "spirit," the most slippery of concepts in *De Doctrina*, to the poet's unwillingness to express directly a relationship to Christ. The anxiety of naming ("May I express thee unblamed?") is more fundamentally an anxiety that has been associated by Geoffrey Hartman with representation itself.[29] The will to represent is the will to figuration, which does not so much deny the literal as indefinitely defer its entrance into language. I can at this point allow the word "literal" to regress into its etymological base, the "letter," but for the critic this would be only a Pyrrhic victory. One hears Milton again in the invocation to Book VII expressing this anxiety ("the meaning, not the Name"), an uneasiness at having to insure a literal presence by means of a *nominal* absence. The transference of power implied by a literal inspiration is represented by a trope, a "fiction of the literal," because there is no literal language for the "meaning." Even the representation of creation itself is dependent upon the inherent contiguity rather than identity of language:

My overshadowing Spirit and Might *with thee*
I send along...

                  (VII.165–66)

To acknowledge the exigency of that odd little prepositional phrase is to recognize the true nature of Milton's problem. The "spirit" here is again not the Holy Spirit but power itself, the only "commodity" in Heaven and the most difficult to "accommodate." The Spirit must go *with* Milton in the verbal act of invocation, and at the same time the act must accommodate this Spirit in the language of men.

The classical invocation is for Milton as for his predecessors a tropological gesture, but for Milton alone the success of invocation as a sequence of *tropes* obscures the *literal* moment of inspiration. At a certain point in the invocation, this phenomenon must seem to represent a failure to the poet himself and he turns to the literal fact of his blindness. It is curious but undeniable that the first half of the invocation fails; the slide into tropes of light or naming is abruptly halted. Whatever is invoked does not answer this call:

> ... but thou
> Revisit'st not these eyes, that roll in vain
> To find thy piercing ray, and find no dawn;
> So thick a drop serene hath quencht thir Orbs,
> Or dim suffusion veiled.

The transfusion of power (spirit) which effects creation ("into thee I have transfus'd") becomes a "suffusion veiled," and the poet must now set about to recover the invocational mode by recourse to some other strategy.

If Milton perceives his blindness to be analogous in some way to the very interposition of the trope between the poetic ego and the nameless, hovering muse, that "blindness" is asserted, almost defiantly, to be only a temporary occlusion in the next lines of the invocation:

> Yet not the more
> Cease I to wander where the Muses haunt
> Clear Spring, or shady Grove, or Sunny Hill,
> Smit with the love of sacred Song; but chief
> Thee Sion and the flow'ry Brooks beneath
> That wash thy hallow'd feet, and warbling flow,
> Nightly I visit; nor sometimes forget
> Those other two equall'd with me in Fate,
> So were I equall'd with them in renown,
> Blind Thamyris and Blind Maeonides,
> And Tiresias and Phineus Prophets old.
>   (III.26–36)

The double negative construction and optative subjunctive highlight an obliquity in these lines that can be associated with the original ambivalence of poet-prophet. Milton is committed to the distinction between sacred and secular text, which surfaces here with peculiar intensity, almost as though the secular "fiction" of invocation were being admitted in the remembrance of classical precedents. Some measure of doubt is being expressed in the very possibility of identification with pagan poets, and I would argue that Milton does not at all desire to be "equalled" with these precursors. The stakes are such that merely to be equalled in renown with the greatest of the pagan poets would represent a failure; the risk of failure is always present in the poet's mind ("nor sometimes forget"). More revealing is the absence of biblical prophets from this list of precursors. The Richardsons, who read these lines with considerable insight, pointed to the significant ambiguity governing the syntax of this period:

> ... tis true Poets are often rank'd with Prophets, they are Nevertheless Distinct Characters, and are accordingly distinguished Here. Milton wishes for the Fame of a Poet, the fame of those two he mentions; he thinks also of the prophets as having been Blind, but his Wish extends not to them, but is applyd to the Other two only.[30]

But I must justify now my own inclination to read the lines as though they said the opposite of what the poet meant. The Richardsons speculate that "too" (meaning "also") rather than "two" was intended by Milton, the mistake being that of the amanuensis; and this "sets the matter right." Without resorting to Milton's blindness to justify emendation of the text, we can at least recognize this blindness as the potentially *ironic* element in the process of identification. Light enters the poem in the literal sense only as an absence and Milton must follow through the implications of this absence before any literal presence can be restored. And this means overcoming the dangerous irony of a partial identification: blindness without the compensatory prophetic vision.

If tropes are signs of absences, the invocation has reached its great crisis of absence in the regression to irony. This juncture is a "crux" in the technical sense, since the remainder of the invocation reverses the topical order of the preceding segment. The result is a chiasmus:

$$\text{Light} - \text{Blindness} : \text{Blindness} - \text{Light}$$
$$\text{1-21} \qquad \text{22-36} \qquad \text{38-50} \qquad \text{51-55}$$

The hinge of the chiasmus (37-38) is a famous grammatical instability:

Then feed on thoughts, that voluntary move
Harmonious numbers...

The status of "move" hovers momentarily as an intransitive before resolving itself as transitive with the unexpected object. Notice, however, that the subject has disappeared altogether (because the sentence is imperative), and Milton no longer needs to specify what mind is feeding upon what thoughts. Merely to have hesitated at this crossing—for a moment *not to go across* (in-transire)—permits the influx of power that turns the invocation around, as Wordsworth would say, with the might of waters. The condition of the ego prior to this moment is genuinely depressed by the blindness that presents itself as a literal fact and only in desire as the signature of divine favor. To have converted this blindness into a favorable trope, into this very signature, is in turn to have restored a literal light to the poet, not physical light as we know it, but real vision. And this is precisely what happens in the second half of the invocation, a re-versing, re-seeing, re-troping:

as the wakeful Bird
Sings darkling, and in shadiest Covert hid
Tunes her nocturnal Note. Thus with the Year
Seasons return, but not to me returns
Day, or the sweet approach of Ev'n or Morn,
Or sight of vernal bloom or Summer's Rose,
Or flocks, or herds or human face divine...

But of course all of these things are "returning," even in the very turning of the verse, and it is somehow with a more acute vision that the day can be seen dawning at the catalectic beginning of the line. This is not a metaphoric vision, and to call it such would be to mistake the sense of chiasmus. The inspiration has taken place, and yet we have not seen it; nor could we see it happening since it took place *between* two lines, and *between* tropes. The blindness which emerges on the other side of this crossing is a sign, welcomed by the poet, triumphing over its own pathos, and the Celestial Light shining in the last lines of the invocation must then be understood, because it is invisible *to us*, as a literal presence to the poet. We may still want to construe this Celestial Light as a metaphor, and yet I want to resist the temptation to take up the inner/outer dichotomy as coterminous with the figurative/literal. The Celestial Light undoes the metonymy opening the invocation by reminding us that this light has real physical priority over the light that comes into being with the creation of our world: "before the Sun, before the Heavens thou wert."

If we have yet a lingering impression of being tricked by what is after all a rhetorical maneuver, we need to remind ourselves at what cost the invocation makes light a presence again for the blind poet. The instability of "move" in line 37 is justified only by the obscuring of the poetic ego in the subjectless imperative "feed." It is here, I believe, that an identification does take place, related to, though distinguishable from introjection. The oral quality of introjection (feeding) points to regression, but this "return" is also an advance, what Ricoeur would call non-regressive identification. The incorporating ego remains unnamed but not unidentified. This is in fact why the model of introjection proves to be inadequate, since it provides for nothing like the establishing of authority by the *willing* transference of power. According to the analytic model the son incorporates the father only upon a predicated loss. Something altogether different is hinted in such a lexical choice as "voluntary," which activates a considerable range of meanings without specifying the originating will.[31] Wordsworth, who understood what Milton did accomplish in this momentary sacrifice of the ego, found another example of this voluntary act, not surprisingly, in the very place where the Messiah "assumes" the authority and power of the Father:

So said, he [Messiah] o'er his Sceptre bowing, rose
From the right hand of Glory where he sat,
And the third sacred Morn began to shine
Dawning through Heav'n; forth rush'd with whirl-wind sound
The Chariot of Paternal Deity,
Flashing thick flames, Wheel within Wheel, undrawn,
Itself instinct with Spirit, but convoy'd
By four Cherubic shapes...

                    (VI.746-53)

Let me quote Wordsworth's allusion to this passage in his *Essay on Epitaphs*; he is commenting on a poem he admires: "The whole is instinct with spirit, and every word has its separate life; like the chariot of the Messiah, and the wheels of that chariot, as they appeared to the imagination of Milton aided by that of the prophet Ezekiel. It had power to move of itself but was conveyed by cherubs."[32]

Milton's lines actually exhibit a greater degree of ambiguity than Wordsworth's reading, which quietly alters "convoyed" to "conveyed," making explicit a paradox (synchronic) where Milton has a temporal instability—precisely like the discontinuous sense of "move" in the invocation to Book III. The chariot of paternal deity is auto-kinetic, self-moved, "but [and this disjunction functions like the false end-stop after "move"] convoy'd / By four Cherubic shapes." Accompanied or driven? The conveyance of the chariot is, if I may borrow another Wordsworthian expression, an example of *redundant energy*. This redundance is precisely where we want to end up, since the transference of power in the poem, *to* the poem, should be accomplished without diminishing authority, without attenuation. To the Messiah belongs a delegated authority but also "all power," and this power is not subtracted from the Father, not wrested away from him. To some readers the distinction between these two powers in action is only too slight, when the Son "puts on" the "terrors" of the Father. Elsewhere we hear a milder voice, whose subtly revisionary cadences ought to be acknowledged for future reference. At this point I want to emphasize the coexistence of authority and power in the Son, as a result of a prior act of deference ("bowing, rose"), analogous to the Miltonic acceptance of literal blindness and the disappearance of the ego as subject in the intransitive moment, the moment of not going across. The ego reconstituted on the other side of the chiastic crossing (and is this ego conveyed or convoyed?) has put on the same power as the Messiah:

So spake the Son, and into terror chang'd
His count'nance too severe to be beheld...
(VI.825-26)

Like the Father, the Son can no longer be beheld; and this is the deeper sense of the severity of his countenance. When Adam and Eve are described in Book IV, this same word is linked to a conception of authority graven into the structure of the poem:

for in thir looks Divine
The image of thir glorious Maker shone,
Truth, Wisdom, Sanctitude severe and pure,
Severe, but in true filial freedom plac't;
Whence true autority in men...

(IV.291-95)

Throughout my reading of these passages I have been resisting the temptation to label as paradox this particular mysterious moment of subjection/freedom ("filial freedom"), or of moved/self-moved. The Son assumes authority in willing the submission to the Father, but the subsequent identification obscures the direction of this willing, that is, the Father wills both the subjection and the elevation of the Son. The moment of bidirectional crossing restores a literal priority to what would have been merely delegated authority, authority by trope: *as if* Christ were God, or *as if* Milton were Christ. The evasion of the trope results in something more than "as if": the poem as an expession of the same power given to the Son. This power can only be severe; it is a disturbing excess in *Paradise Lost*, and reminds us of something potentially darker in the process of identification. The relation of the Messiah to the Father is by no means simple, nor is authority to be achieved without the risk of a severity that can become a severing. Miltonic authority is increasingly defined in opposition to, and isolation from, the human community. We remember, too, that chiasmus is a device as available to Satan, whose loneliness is absolute, as to Milton or Christ. When we read perhaps the most famous chiasmus in the poem, the sense of isolation is unbearably intense:

More safe I Sing with mortal voice, unchang'd
To hoarse or mute, though fall'n on evil days,
On evil days though fall'n, and evil tongues;
In darkness, and with dangers compast round,
And solitude...

(VII.24-28)

"Yet not alone" the invocation continues, assuring continuity itself in companionship with the unnamed muse.

Another continuity, already noticed by Wordsworth, returns Milton to the domain of literary (or textual) history, even while it paradoxically highlights his tremendous effort to escape from this more human lineality of descent. The chariot of paternal deity, emblem of self-moving itself, is derived from Ezekiel, and there is a significant principle here for literary history. The moment of inspiration seems to transcend any problem of human priority by overleaping texts altogether to receive as spoken word, literal and present, the poem of the muse. The ambivalence of Milton's identity as poet-prophet, one might think, ought to be resolved in the reception of this word, and yet this is not the case. The poem remains full of regressive and residual material, for which we can give the name of Milton's most complex trope: allusion. And not all of these allusions have the built-in safeguard of deference to the sacred text. Between Christ (or Ezekiel's "muse") and *Paradise Lost* intervenes the whole of Western literature; and the heavenly muse is surprisingly not averse to speaking again words whose authority is fundamentally suspect. As much as Milton desires continuity with the prophetic line, so much does he desire the "severing" of the poetic tradition, and his authority is incomplete without proof of this severance. I am less concerned with the obvious declarations of this severity (for example, the deprecation of epic convention in the invocation to Book IX) than with the complex moment of allusion, where the poetic voice seems condemned to repeat against the counterpressure of denial and renunciation.

4. *The Better Teacher and the Belated Peasant*

Allusion, as I have argued in chapter 4, is the poet's own version of literary history, written, as it were, from the interior. Critics perceive the literary work from an exterior position, but what they interpret, because this matter is already interpretation, gains only an illusory objectivity. One senses that current dissatisfaction with literary history derives more from this inability to perceive its interior existence, as though bodies of poetry, or poets, were the unitary structures of poetic history.[33] One purpose of my own argument, beginning with a more interior history of imagination, has been to revise the notion of a line descending from Spenser to Milton, because this notion is founded upon an anachronism and a questionable assumption about the nature of influence. Although much of what has been presented as cultural background indicates that Spenser and Milton shared a problematical relation of religious and poetic identities, and that both poets therefore are uncertain about the distinction between a sacred and a secular text, this does not mean that Spenser must necessarily have been the major influence upon Milton, or even that influence need be conceived in such interpersonal terms. Milton's own testimony notwithstanding, the evidence of *Comus* produces a much more complex picture of influence than is generally accepted. Spenser himself, if the *Mutabilitie Cantos* are read as his crisis poem, contended more deeply with the spirit of Ovid than with his acknowledged original, Chaucer. Such histories are inevitably revisionary.

The most recent and sophisticated model of literary history, formulated by Harold Bloom, happens to find its literary analogue in the fall of Satan, whose complicity in the history of imagination can be indisputably established. Bloom's view of Milton's "debt immense," however, turns out to confirm what literary historians have always said with far less reason, and there is something curiously conservative in the restriction of influence history to the Protestant family.[34] Bloom's sophistication of literary history is nevertheless precisely what we need at this point in order to move beyond the intertextual dialogue of *Comus*, and the antitextual movement of invocation, because the model he proposes can be interiorized by means of tropes. Whether or not we adopt psychoanalytic, semiotic, phenomenological, or any other extrinsic model, we can be reasonably certain that an interior literary history can be written tropologically, which is in effect what Bloom has shown to be possible. It seems to me, therefore, that the most important discovery of recent years (initiated by Angus Fletcher) is the significance of transumptive allusion as the trope *of* literary history, and it is by reading this trope that we shall be able to modify further the current conception of Renaissance lines of influence.[35]

I must preface this discussion, however, with consideration of a text that is not an example of transumptive allusion, because this text has become the *locus classicus* of discussion concerning the influence of Spenser on Milton:

> It was from out the rinde of one apple tasted, that the knowledge of good and evill as two twins cleaving together leapt forth into the World. And perhaps this is that doom which Adam fell into of knowing good and evill, that is to say of knowing good by evill. As therefore the state of man now is; what wisdome can there be to choose, what continence to forbeare without the knowledge of evill? He that can apprehend and consider vice with all her baits and seeming pleasures, and yet abstain, and yet distinguish, and yet prefer that which is truly better, he is the true warfaring Christian. I cannot praise a

fugitive and cloister'd virtue, unexercis'd & unbreath'd, that never sallies out and sees her adversary, but slinks out of the race where that immortall garland is to be run for, not without dust and heat. Assuredly we bring not innocence into the world, we bring impurity much rather: that which purifies us is triall, and triall is by what is contrary. That vertue therefore is but a youngling in the contemplation of evill, and knows not the utmost that vice promises to her followers, and rejects it, is but a blank vertue, not a pure; her whitenesse is but an excrementall whitenesse; Which was the reason why our sage and serious Poet *Spencer*, whom I dare be known to think a better teacher then *Scotus* or *Aquinas*, describing true temperance under the person of Guion, brings him in with his palmer through the cave of Mammon, and the bowr of earthly blisse that he might see and know, and yet abstain. (2:514ff.)

What interests literary historians in this passage is not only the tribute to Spenser, but perhaps more, the curious lapse of memory, since Guyon is not accompanied by the Palmer in the Cave of Mammon. The prevailing explanation for this lapse was argued by Ernest Sirluck, who believes that Milton misinterpreted the Aristotelianism of Spenser's moral scheme, according to which "the mere habit of temperance is sufficient to withstand the solicitations" of Mammon.[36] This statement would be true from Spenser's point of view, as though Spenser were reading Milton: yet the origin of the memory lapse remains unexplained. One can say only that *if* Milton simply forgot the exact details of Canto vii, this is how he might have written the episode. From another point of view, however, there is no such thing as "simply forgetting," and Harold Bloom posits a stronger, re-pressed motive compelling the revision:

> Milton's is no ordinary error, no mere lapse in memory, but is itself a powerful misinterpretation of Spenser, and a strong defense against him. For Guyon is not so much Adam's precursor as Milton's own, the giant model imitated by the Abdiel of *Paradise Lost*. Milton re-writes Spenser so as to *increase the distance* between his poetic father and himself. St. Augustine identified memory with the father, and we may surmise that a lapse in a memory as preternatural as Milton's is a movement against the father.[37]

If, as I shall argue now, Milton is writing to *decrease the distance* between himself and Spenser, it is with great respect for the revisionary genius of Bloom's argument. It is difficult to believe that Guyon is anyone's "giant model," Abdiel's or Milton's, neither of whom suffers from the weakness of his precursor. Milton's desire to co-opt this example for an argument in which it does not quite fit gives us a passage quoted, as it were, "out of context," and the result is quite different from the effect of allusion. It is all the more remarkable, then, that the passage introduces Bloom's analysis of transumptive allusion in *Paradise Lost*. The same motive is being attributed to both the lapse of memory and the mode of allusion, and it is here that I would like to make some distinction. If Bloom's interpretation were correct, Milton would have written the Mammon episode *as Spenser did*, with Guyon unaccompanied, and he misremembers the fact of the Palmer's absence to reserve for himself the heroic model of virtue standing alone against temptation. This model, however, is manifestly retrospective; we read *Areopagitica* having read *Paradise Lost*. The more nearly contemporary of Milton's protagonists is the Lady of *Comus*, who cannot stand alone except in passive resistance. She too needs the accompaniment of someone like the Palmer, and there is more reason to assume that Milton is remembering *Comus* (where "sage and serious" also appears) than that he is looking forward to Abdielian greatness.

There is one other fact to consider, Milton's interpretation of Acrasia's Bower as the bower of *earthly* bliss; this epithet does not appear anywhere in Book II of *The Faerie Queene*. The conditions of our earthly existence are uppermost in Milton's mind at this point, obscuring the difference between the Cave of Mammon and the Bower of Bliss. *In context* it is more important for Milton to allow the Cave of Mammon to function as another emblem of our earthly existence than to acknowledge its status as an underworld. The reading Harold Bloom gives to this passage is itself a transumption, where none is yet necessary, since the syntax governs both prepositional objects with the same adjectival condition: "brings him in with his palmer through the cave of Mammon and the bowr of earthly blisse."

If we were to propose, nevertheless, that at some level Milton is disturbed by this difference, we would still have to understand the rewriting of Book II as an attempt to decrease the distance between his position and Spenser's, in order to enlist the aid of Spenser's name in the argument of *Areopagitica*. It is not without some hesitation however, that I deplete the passage of a meaning that Bloom finds so astonishing and indicative. An allusion at this point would have given us safer ground upon which to argue that Milton feels Spenser is too near him. The absence of allusion (or the willingness to call openly on the name) suggests, though it does not prove, the absence of anxiety. The trope employed in the passage from *Areopagitica* is still metonymy (Guyon/temperance, Spenser/choice), or what Bloom calls, following Harry Berger, "conspicuous allusion."[38] As we have already seen in *Comus*, not until the name is suppressed does allusion begin to function transumptively, or in Bloom's tropology, as a trope-reversing trope. It may be, then, that the memory lapse is not necessarily or only an effect of intersubjective tension. But this is only to say that we have not advanced beyond *Comus* in our understanding of Spenser's position in Milton's work.

It should be possible to advance this understanding, given the conspicuous entrance of Spenser at so crucial a point in Milton's argument. We can begin by setting Milton's acknowledgement in its rhetorical context: the determining metaphor of master and pupil. That Milton should see himself as Spenser's pupil tells us not that he suffers from the usurpation of his "doctrinal" ambitions (which he indulged relentlessly), but that he has the guilty conscience of the student who has diverged from his teacher. *Areopagitica* finds its true voice neither in the quiet subservience of the "better pupil," nor in the anxious stretching of a too crowded mind, but rather in the ambivalent pleasure of resistance, in the enjoyable outrage against the "overseeing fist," which must first be invoked in order that the claim of the pupil to mastery be put forward:

> And how can a man teach with autority, which is the life of teaching, how can he be a Doctor in his book as ought to be, or else had better be silent, whenas all he teaches, all he delivers, is but under the tuition, under the correction of his patriarchal licencer to blot or alter what precisely accords not with the hidebound humor which he calls judgment. When every acute reader upon the first sight of a pedantick license, will be ready with these like words to ding the book a coits distance from him. I hate a pupil-teacher, I endure not an instructer that comes to me under the wardship of an overseeing fist. (2:532-33)

The highly wrought anger of Milton's polemic is congenial to us now because we happen to agree with his position (or we should). And yet his choice of metaphor is not a necessary one, and his anger reaches beyond the figurative status of instruction to touch a complexity in the nature of discipleship. The problem of the Licensing Act, though it is real enough, and not to be diminished, occasions Milton's more general declaration of independence: the freedom to choose his own teachers. Obviously no one has this freedom except retrospectively, in the power to *reject* what has already been taught. *Areopagitica* argues the right of the individual to this power of negation. If Milton has established his title to mastery, however, he does not come to that authority by rejecting Scotus or Aquinas; it is only too easy for Milton to reject such teachers. I take it that he cannot so easily justify his divergence from his "better teacher," and that his acknowledgment of Spenser has the economic advantage of discharging the residual guilt of this divergence. Milton has already moved too far away from Spenser, and the danger of this self-reliant posture is acknowledged in the allusion (via *Comus*) to Guyon, who really can do no more than stand without his Palmer. Milton must "bring in" the Palmer even as he brings Spenser into his argument, because it is the absence of both that signifies danger.

But can Milton, after all, do without Spenser? I would like to suggest that for Milton this question should be read as "Can the sacred poet do without allegory?" It is also in the realm of representational choice that we must locate the origin of Milton's remembering and misremembering of Spenser. The authority of allegory is established by its guarded and self-qualified relation to truth. Allegory cannot err because it represents error itself, endlessly circumscribing the domain of truth. Milton knows that his argument in *Areopagitica* is implicitly a defense of heresy, of that statement of truth which *can* be wrong because it ventures to *state*. The difficulty of the way Milton chooses as his own also tells us something about the persistence of allegory in his work. Consider, for example, the reworking of the "error" about Spenser's Palmer into the climactic "allegory of truth":

> Truth indeed came once into the world with her divine Master, and was a perfect shape most glorious to look on; but when he ascended, and his Apostles after him were laid asleep, then strait arose a wicked race of deceivers, who as that story goes of the *AEgyptian Typhon* with his conspirators, how they dealt with the good *Osiris*, took the virgin Truth, hewd her lovely form into a thousand peeces, and scatter'd them to the four winds. From that time ever since, the sad friends of Truth, such as durst appear, imitating the carefull search that *Isis* made for the mangl'd body of *Osiris*, went up and down gathering up limb by limb still as they could find them... (2:549)

The allegory tells us, incredibly, that though our truth may be *partial* (synecdochic) it is not, as in allegory, *substitutive* (metaphoric). The first clause of this passage recollects the earlier "brings him in with his Palmer," but the repetition of the master/student paradigm is significantly revised. If the Truth that is the word of the Master (Christ) must stand alone after the Master's departure, this autonomy collapses almost immediately, as the Truth begins to wander, or simply, is disseminated. The wicked deceivers who receive the word (the Catholic Church!) in turn mangle it, and so become bad teachers. I do not doubt that Milton thought the fragmentation of the original Truth a great tragedy, and its "re-collection" a wonderful thing. And yet this allegory, however powerfully idealizing, is overdetermined by the guilt Milton has accumulated in his revolt against his teachers. This guilt is displaced upon the safely unequivocal villain, the Catholic interpreter. The allegory is opened more truthfully by Milton himself in the next paragraph, where it is his intention less to remind us again that the meaning of Christianity is not to be found in its traditional *doctors*, than to free us from the *better teachers* of the Reformation itself:

> The light which we have gain'd, was giv'n us, not to be ever staring on, but by it to discover onward things more remote from our knowledge. It is not the unfrocking of a Priest, the unmitring of a Bishop, and the removing him from off the Presbyterian shoulders that will make us a happy Nation, no, if other things as great in the Church, and in the rule of life both economicall and politicall be not lookt into and reform'd, we have lookt so long upon the blaze that *Zuinglius* and *Calvin* hath beacon'd up to us, that we are stark blind. (2:550)

Spenser too possesses light, which, if it did not blind his student, illuminated the path he chose not to follow. When we turn to the first book of *Paradise Lost*, we are not surprised to find this light still shining, not blindingly, but as a "darkness visible." The Cave of Mammon, as Bloom rightly argues, *is* Milton's hell. We see many things by the Spenserian light, but most of all we see how *Paradise Lost* came *not* to be written as an allegory. Here, then, are the stanzas alluded to in *The Faerie Queene,* and the allusive passages from Book I of Milton's poem:

Thence forward he him led, and shortly brought
  Vnto another rowme, whose dore forthright,

To him did open, as it had beene taught:
Therein an hundred raunges weren pight,
And hundred fornaces all burning bright;
By euery fornace many feends did bide,
Deformed creatures, horrible in sight,
And euery feend his busie paines applide,
To melt the golden metall, ready to be tride.

One with great bellowes gathered filling aire,
And with forst wind the fewell did inflame;
Another did the dying bronds repaire
With yron tonngs, and sprinckled oft the same
With liquid waues, fiers Vulcans rage to tame,
Who maistring them, renewd his former heat;
Some scumd the drosse, that from the metall came;
Some stird the molten owre with ladles great;
And euery one did swincke, and euery one did sweat.

$$\text{(II. vii. 35–6)}$$

Mammon led them on
Mammon, the least erected Spirit that fell
From Heav'n...

... by him first
Men also, *and by his suggestion taught,*
Ransack'd the Center, and with impious hands
Rifl'd the bowels of thir mother Earth
For Treasures better hid. Soon had his crew
Op'n'd into the Hill a spacious wound
And digg'd out ribs of Gold. *Let none admire*
That riches grow in Hell; that soil may best
Deserve the precious bane...

Nigh on the Plain in many cells prepar'd,
That underneath had veins of liquid fire
Sluic'd from the Lake, a second multitude
With wondrous Art founded the massy Ore,
Severing each kind, and scumm'd the Bullion dross...

$$\text{(I.679–80.684–92.700–4; italics mine)}$$

The depth of the allusion is patent, even the continuation of *Areopagitica's* great trope of master/guide: Mammon is a *teacher* of men. And yet, when we ask what else Milton has taken from Spenser here, we must acknowledge that the allusion to the Cave of Mammon is essentially complete by line 710, when the Palace of Pandemonium *begins* to rise from the ground. The severe context within which Mammon is reborn in Milton's text does not extend to particularities in the description of the edifice itself, whose massiveness (contemporary baroque) is immediately and continually denied by an altogether different allusive context:

Anon out of the earth a Fabric huge
Rose like an exhalation, with the sound
Of dulcet symphonies, and voices sweet,
Built like a Temple...

(I.710-13)

The allusion here, as John Hollander points out, is to the genre of the masque, particularly to the "transformation scene," the most technically advanced form of dramatic illusion in Renaissance stagecraft.[39] There is yet another sense in which we are witnessing a transformation, since the rise of Pandemonium from the infernal soil also marks the temporary disappearance of the unambiguous interpretive voice. This voice is replaced by a series of allusions and allusive similes, which are themselves little transformation scenes. The textual discontinuity is effected with only the slightest disruption in the movement of the verse; we really do not mark the absence of the narrator's voice until the much greater disruption of its return after Mulciber's fall: "thus they relate / Erring." I emphasize the importance of this absent/present voice in its comings and goings because I believe it derives in its *presence* from the continuity Milton feels with the Spenserian moral allegory, and in its *absence* from his resolve not to "relate" his story *as allegory*. The problem here is not that Spenser has already done what Milton desires to do but rather more deeply an anxiety about the possibility of a text both sacred and *mimetic*. The voice that tells us "thus they relate / Erring" exposes the false mimesis of classical literature, but the true mimesis of *Paradise Lost*, discontinuous with the secular text, cannot veil itself in allegory.

What Milton fears as perhaps too near him belongs to the great mimetic success of Renaissance literature, to its very illusionistic power, preemi-

nently to the drama and the drama's greatest poet. The subtle transformation of Pandemonium into a masque inaugurates what Bloom rightly sees
as a "continuous and unified allusion to the very idea of poetic tradition,"
but the transumption exempts Spenser from the very beginning. Milton is
not, as in *Comus*, using Spenser to annul the power of the Shakespearean
voice; something else is at stake here, a problematical relationship of sacred
voice to secular text. Even after we have understood how the literal,
transcendent muse speaks to Milton, we remain perplexed at the persistence of the secular form, to which the Spenserian voice can respond but
not, as in *Comus, transform*. Where this voice is strongest it is *almost*
internalized, and this partially internal accompaniment is the sense in
which Spenser can go "with" Milton: "Let none admire that riches grow
in hell . . ." These are the words the Palmer would have spoken *if* he had
descended with Guyon to the Cave of Mammon. That readers have expressed uneasiness at the ventriloquism testifies to the incomplete nature
of Milton's introjection of Spenserian authority (and so to the limits of his
investment in his *auctor*). Spenser enters Milton's poem now *with Mammon*,
as the antithetical image of Mammon as teacher. Both Mammon and
Spenser can only lead the way, preparing the ground of transumption,
its soil.

   It is the more mysterious Mulciber who preempts the great achievements
of classical and contemporary art by surpassing them, as Milton must link
his poetic achievement to the literal preemption of Mulciber himself. The
reduction of human art consequent upon the fall of the archetypal artificer
(Mulciber's fall) turns out to be surprisingly equivocal, since this human
power returns more forcefully with every allusion, finally in the very
reduction of the devils themselves, the greatest of the transformation
scenes in the epic. It is often said that Milton "killed" the epic form in
English literary history, but his greater victory was against the drama, the
secular triumph of his native tradition. Great long poems continue to be
written, but no great poet (with the exception of Milton himself in *Samson
Agonistes*) would speak again in the form of the drama.[40] In this overcoming
Milton takes up both the blank verse medium, the Parian marble of
Renaissance drama, and the allegorical play that was the seminal form of
Paradise Lost. The allegory returns when it is called, but the dramatic
impulse returns of its own will, a much more powerful voice that must be
re-versed into sacred epic. I would like to examine now the final simile of

Book I, which responds to the power of that voice, by further descending into an underworld beneath Hell itself:

Behold a wonder! they but now who seem'd
In bigness to surpass Earth's Giant Sons
Now less than smallest Dwarfs, in narrow room
Throng numberless, like that Pigmean Race
Beyond the Indian Mount, or Faery Elves,
Whose midnight Revels, by a Forest side
Or Fountain some belated Peasant sees,
Or dreams he sees, while over-head the Moon
Sits Arbitress, and nearer to the Earth
Wheels her pale course; they on thir mirth and dance
Intent, with jocund Music charm his ear;
At once with joy and fear his heart rebounds.
                            (I.777-88)

The energy expended in this transumption, the force that propels us so far away from Pandemonium, is the first indication we have that some extraordinary poetic event is taking place. The trope of transumption, or *metalepsis*, was translated by Puttenham as "the far-Fetcher," and these elves have indeed been fetched from afar. The voice speaking here derives, via *Comus*, from the pre-text of that masque, *A Midsummer Night's Dream*, and we are left once again with the necessity of reflecting upon the importance of that play to Milton. Why, at this moment, should the devils be likened to Shakespearean fairies? The motive of reduction is inadequate to explain the simile-allusion, since the stature of the devils is in some way *aesthetically compensated* even while they are being physically reduced. Neither do the fairies of Shakespeare's play suffer from their sudden displacement into an infernal context. One hears the *effort* to reduce, directed both against Shakespeare and against the devils themselves, but what we see is an allusion that establishes its own autonomous poetic law. Geoffrey Hartman understands this autonomy as a "counterplot" whose hermeneutic first principle is Milton's "feeling for divine imperturbability . . . the knowledge that creation will outlive sin and death."[41] The reader can detect this counterplot in many allusions, including this one, though I am interested in another kind of survival, working perhaps against the counterplot itself. The context of the Shakespearean allusion is, as in *Comus*, the quarrel of Oberon and Titania, which must have had some extraordinary but partially inexplicable significance for Milton. Titania invites Oberon to "dance in our round / And see our moonlight revels, go with us." Oberon refuses, since Titania will not give him the "Lovely boy, stolen from the Indian king" (perhaps touching off the memory link, "Beyond the Indian mount"). The fact of the quarrel "fetches" from *Comus* once again the pre-text from *A Midsummer Night's Dream:*

And now they never meet in grove or green
By fountain clear or spangled starlight sheen
But they do square...

(II.i.28–30)

Oberon is transformed into the "belated peasant," equally aloof from the midnight revels, but for different reasons. Milton is closer to this peasant, as he did not, like Oberon, have the chance to join in the Titanian revelry; but he must recreate this possibility poetically in order to choose to be apart, where the choice and not the belatedness determines his position, as Hartman says, *ab extra*. Nevertheless, we are as impressed by the belatedness itself, which has given the peasant this vision, as we are by the possibly chosen alienation from the scene; if this peasant is at all like his creator, we might say that he chooses to linger in this way. It is a belated peasant indeed who sees such an archaic vision; and this vision, *because* it is archaic, brings to a point of crisis the development of Milton's enlightened hermeneutic. The reader encountering these fairies must choose to remain apart, in his enlightened present; he must choose Milton's mimesis over the powerfully real illusions of Renaissance drama.

Just as we begin to understand, however, the necessity of this choice, the allusion is compounded strangely with a recollection of Virgil, a further regression to an even more "obsolete" text. The context of the second allusion resonates harmoniously with the Shakespearean context because the phrase "sees, or dreams he sees" leads us to another disunited couple, Dido and Aeneas, even while the doubling of pre-texts complicates the focusing of vision; we are less and less sure of what we are seeing. The link between the two uncertain visions is the moon, another observer *ab extra*,[42] but in Virgil a simile for Dido herself. Aeneas meets her, of course, in Virgil's underworld, where she is really being met again.

inter quas Phoenissa recens a volnere Dido
errabat silva in magna. quam Troius heros
ut primum iuxta stetit adgnovitque per umbras
obscuram, qualem primo qui surgere mense
aut videt aut vidisse putat per nubila lunam,
demisit lacrimas ducique adfatus amore est...
(Aeneid VI.450-55)

> Among them, with wound still fresh, Phoenician Dido was wandering in the
> great forest, and soon as the Trojan hero stood nigh and knew her, a dim form
> amid the shadows—even as, in the early month, one sees or fancies he has seen
> the moon rise amid the clouds—he shed tears and spoke to her in tender love;
> (Loeb translation)

Overleaping Shakespeare's fairy world, we are once again in an underworld, but only to find ourselves in the midst of a very human scene. The
moon is the slender link holding the two visions together, and it too is in
motion, inherently unstable. This moon, wheeling her course "nearer to
earth," is less obscure in Milton than in Virgil, but at the cost of making
problematic the earth itself. This is not *where we are* in either Virgil or
Milton, although it is perhaps where Shakespeare is, where even his fairies
may reside. We are nearer to earth in this passage than Milton will permit
us to be for quite some time, if ever. Wallace Stevens would say that *Paradise
Lost* is not a poem of the earth. Nor is Milton a poet of the earth, if that
means a Mulciberian fall into the secular, the *worldly*. The allusion here
may be said to "transume" Shakespeare, but not without its own tragic
irony, borrowed from Virgil. Milton rejects the Shakespearean, the world
of moonlight, imagination, fairies, paganism, and Elizabethan drama. All
of these rejections are here in the alienation of the belated peasant, who is
really in context watching a dance of devils, hard though it may be to credit
this.[43]

Like Aeneas, Milton has made his choice, and he is not yet certain that he
has been recompensed for the Dido he was forced to give up. She returns
to him now, as the poems of the earth return, *to reject him*, as though he had
not undertaken the first renunciation:

talibus Aeneas ardentem et rorva tuentam
lenibat dictis animum lacrimasque ciebat.

illa solo fixos oculos aversa tenebat
nec magis incepto voltum sermone movetur...
(VI.467-70)

> With such speech amid springing tears Aeneas would soothe the wrath of the
> fiery, fierce-eyed queen. She, turning away, kept her looks fixed on the ground
> and no more changes her countenance as he essays to speak.
> (Loeb translation)

Dido's silence is tearingly pathetic in Virgil's text, and it is this silence that
Milton most fears. He must reject Dido, renounce what she represents, and
yet she must continue to speak to him, as the voice of allusion itself (the
literary function of the underworld is disclosed to us here as the housing of
these echoes, the verbal analogues of shades). So the peasant continues to
hear the music of the fairies, genuinely charmed by what is genuinely
"charming," a word we know to be saturated with the Miltonic ambivalence to literary tradition. "At once with joy and fear his heart rebounds"—
this is unmistakably the ambivalence itself, a "rebounding" between past
and present, secular and sacred, text and text, as much ambivalence as
Milton can admit into his poem.

The transumption, then, is curiously equivocal. Milton does not establish his priority to literary tradition without acknowledging a deep sense
of loss; and the loss must express itself as an acknowledgment *of Shakespeare*. I believe this fact accounts for the apparent incongruity of the scene
depicted; the belated peasant pauses to admire the very siren song that
might be, if he were to linger too long, captivating. Milton's effort to
establish his poem as a rupture in the literary tradition, a point of vertical
descent by the Muse, is also like what *might* have happened had Adam not
chosen to fall with Eve. Adam can choose as Aeneas does, that God may be
obeyed, but Milton cannot recollect this precedent at the moment of
Adam's choice without upsetting the moral balance of the poem. And yet
he does remember elsewhere in *Paradise Lost* this traumatic sense of loss.
Eve herself remembers, as it were, prospectively:

... back I turned
Thou following cridst aloud, Return fair Eve.
Whom fli'st thou? whom thou fli'st, of him thou art...
(IV.480-82)

And we hear Aeneas say to Dido: "*quem fugis*? extremum fato, quod te adloquor, hoc est."[44] These are the last words Aeneas is permitted to say to Dido, and they are the first words Adam says to Eve. He has already lost her when he speaks the word "Return," and when she returns to him, he will never lose her again. In Adam's retelling of Eve's creation to Raphael, this incident is omitted (we would say, repressed). If Adam does not lose Eve a second time, Milton must surely have experienced a tremendous (albeit ambivalent) relief in this fall through continuity ("whom thou fli'st, of him thou art"). As a poet, Milton chooses differently: not to fall. He can say to the great spirits of the past, Return!, but it is more important that he know how to say, *nunc dimittis*. I recur to the sense in which Milton believes authority to be severe. Adam loses precisely this authority in his unwillingness to sever himself from Eve:

Bone of my Bone thou art, and from thy state
Mine never shall be parted...

Our state cannot be sever'd...

                    (IX.915-16.958)

The simile I have been discussing is complex enough to make it difficult for us to measure the profit and the loss. Whatever Milton may have lost seems more than recompensed in the return of departed spirits, even when they come back to reject him. My point is that transumptive allusion does not merely reverse a temporal relationship in order to establish the authority of the later poet. These reversals are subject to more intricate motions of "rebounding," since they are responsive to an ambivalence within the poet himself. Milton's relation to his tradition is not exhausted by terminologies of continuity or discontinuity, or even of tropes, like transumptive allusion, that fuse these terms in a dynamic fashion. A better sense of what happens temporally in Milton's interior literary history is given us by that most originary of allusions, to the Homeric fall of Mulciber:

                    from Morn
To Noon he fell, from Noon to dewy Eve,
A Summer's day, and with the setting Sun
Dropt from the Zenith like a falling Star.
                    (I.742-45)

I cannot see Milton here "mocking" Homer, as Bloom argues, by over-accentuating the idyllic nature of Mulciber's fall.[45] This fall seems to me deliberately prolonged, Milton's *verweile doch* to the spirit of Homer. The fall of the original artist into secularity, temporality, is ambiguously ex-tended as time becomes the precondition of human value. This experience of time is the medium of human existence, what Milton elsewhere calls "process of speech." When the motion of Mulciber's fall is suddenly speeded up to the image of a falling star, the splendor of the dissolution is not qualified aesthetically by its untruth. So long as this artist can be kept falling, so long can he remain in the poem. When we come to the harsh "thus they relate / Erring," we are reminded of how difficult a choice this is for Milton, how enjoined to harshness he is by the very allure of what he renounces. Homer is not easy to mock, much less to give up, despite his error. This is also Dido wandering in the wood ("errabat silva in magna"), and every other wanderer in the poem. Excepting God the Father, this is every character and every "spirit" in *Paradise Lost*.

Miltonic authority as writer of a sacred text, speaker for the heavenly muse, is guaranteed by the source from which it emanates, and the literal power of that source. Milton's humanity, however, remains as complex and troubled as the interior literary history of *Paradise Lost*, because Milton shares with his poetic predecessors what he cannot give up or deny: that very humanity. The impulse behind invocation would remove the poem altogether from literary history, as it would elevate the Miltonic voice above the merely human process of speech. To return that voice, like fallen Adam, to its place of poetic birth, a "fitter soil," is not to deny the success of invocation but to maintain the human priority of fiction, the trope of allusion over the power of invocation. My reason for making this choice, only apparently against the manifest intention of the poem, has something to do with what I feel to be an ethical imperative, but even more with the neglected historicity of *Paradise Lost*. The most belated of all epics exploits its disrelation to a contemporary setting as a means of assuring the purity of its sacred subject. The failure of this intention is a *poetic* success, indeed, the source of the poem's sublimity. We begin to understand this sublimity when we return *Paradise Lost* to history, this and every epic's "native soil."

CHAPTER SIX

Ithuriel's Spear:
History and the Language of
Accommodation

Thought can as it were *fly*, it doesn't have to walk. You do not understand
your own transactions, that is to say you do not have a synoptic view of
them, and you as it were project your lack of understanding into the idea of
a medium in which the most astounding things are possible.

Wittgenstein, *Zettel*

1. *"Thir own dimensions like themselves"*

The simile-allusion concluding Book I of *Paradise Lost* complicates the
idea of literary history by pushing to a further limit the notion of reduction,
which is the structure of both metonymy and its more complex successor,
transumption. When the simile spends itself, however, there remains
something more to be said, and this supplementary matter is untouched by
both the rhetorical reductions taking place within the lines of verse, and
the physical reductions of bodies within the palace of Pandemonium. I
would like to place some pressure on these additional lines in order to open
a pathway from literary history to history itself, which seems to have been
virtually excluded from the poem but which remains "left over" at precisely those points where transumptive allusion reaches a zenith of complexity. There are uneasy currents of contemporary allusion in the final
paragraphs of Book I, ranging from an almost certain reference to St.
Peter's Basilica, to more uncertain allusions to the Barberini pope, and
perhaps to the Long Parliament.[1] These contemporary allusions are in-
versely related to the literary allusions; as the past is idealized, the present

carries a greater weight of negative judgment. At the least, an air of political and religious decay hangs over this passage, whether or not we care to specify the topical references. The upper echelons of the infernal hierarchy are therefore "unreduced," as power flows away from the lesser devils to be concentrated in a more privileged elite, here an object of Milton's scorn. Within this surprising revelation Milton insinuates an even more difficult notion, which, though it seems at first quite removed from the matter of history, will eventually lead us back to the "native soil" of *Paradise Lost*:

> Thus incorporeal Spirits to smallest forms
> Reduc'd thir shapes immense, and were at large,
> Though without number still amidst the Hall
> Of that infernal Court. But far within
> *And in thir own dimensions like themselves*
> The great Seraphic Lords and Cherubim
> In close recess and secret conclave sat...
>   (I.789–95)

The line I have italicized is puzzling because we are never told what the dimensions of these devils are. Milton is saying only, "However big they are, that is how big they are." Tautology displays an inherent tendency toward conundrum. Similes of size in Book I, far from clarifying dimensions, permanently confuse them, a fact generally noted.[2] This confusion seems to be their purpose, or at least an intermediate intention. I would like to consider the poet's deliberate lack of specificity about such matters as the size of the devils, an indication of more fundmental difficulties of representational language. The uncertainty noted above seems to be embedded in the language itself, in the non–simile "like themselves." If there can be no similitude without difference, this is not a simile, but the spurious simile does not point to a purely mimetic representation (as though we had been given not a picture but the thing itself). There is still one remove between the absence of simile and the undistorted perception of the devils themselves, and much of the poem is located in this mysterious distance. This much was recognized as long ago as Dr. Johnson, whose formulation of the problelm remains perhaps the best and most useful:

Another inconvenience of Milton's design is, that it requires the description of what cannot be described, the agency of spirits. He saw that immateriality supplied no images, and that he could not show angels acting but by instruments of action; he therefore invested them with form and matter. This, being necessary, was therefore defensible; and he should have secured the consistency of his system, by keeping immateriality out of sight, and enticing his reader to drop it from his thoughts. But he has unhappily perplexed his poetry with his philosophy. His infernal and celestial powers are sometimes pure spirit, and sometimes animated body. When Satan walks with his lance upon the *burning marle*, he has a body; when in his passage between hell and the new world, he is in danger of sinking in the vacuity, and is supported by a gust of rising vapours, he has a body; when he animates the toad, he seems to be mere spirit, that can penetrate matter at pleasure: when he *starts up in his own shape*, he has at least a determined form; and when he is brought before Gabriel, he has a *spear and shield*, which he had the power of hiding in the toad though the arms of the contending angels are evidently material.[3]

These objections have a markedly post-Cartesian ring, and the entire statement must be cleared of the charge of anachronism before the substance of Johnson's criticism can be redeemed for contemporary use. If Milton did not distinguish between spirit and matter, except as degrees in a scale of being, there remains a point of divide beyond which *representation* does not reach. The ideological monism can be credited without resolving the dualistic problem at the level of representation. Johnson was particularly fortuitous in his choice of examples, many of which cannot be dismissed as simply illustrative of the more exalted Miltonic monism, or of a supposed Renaissance transcendence of our divided modern consciousness. Milton seems to emphasize this division between spirit and matter precisely where the "philosophy" would demand the blurring of distinctions. Let us take one of Dr. Johnson's examples, Satan at the ear of Eve, "squat like a toad." The phrase does not specify that Satan has actually taken the form of a toad, and Johnson would say that Milton ought to have decided one way or the other; but in fact the uncertainty is resolved in the following lines:

Him thus intent Ithuriel with his Spear
Touch'd lightly; for no falsehood can endure
Touch of Celestial temper, but returns
Of force to its own likeness: up he starts

Discover'd and surpris'd. As when a spark
Lights on a heap of nitrous Powder...

....

So started up in his own shape the Fiend.

(IV.810–20)

The proper point is surely that Satan's shape-changing has coincided with a trope, and that Milton sees no need to distinguish between the two so long as Ithuriel's spear happens to be around. I would like to elevate this spear to something like a poetic principle and say that it represents an ideal relation between the object and the process of representation. The touching of Satan is recognizably an apotropaic ritual, a warding off of the evil spirit, as well as a translation or revelation of truth. Ithuriel's spear translates, as it were, the simile "like a toad." Although it has become conventional to emphasize the anti-poetic element of Milton's discipline, as though all rhetorical devices were suspect as Satanic, it is just this conclusion which can be avoided by the notion of translation. The simile is undone by Ithuriel, or revealed as literal. The thing we thought we saw is what we really saw; but this is not to say that the first vision was unnecessary. The whole of creation, Milton believes, moves (*translatio*) toward the condition of becoming like itself. This is not an infernal process at all, but one to which Satan is as subject as any other creature.[4] This "becoming" can also be conceived as a paradoxical return, or, within language, as the trope's return to the literal from which it has diverged. Tropes can then be associated with the earlier stage of a progression from one state of being to another.

Readers of Milton, or of Protestant theology, will of course recognize an analogy to the doctrine of typology, whose importance is now fully acknowledged.[5] My own concern is both narrower and broader. Dr. Johnson did not understand that Satan could be either spirit or matter because he did not have Milton's "typological" interpretation of matter itself: from "shadowy types to truth" coincides in *Paradise Lost* with from "Flesh to Spirit." But there is also something very right about Johnson's sense of incongruity because we still do not have a clear picture of Satan, even after he has been transformed into his "own shape." Again we have only the tautology, "he looks like himself." I said that Ithuriel's spear represents an ideal relation and by that I mean to reduce the spear to an emblematic status, an image of a terminal state that is never completed in the poem. The ideal is expressed more abstractly by Raphael in his speech about "subliming"—the distinction between matter and spirit works like a sliding bar in Raphael's scale—but we never manage to see the "thing itself" when we are speaking of "spiritual" beings. This might be a vain quest, after all, and yet Milton worries the notion in every instance where the figurative is allowed to slide into the literal.

I propose to work out an understanding of this process of literalizing in order to assimilate its greatest failure into the achievement of the poem. Ithuriel's spear, we discover, does not always work. Milton touches history itself with this spear, and recoils when nothing happens. This assertion might seem at first perverse, when every reader knows that Milton succeeded so well in submerging contemporary reference beneath an almost opaque layer of literary allusion. The sense of troubled contemporaneity pervading the close of Book I, while it is an undeniable presence, is quite difficult to specify. This is a transformation of sorts, but precisely what does not happen at the touch of Ithuriel's spear, which translates the figurative into the literal, the type into the anti-type. History, if it is the medium of the Providential God, is already a language, already a system of figures. The poem ideally restores a more essential "likeness" in a further translation out of the language of historical fact, but the translation ought to produce a less ambiguous picture, a univocal interpretation. This does not at all describe the relation of *Paradise Lost* to its historical context, which is anything but perspicuous. The apparent expelling of history from the poem is a consequence of a prior failure and determines a number of compensatory strategies, for example, the use of epic conventions against the generic premises of epic itself—the poem of national origins. This is not merely to say that Milton is reacting to the failure of the English revolution. The omission of contemporary reference already constitutes a reaction, but oblique reference is not difficult to discover; Christopher Hill enumerates these responses in what he calls "political analogies."[6] Yet the analogies tell us disappointingly little about *Paradise Lost*, which is to say that merely uncovering a "veiled reference" might be a beginning but cannot be an end of criticism. The notion of reaction to failure is more inherently meaningful in that such reactions affect the process of representation where least expected. The most authentic intentions, connoisseurs tell us, are discernible in the minutest of particular details. Milton's largest intentions have to do with the peculiar position he and his nation occupied in a historical process, but all of that "intentionality" seems to have been displaced with the decision not to write a national epic. My supposition is that this burden of meaning has not disappeared from the poem. Rather it has been dispersed throughout, saturating the epic even at the level of individual phrases and rhetorical devices. I will take up first, however, the larger intention, returning to Dr. Johnson's objection because it illuminates, from his very commonsensical perspective, the concept that virtually defines the largest intention of *Paradise Lost*: accommodation.

2. *The Language of Accommodation and Galileo's "Optic Glass"*

If Dr. Johnson had sought to ground his objection in the language of theology, he would have said that Milton's "confusion of spirit and matter" is an example of an accommodation that concedes too little to the understanding of the poem's auditors.[7] This is to assume the commonplace notion of the doctrine of accommodation, which is basically quite simple: Revelation cannot be expressed except in human language, whose intrinsic limitations prevent an exact description of divine events or personages, hence necessitating figurative or "anthropomorphic" representations. Dr. Johnson could not have known that Milton's understanding of this idea was peculiar in several respects. He did not, for example, believe that the "accommodating" was done by the prophets themselves, who were conventionally supposed to have had a vision of naked truth. Rather the accommodating was done by the divine mediator speaking to the prophets. Nor did Milton believe that the language of the Bible need be historically accommodated, that is, adjusted to the understanding of a reader's particular time or place. Johnson's remarks, in focusing upon the problem of spirit and matter as a question of representation, imply that Milton ought to have accommodated the language of the Bible just as this language had earlier accommodated the vision of the prophets. We are better able, it would seem, to conceive of immateriality than to accept the too physically weighted depiction of Miltonic angels. To Johnson, Milton's representation seems strangely archaic. In truth, Milton's hermeneutic was by the standards of his own time remarkably enlightened. He applied to the Bible a principle that H. R. McCallum, his best interpreter on this subject, calls Kantian. Here is *De Doctrina* on the representation of God:

> Our safest way is to form in our minds such a conception of God, as shall
> correspond with his own delineation and representation of himself in the
> sacred writings. For granting that both in the literal and figurative descriptions
> of God, he is exhibited not as he really is, but in such a manner as may be
> within the scope of our comprehensions, yet we ought to entertain such a
> conception of him, as he, in condescending to accommodate himself to our
> capacities, has shewn that he desires we should conceive. For it is on this very
> account that he has lowered himself to our level, lest in our flights above the
> reach of human understanding, and beyond the written work of Scripture, we
> should be tempted to indulge in vague cogitations and subtleties.[8]

Several extraordinary conclusions follow from so radical a statement,
the most obvious being the flattening out of biblical language: it no longer
makes sense to distinguish between the literal and the figurative, since no
literal basis can be specified for any figurative depiction of deity. It should
be evident already that such a doctrine will have a huge effect upon the
status of figurative discourse in *Paradise Lost*, lending impetus to what
might be called the literal drift of Milton's tropes. A second, "Kantian"
conclusion is determined by the "noumenal" status given to God in this
argument. The language of the Bible expresses as much as we can know of
God; our understanding is therefore limited by language itself. A third
conclusion touches upon the status of the poet in a poem aspiring to the
condition of the sacred text, and reintroduces into this larger context all of
the problems of authority and inspiration structuring this essay.

If indeed the Muse responds to the gesture of invocation, as Milton
evidently believed, this would have to mean that the language of *Paradise
Lost* is *already accommodated*, and that Milton's own intentions can only
coincide with, not precede or succeed, the intentions of the "superior
power" speaking through him. When we speak of intentions, then, under
the rubric of accommodation, it follows that the intentions of the poet are
qualified out of existence. There is no sense in which the poet can be said
to have intentions, since that would imply at the least some accommodation
on his part. The oddity of such a stance demands an equally unusual
interpretive posture, even something of a contortion, because we feel that
the poem can only be an intentional act, and that this act is really Milton's.
Let me offer as an example of how this problem has affected criticism, the
difference between two very fine critics of *Paradise Lost*, William Madsen
and William Kerrigan. First Madsen, whose text is the passage from *De
Doctrina* quoted above:

Here and here only Milton refuses to conceptualize the figurative language of the Bible, and in this respect (it may be added) he is almost alone among his Protestant contemporaries. In interpreting biblical passages that do not refer to God Himself, however, Milton consistently distrusts metaphorical statements of doctrine and seeks to go behind them by referring to other, literal statements, even in passages referring to Christ and the sacraments. It is therefore difficult to understand what it means to say that Milton uses the *method* of accommodation in *Paradise Lost*, since he would hardly arrogate to himself a mode of understanding and expression that he denies to the human authors of the Bible and reserves to God alone. He of course uses the biblical *language* by which God has accommodated Himself to our understandings, but this does not make him a Moses who has "looked on the face of truth unveiled." Nor does the fact that Raphael, as a fictional character, tells Adam that he must use the method of accommodation in describing the War in Heaven mean that Milton thought that he himself was in possession of truths so ineffable that he had to "accommodate" them to ordinary human understanding by veiling them in myth and allegory. As a fictional character the narrator does indeed lay claim to such knowledge, but unless we are willing to grant that John Milton was literally inspired, there seems to be no meaningful way to relate this fictional claim to the language of *Paradise Lost*.[9]

Madsen is disputing here and throughout his study a Neoplatonic view of Miltonic representation, and on this point he is on safe ground. There is no evidence that Milton is accommodating an ineffable visionary experience; this style of mysticism is incompatible with what we know of both his theological allegiances and his character. The logic of Madsen's argument is virtually hermetic until the final sentence, when the troublesome notion of "literal inspiration" enters the discussion as a foreign element, a term belonging to a different category of discourse. Surely the validity of the argument ought not to be contingent upon our discrediting the literality of Milton's inspiration? Madsen goes on to stress the fictionality of the poem, which leads to the conclusion that Milton is writing exegetically, not in the manner of scripture itself but of scriptural interpretation. For Madsen this means *typologically*, where the intention of retelling a biblical story implies the elucidation of anti-types. I am inclined to accept the construing of Milton's "figurative" intentions as typological, but I am by no means assured that Milton himself always equated a type with a figure of speech. Tropes in the Bible, as Madsen himself reminds us, were set apart by Milton (he "distrusts metaphorical statements and seeks to go behind them to other, literal statements"), in contradistinction to types, which define a relation between literal events. In short, a type can only be considered a trope from a certain point of view, and we have not as yet determined where Milton stands in the reading of types. In this light, let us consider Kerrigan's comment on Madsen's paragraph:

> I can find no place in the poem where the narrator "does indeed lay claim" to knowledge that he cannot communicate to the reader. There is only one accommodation in the epic: the Muse accommodates divine truth for the narrator, who then transcribes this accommodation for the reader. Both poet and reader are spectators at the heavenly court. Aside from this defect, Madsen seems to emerge victorious.[10]

Again a question of the reader's belief seems to affect radically the object of representation, where every canon of readerly objectivity argues against this confusion. I have already tried to demonstrate how deliberately Milton seeks to evade tropes in representing himself at the moment of inspiration, but as yet a larger question of intention remains unanswered. Why does the writer of *Paradise Lost* need to be inspired if he only repeats or reinterprets the matter of the Bible? Both Madsen and Kerrigan seem to be arguing against any Miltonic intention to accommodate divine truth, although both positions, as critical postures, are involved in an inexplicable difficulty of language. I want to suggest an analogy here between the idea of accommodation and a reflection by Ludwig Wittgenstein on the subject of "intention":

> By "intention" I mean here what uses a sign in a thought. The intention seems to interpret, to give the final interpretation; which is not a further sign or picture, but something else—the thing that cannot be further interpreted. But what we have reached is a psychological, not a logical terminus.
> Think of a sign language, an "abstract" one, I mean one that is strange to us, in which we do not feel at home, in which, as we should say, we do not *think*; and let us imagine this language interpreted by a translation into—as we should like to say—an unambiguous picture-language, a language consisting of pictures painted in perspective. It is quite clear that it is much easier to imagine different *interpretations* of the written language than of a picture painted in the usual way. Here we shall also be inclined to think that there is no further possibility of interpretation.[11]

Insofar as the idea of "accommodation" implies the difficulty of comprehending the matter being accommodated, we can say that the theological problem recapitulates the linguistic situation of relating intention (here,

Wittgenstein's "strange" language) to the accommodation (here, the "picture language"). When we discuss the notions of accommodation and inspiration in Milton, we experience something of the futility of guessing at intentions. At the same time, as Wittgenstein very cannily observes, interpretation makes just this claim: to have guessed rightly about intentions and hence "rested" (in a psychological sense). We demand further of interpretive language that it be reductive, that it give us the "unambiguous picture language," which in turn recapitulates the linguistic situation of the translation of tropes into original literal significations. This would coincide in my own argument with the touch of Ithuriel's spear. I do not believe that any interpretation can free itself from the tangles of intentionality, and I find it possible to move past Madsen and Kerrigan's dilemma only by making a further "guess" about Milton's intentions.

Milton's predisposition to deny having intentions is evident from the very first lines of the poem, where the subject of "intends to soar" is not "I" but "song":

> I thence
> Invoke thy aid to my advent'rous Song,
> That with no middle flight intends to soar
> Above th'Aonian Mount...

Of course we remember these lines as an expression of personal intention, even though the grammatical evasion is a consistent feature of Miltonic invocation. Milton intends only the intermediacy of his act, and the ultimate intention, the "meaning," belongs to the ultimate intender, the Muse. The one easily identifiable intention—the self-effacing of the ego in the act of invocation—ought to result in the kind of text Milton would have believed to be sacred. To that extent, Kerrigan's argument ought to be credited. But if the idea of accommodation implies the noumenal status of divine intention, the concept itself becomes almost superfluous. We cannot interpret at all where intentions are asserted to be unknowable. It is typical of both Milton and radical Protestant theologians that they deny interpreting the Bible, which is supposed to be the one text that means exactly what it says. [12] The sacred text seems to have a double nature as both accommodated, and therefore possessing a secret meaning, and utterly perspicuous. When the reader of Milton's epic declines to read the poem as scripture

(Kerrigan reads Milton *programatically* as scripture), a host of specifically personal intentions, ranging from a desire for literary fame to the possibility of reaction to the failure of the English revolution, reenter the poem. These intentions are not compatible with the primary intention of acting only as the inspired agent, the voice of the "superior power." Critics will at this point (though they have not yet analyzed this moment of choice) throw out one set of intentions or the other (Kerrigan's inspirationalism versus Madsen's anti-inspirationalism), or falsely reconcile conflicting elements by resorting to a hypothetical "unconscious intention" (Tillyard, Hyman, Empson).[13]

To the question, does Milton write *Paradise Lost* for reasons not explicit in either the subject, genre, or the personal statements of invocation, the answer would have to be, yes. Recovering the inexplicit intention, however, has proven to be a game without rules, or rather, a haphazard "accommodation" of the language of *Paradise Lost* by literary exegetes. It is more important at this point to acknowledge the confusion pervading discussion of this issue, than to clarify the notion of intentionality, which is beyond the scope of this, or perhaps any, essay. All that we can say, with Wittgenstein, is that the interpretation which is an "unambiguous picture language" remains unavailable to us. It is only an idea, like the unimaginable image of Satan touched by Ithuriel's spear, or the face of God. The problem of accommodation is a persistent concern for Milton the poet, because it expresses the effort to represent both "things invisible to mortal sight" and things which are too visible, but which have disappeared behind the surface of the poem: the matter of history itself. The two problems, of divine intention and of historical circumstances, are therefore both expressed in the poem as the *single* problem of representing the invisible. In order now to "see" how these two problems are conflated, we shall need not Ithuriel's spear, but an instrument of human vision, the "optic glass" of Galileo.

My developing "guess" about Milton's intentions is founded in part upon the curious circumstance that Galileo happens to be the only contemporary name, or overt topical reference, in *Paradise Lost*. If contemporary history is related to what critics have regarded as "unconscious intention" in the poem, then the appearance of Galileo might be considered a return of the repressed, Milton's failure to keep history wholly purged from his redaction of the biblical story, which is intended, after all, to tell us what *precedes* history. This hypothesis is worth considering, tentatively, because it highlights so conspicuously the absence of contemporary reference. A more complete absence might have gone unnoticed, which is to say that the return of the repressed is the only evidence of the presence which is also an absence: the repressed content. In a moment, we shall be able to discard the notion of repressing as not entirely adequate. Galileo makes his way into the poem initially through the front door; Milton seems to believe that it is safe to bring him in. This first mention concerns the shield of Satan:

> his ponderous shield
> Ethereal temper, massy, large and round,
> Behind him cast; the broad circumference
> Hung on his shoulders like the Moon, whose Orb
> Through Optic Glass the Tuscan Artist views
> At Ev'ning from the top of Fesole,
> Or in Valdarno, to descry new Lands,
> Rivers or Mountains in her spotty Globe...
> (I.284–91)

Although we learn later that this particular aid to vision is limited in efficiency, there is something in Milton's metaphysics that might lead us to wonder, if only momentarily, whether a powerful enough telescope could bring heaven itself before our eyes. That is, so long as we believe heaven to be a place. Among its contemporaries the telescope seemed to provoke a great anxiety; it signified forbidden knowledge and forbidden aspirations, a more intellectualized version of the Tower of Babel.[14] What is the relation between this kind of augmented vision, and the "vision" of inspiration? Possibly Milton had worked this problem through in the invocation to Book III, but at the expense of reinstating the distinction between a corporeal and spiritual sight, of fixing the bar where ideally it should slide up and down. When Raphael (Milton's *Siderius Nuncius*, more authoritative than Galileo's)[15] argues for the necessity of accommodation in relating the war in heaven, he too is compelled to reinstate this boundary, but not without two interesting qualifications:

> how last unfold
> The secrets of another World, perhaps
> Not lawful to reveal? yet for thy good

This is dispenst, and what surmounts the reach
Of human sense, I shall delineate so,
By lik'ning spiritual to corporal forms,
As may express them best, though what if Earth
Be but the shadow of Heav'n, and things therein
Each to other like more than on Earth is thought?
                              (V.568-76)

If there is an analogy in Milton's language between the telescope and the method of accommodation, a similar anxiety attaches to both. The descending movement of accommodation corresponds to, or passes along the way, the ascending "reach" of human vision, and at the place of coincidence, a doubt arises. Leslie Brisman suggests that the voice we hear in these lines is more Milton's own than elsewhere in Raphael's speech; for a moment the anxiety is great enough to force the poet into speaking *in propria persona*.[16] If Milton is truly compelled by his understanding of accommodation to deny his own initiation of this process, then it follows that he can no more know what Raphael is "translating" into human language than his readers; and this is difficult to believe. The introduction of typology in the last lines of the passage answers the doubt about the "lawfulness" of this translation by permitting the distinction between corporeal (earthly) and spiritual (heavenly) to fade. The narrator need not claim a visionary experience, nor need he be defended for revealing secrets "not lawful."

Nevertheless an element of uncertainty remains. The same uncertainty is intimated in the first reference to Galileo, not so much in defects of vision attributable to the telescope as in the object whose true nature is being revealed: the moon. The notion of "new Lands" recurs in the voyaging of Satan and Raphael, always attended with a measure of uncertainty. And of course the moon itself is an image of both instability and (as in Spenser) the threshold between two orders of reality. The telescope reveals, as it were, uncertainty itself. With each succeeding appearance of Galileo, this focus on the lack of focus evolves into the thematization of cosmological uncertainty. Satan travels in Book III through the "calm Firmament; but up or down / By centre or eccentric hard to tell." This line is taken by editors to indicate Milton's hesitation between Ptolemaic and Copernican systems, but I read this hesitation as the sign of a much greater doubt.

Knowledge of local astronomy seems a rather trivial secret to keep after revelations of war in heaven, and it is more likely that the uncertainty attending the latter is transferred to a less sensitive area. At any rate, in the next few lines Milton is striving to assert the priority of his accommodated text to the discoveries of the telescope, as though the method of transumption were needed to preempt Galileo:

There lands the Fiend, a spot like which perhaps
Astronomer in the Sun's lucent Orb
Through his glazed Optic Tube yet never saw.
                    (III.588-90)

Galileo has not, nor can he ever, see what we are seeing here. The discovery of sunspots is transformed into another myth of Satanic origin, an ironic deflation of what Milton's editor calls "one of the most exciting astronomical events of the century."

The last, and perhaps the most interesting, mention of Galileo (this time, by name) forms part of an elaborate description of Raphael's descent to Earth, and with these lines, there is no longer any question of Milton's resistance to the meaning the telescope is beginning to possess:

From hence, no cloud, or, to obstruct his sight,
Star interpos'd, however small he sees,
Not unconform to other shining Globes,
Earth and the Gard'n of God, with Cedars crown'd
Above all Hills. As when by night the Glass
Of Galileo, less assur'd observes
Imagin'd Lands and Regions in the Moon...
                    (V.257-63)

Raphael's vision, as the reader expects, can only be more accurate than Galileo's, but the point of interest is that the problem of accommodation has finally, very explicitly, intersected with the upward aspiration of human vision. This is the great accommodative moment in the poem, when divinity condescends to explain its intentions to the limited reason of man. The limitation which makes this condescension necessary is then associated with the defects of even the augmented vision of Galileo, who is first slighted ("less assur'd") and whose discovery of "new Lands" in Book I is then glossed as "imagin'd Lands." Geoffrey Hartman has commented on the way in which the idea of accommodation is worked into the description of Raphael's wings, which "shade / His lineaments divine," figuring in that "shadow" the "self-veiling nature of divine light."[17] This is as perfect an emblem of accommodative representation as Milton conceived, and within the emblematic portrait Raphael can move freely from the shape (representation) of a phoenix ("to all the Fowles he seems / A phoenix") to his "proper shape" as a winged seraph. The impacted image allows the fusion of literal and figurative to stand for the much more desired effacing of the boundary between heaven and earth. Ithuriel's spear is at such moments an internalized principle of representation.

There is also an analogy in these lines to the psychological terms Milton worked so hard to keep apart: If inspiration is associated with the method of accommodation, then imagination is inevitably linked to the failure of the method, or anxiety about the possibility of failure. The "imagin'd" is once more devalued and set against the authority of inspiration, the non-usurping *nuncius*. When Raphael worries about the possibility of usurping the authority whose message he is delivering, he casts himself momentarily in the role of imagination as it was conceived by Bacon or Hobbes. But the moment passes. The major anxiety continues to be projected onto Galileo, whose "imagin'd Lands" hint at the distortion of imagination itself. Galileo emerges as one of the more overdetermined figures in the poem, carrying with him a burden of meaning deeply involved in Milton's complex theologico-poetic.

If it was inevitable, then, according to the inner logic of this system, that Raphael and Galileo should be brought together, the significance of their juxtaposition is even more extensive than has yet been indicated. I have suppressed, of course, the personal significance of Galileo, whose name is often read as a metonymic signature for John Milton. Certainly his status as blind prisoner of the Inquisition is initially responsible for his safe entry into the poem, though not for his involvement in the representational problems of the accommodated text. The latter development has more to do with the meaning Milton has already given to Galileo in the pages of *Areopagitica*, and which he is evidently remembering in *Paradise Lost*:

> There it was that I found and visited the famous Galileo, grown old, a prisoner of the Inquisition for thinking in astronomy otherwise than the Franciscan and Dominican licencers thought. And though I knew that England then was groaning loudest under the prelatical yoke, nevertheless I took it as a pledge of future happiness that other nations were so persuaded of her liberty. (2:538)

If Milton did remember the context of the earlier passage, that memory must inevitably have suggested to him an unwelcome pattern of repetition. His identification with Galileo is only possible because the "pledge of future happiness" was not fulfilled. The Inquisition is a principle of historical repetition over which revolution has not triumphed. The resonance of identification is easy to detect, and we are in a position now to understand what this resonance means: History and accommodation share a repetitional structure denied alike by both the Galilean discovery of "new Lands" and the promise of revolution, a new earth, if not a new heaven.

3. The Third Temple

To insist longer upon the "already accommodated" text of *Paradise Lost* would be to surrender the poem to an evasive theological concept, to read it as though it were a sacred text. The method of accommodation translates intentionality into theological language by transferring intention itself to the mind of divinity, and this method can be used equally for "things invisible to mortal sight" and things purged from the poem's field of reference—the matter of history. Both are *things not seen*. And this is why Kerrigan's reading of Milton as scripture effectively de-historicizes the poem, as does Joseph Wittreich's, whose prophetic Milton also denies repetition in history: "For Milton, it is not especially important that history repeats itself but that, as Mark Twain once wrote, it rhymes, and through its rhymes holds out the possibility of progress."[18] This might have been true for Milton in the 1640s but not for the poet of *Paradise Lost*. In reacting now against the current and very valuable conception of the "prophetic" Milton, I would also want to avoid the opposite error of hypothesizing an "unconscious intention," which restores Milton to history by evading the explicit intentions altogether. For that reason, I do not consider the figure of Galileo so much a return of the repressed as a cryptic self-portrait. The Milton who accommodates his poem to the vast failure which is historical repetition knowingly conceals this accommodation. The concealment itself is only covertly admitted in the negative reflection of accommodation in Galileo's glass. The hiddenness of Milton's meaning need not be considered bad faith; I am more impressed by Milton's painful honesty in dwelling at length upon difficult subjects. I refer instead to Angus Fletcher's remark that Milton "could not afford the Shakespearean openness," and that the "burying" of his meanings was necessitated by the very age in which he lived.[19] It is possible now to explain why this is so.

Let me begin with an image drawn from an early text on the theme of historical repetition, from Book I, Chapter ii, of *The Reason of Church Government*:

> As therefore it is unsound to say that God hath not appointed any set government in his Church, so is it untrue. Of the time of the Law there can be no doubt; for to let passe the institution of Priests and Levites, which is too cleare to be insisted upon, which the Temple came to be built, which in plaine judgement could breed no essential change either in religion, or in the Priestly government; yet God to shew how little he could endure that men should be tampring and contriving in his worship, though in things of lesse regard, gave to *David* for *Solomon* not only a pattern and modell of the Temple, but a direction for the courses of the Priests and Levites, and for all the worke of their service. At the returne from the Captivity things were only restor'd after the ordinance of *Moses* and *David*; or if the least alteration be to be found, they had with them inspired men, Prophets, and it were not sober to say they did ought of moment without divine intimation. In the Prophesie of *Ezekiel* from the 40 Chapt. onward, after the destruction of the Temple, God by his Prophet seeking to weane the hearts of the Jewes from their old law to expect a new and more perfect reformation under Christ, sets out before their eyes the stately fabrick & constitution of his Church, with al the ecclesiasticall functions appertaining; indeed the description is as sorted best to the apprehension of those times, typicall and shadowie, but in such manner as never yet came to passe, nor never must literally, unlesse we mean to annihilat the Gospel. (1:756-57)

The passage gathers together a number of Miltonic leitmotivs, most impressively working the concept of Reformation into the story of the "second temple" built after the return from Babylon—or at least, Reformation seems to hover over the interpretation of this part of the Old Testament history. The second temple, as Dryden reminds us in another, rather loaded context, "was not like the first."[20] In fact it was not so splendid as its original and this entropic repetition must have been vaguely disturbing for Puritan readers of the Bible. Similarly, the Babylonian captivity is a dreary repetition of bondage in Egypt and difficult to interpret as in any way "progressive." Yet this is exactly what Milton proceeds to do, resorting to a typological reading in order to discern retrospectively a progress that can hardly have meant anything to the Jews themselves. Were their hearts at all "weaned from the Old Law" by the divine ordinance of the second temple? Rather, it is only in the dispensation of the Gospel that the weaning process can be detected, an origin of the sort where meaning catches up with

memory. Once the typological significance of the second temple is established, however, the building of that temple in its own time must be
distinguished from the fulfillment of the type set out in the text from
Ezekiel. The type is reduced to figural status because it happens to be
attached to a physical structure, and that structure is not what Milton really
wants to talk about. Implicit also is the portending of this apocalypse in
the success of the Reformation.

The argument in the *Reason of Church Government* charts a very complex
movement of Milton's mind, a rapid arc from a point of origin in the past
to a moment of apocalyptic annihilation; also from that "typical" origin to
a time when those types must be taken "literally." Thus far I do not believe
that I have said anything we do not already know about a certain kind of
Reformation temperament. The next assertion is more polemical: From
the stance of *Paradise Lost*, this concept of Reformation is a Satanic error.
Here is Satan in a typological mood:

O Earth, how like to Heav'n, if not preferred
More justly, Seat worthier of Gods, as built
With second thoughts, reforming what was old!
For what God after better worse would build?
                    (IX.99-102)

Earlier in his career Satan has mistaken priority for the basis of an authority
more absolute than God ordains, and he clings to this literal priority. The
inversion of temporal valuations provides a very powerful defense against
that earlier mistake by devaluing earliness itself as the "type" of what comes
later. Satan would have "preferred" (put before) the second temple, and it
devolves upon us to explain why God "after better worse would build." If
this passage does indeed comment obliquely on a difficulty in the progres-
sivist impulses of Reformation, the mysteriousness of the image in *The
Reason of Church Government* is clarified. Satan is the agent of historical
repetition masquerading as an advocate of progress. Eve is later persuaded,
and Adam persuades himself, that she is "last and best" of God's creation.
Milton perhaps mistook the second temple for this apocalyptic emblem
when a truer image would be one of destruction, even the destruction of
the temple. The "second temple," like Satan's "second thoughts," betrays
the promise of Reformation to the binding down of historical repetition.

The first temple of the human spirit was Paradise itself, and the image of its destruction is to be found in Book XI of *Paradise Lost*, where its removal from Eden is given a pedagogic significance by Michael. In fact, the notion can be expanded now to comprise the thematic boundaries of the epic, which revises the concept of a third temple along apocalyptic lines; that is, the final temple, which the Book of Revelation identifies with the New Jerusalem, is not identical to the first but a thorough displacement into what looks like the category of the trope. We have been taught to regard this displacement ("thou dost prefer / Before all Temples th'upright heart and pure") as the thematic center of the poem, but it has not been sufficiently emphasized that the typological system producing this displacement is aberrant. Normal typology asserts only the correspondence between the type in the Old Testament and the antitype in the New. H. R. McCallum establishes the dominantly radical style of Milton's typology, which relegates all of the Bible to typological status.[21] The antitype then is construed as either a present historical condition or a spiritual condition of the individual. The latter revisionary antitype seems to be figurative, but there is a curious wavering between the historical antitype (predictably, this as a literal event: apocalypse) and what might be called an apocalyptic state of mind. This shifting between significations of apocalypse corresponds to the distinction between the temple and the destruction of the temple as alternative typological emblems. Milton's stance as a prophet might be considered apocalyptic, a hypothesis evidently confirmed by recent studies uncovering the use of the Book of Revelation as a structural model for *Paradise Lost*.[22] This textual repetition bears another interpretation, however, in the light of the larger historical failure within whose shadow the poem is written. There is, I believe, a conflict between apocalyptic and nonapocalyptic typologies enforcing a very un-Hebraic separation of history and prophecy. The conflict is inscribed in various subnarratives of *Paradise Lost*, one of which I will consider here, the story of Noah and the Flood.

Noah's story expands to fill a large part of Book XI, and this fact is worth pondering because it so strangely unbalances the recounting of Old Testament history, overshadowing the more typologically significant covenant with Abraham. Milton is more interested in this narrative, certainly because it is the pretext for the destruction of Paradise, but even more for its apocalyptic resonance. Adam believes he has seen the end of the world,

a mistake which logically extends the Satanic error in the Reformation
mentality. But this is not to say that Milton is adopting the stance of
historical disillusion; this would also be too reductive a "guess" at the heavy
burden of the poet's intentions. I do not find that the angel Michael, if he is
speaking for Milton, has entirely detached himself from his text of origin,
John's *Apocalypse*, since he too eagerly moves on to the last days immediately upon concluding the story of Noah:

> but then he brings
> Over the Earth a Cloud, will therein set
> His triple-color'd Bow, whereon to look
> And call to mind his Cov'nant: Day and Night
> Seed-time and Harvest, Heat and hoary Frost
> Shall hold thir course, till fire purge all things new,
> Both Heav'n and Earth, wherein the just shall dwell.
> (XI.895-901)

While this transition is warranted by Genesis, several other times in the
course of his narrative, Michael suddenly overleaps whatever intervening
historical time remains between the temporal present and the apocalyptic
restoration of Paradise. Again, for example, at the story of Joshua:

> But Joshua whom the Gentiles Jesus call,
> His Name and Office bearing, who shall quell
> The adversary Serpent, and bring back
> Through the world's wilderness long wander'd man
> Safe to eternal Paradise of rest.
> (XII.310-14)

And again at the return of Christ to Heaven:

> Then to the Heav'n of Heav'ns he shall ascend
> With victory, triumphing through the air
> Over his foes and thine; there shall surprise
> The Serpent, Prince of air, and drag in Chains
> Through all his Realm, and there confounded leave;
> Then enter into glory, and resume
> His Seat at God's right hand, exalted high
> Above all names in Heav'n; and thence shall come,
> When this world's dissolution shall be ripe,

With glory and power to judge both quick and dead,
To judge th'unfaithful dead, but to reward
His faithful, and receive them into bliss,
Whether in Heav'n or Earth, for then th'Earth
Shall all be Paradise, far happier place
Than this of *Eden*, and far happier days.
                                        (XII.451–65)

Not until line 539 does the narrative catch up with Michael's proleptic urgency:

                                        till the day
Appear of respiration to the just,
And vengeance to the wicked, at return
Of him so lately promis'd to thy aid,
The Woman's seed, obscurely then foretold,
Now amplier known thy Saviour and thy Lord,
Last in the Clouds from Heav'n to be reveal'd
In glory of the Father, to dissolve
Satan with his perverted World, then raise
From the conflagrant mass, purg'd and refin'd,
New Heav'ns, new Earth, ages of endless date
Founded in righteousness and peace and love,
To bring forth fruits Joy and eternal Bliss.

These passages establish a rhythm of their own, quite discontinuous with the dismal repetitions constituting history. In fact Michael is rather reluctant to return to his primary narrative after his earlier apocalyptic flights, and he gives surprisingly short shrift to the New Testament "law of Faith" that seems so fundamentally involved with the progressive historical notions of Radical reformers. The two narrative postures exist in a state of tense disparity, but insofar as apocalypse is deferred, the rule of repetition prevails.[23] Even the Story of Noah, with its thrilling prolepsis, is told twice (712–62, and again at 787–839). The retelling is of course different, but this difference, as we shall see, is more an attempt to understand, than to deny the fact of repetition. Apocalypse cuts transversely across the primary narrative structure, without establishing itself within that rhythm. The accommodative moment in *Paradise Lost* locates itself somewhere in between, in an undefined space between repetition (history) and the event (apocalypse) which is always outside. It is the very sense of being halted, of not breaking through to an apocalypse, which builds up sufficient energy for the rhetorical release of sublimity. I think that English models of the sublime tend to emphasize this blockage (which is so conspicuous in Wordsworth) less for the peculiar turn taken by poetic theory in England than for the massive displacement of Miltonic energy from apocalyptic yearning for an end to history *into* the rhetoric of *Paradise Lost*. Later writers as a consequence receive Milton as the model of sublimity in English, even before there becomes generally available any theory, Longinian or otherwise, to analyze this model.

One other fact is illuminated by this recognition, the flattened tonality of the final two books of the epic, the occasion of so much registered disappointment. No longer should we identify the source of the problem with the reentry of history into the poem. On the contrary, history has up to this point saturated *Paradise Lost*, and in the final two books this matter has precipitated out. The sublime moment occurs not in the attenuations of historical chronology, but in rhetorical compressions that are charged with the premonitory rumblings of apocalypse: "He onward came, far off his coming shone." The condensation of temporality in such a line should be understood in this sense, gathering in one phrase a first coming, a *second* coming, and the feeling that this coming is both now and "far off."[24]

If the possibility of sublimity is lost in the last two books of *Paradise Lost*, with their obsessive historical repetitions and equally obsessive proclamations of apocalypse, the analytical extension of the sublime moment is an invaluable aid for the interpreter. I would like to examine the historical paradigm as it disintegrates before our eyes, in the one place where that disintegration is most explicit: Michael's explication of typology in Book XII. The passage is redolent with the self-inflating Puritan conviction of living in apocalyptic time, after the law has been abrogated:

So Law appears imperfect, and but giv'n
With purpose to resign them in full time
Up to a better Cov'nant, disciplin'd
From shadowy Types to Truth, from Flesh to Spirit,
From imposition of strict Laws to free
Acceptance of large Grace, from servile fear
To filial, works of Law to works of Faith.

This was the great guess about God's intentions, his historical "purpose," but history does not confirm this guess. What follows is another false apocalypse:

And therefore shall not Moses, though of God
Highly belov'd being but the Minister
Of Law, his people into Canaan lead;
But Joshua whom the Gentiles Jesus call,
His Name and Office bearing, who shall quell
The adversary Serpent, and bring back
Through the world's wilderness long wander'd man
Safe to eternal Paradise of rest.
                            (XII.300-14)

It is as though Joshua *did* bring the Hebrews back to Paradise and not merely to Canaan. The typology works quite lucidly to indicate the significance of Joshua's name, but the grammar interrupts the historical rhythm with such a proleptic ambiguity that Michael must forcefully reinstate the repetitional narrative by the egregious reminder that the place of rest is to be distinguished from *earthly* Canaan: "Meanwhile they in thir earthly *Canaan* plac't."

Each of these moments of historical crisis fails to precipitate an apocalypse; even the death of Jesus, while it completes the *typology*, does not yet bring long wandered man to Paradise. The world proceeds from bad to worse. The structure that disintegrates here can be diagramatically expressed as follows:

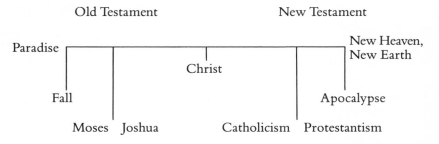

The typological sign, Moses-Joshua, even though it points to the antitype Jesus, corresponds *in context* to the transition from Catholicism to Protes-

tantism, an antitype fully explicable after taking into account the accusations of regressive Hebraism leveled at the Catholic Church, as well as at
backsliding Protestants. Types for Milton tend to locate themselves at such
points of transition, which function much as the caesura at the center of a
chiasmus. Indeed the entire structure is ideally a chiasmus, ABBA, but
history seems lodged in the repetitions before the final reversal of BA. I
have already associated the scheme of chiasmus with moments where the
poet, or his epic characters, gather power to themselves after being stopped
momentarily between the terms AB and BA. This hypothesis can be
extended now to reconnect the end of this essay with its beginning.
Chiasmus is the infrastructure of *Paradise Lost*, more important than any
trope but functioning tropologically because the element of repetition is
also a turn from an original signification. Schematically, a chiasmus
"moves" or "turns" as follows:

           A   B   B   A
        Origin— Divergence — Repetition — Return

History can indefinitely extend the B term, innumerably multiply "second
temples," but the basic pattern assures in some sense the inevitable return.
Milton stands poised at one of these junctures, but the choice that presents
itself is in the representation of the final A term: either a literal restoration
of Paradise, or something different, a displacement into tropological language. Michael evidently chooses the latter ("paradise within") after some
vacillation, a choice which lends particular interest to Milton's choice of
him: the angel of John's *Apocalypse.* The reworking of the Book of Revelation
is more thoroughly revisionary than Milton's current interpreters believe,
especially as the structure of *Paradise Lost* is said to "imitate" the seven-part
structure of John's book. "Paradise within" is a metaphoric displacement
but it is also a transumptive allusion, revising its pre-text with a final
structural echo of John's displacement of the temple into figuration: "And I
saw no temple therein: for the Lord God Almighty and the Lamb are the
temple of it." Milton goes just a little further: A visionary poet might have
chosen to bring down the New Jerusalem; he does not.
    The two possibilities for construing chiasmus should finally elucidate
the difficulty in Milton's representational language so vexing to readers

like Dr. Johnson. The impulse to literalize is in a hidden sense apocalyptic, and Ithuriel's spear, as it touches off Satan's explosive return to "his own likeness" is a small rehearsal for the final conflagration out of which New Heaven and New Earth will arise; one assumes that Satan will be fixed thereafter in his true shape, eternally innocuous. Apocalypse comes in God's own time. When chiasmus is read in the time of "meanwhile" (and I interpret this temporality, of course, as the return of the *secular*), the restored Paradise becomes a trope for a state of mind as available to fallen Adam as to the society of Saints. We have only to distinguish now between this displacement and its Satanic parody, though I will always insist that these structures are more fundamental than any individual character's responses. Satan's parody of displacement ("the mind is its own place") precedes by the length of the epic Michael's turn to the "trope" of Paradise, but his reaction is no less a response to a failed revolution than Milton's poem is to its contemporaneous national failure. Satan's failed attempt to depose God cannot be so easily compensated by a turn to figuration. It makes a great difference that we have suffered through the turbulence of the epic, and even more that we have worked through a repetition of the apocalyptic text. The legitimacy of Michael's trope inheres not simply in its being a metaphor, but in its transumptive engagement with its biblical model, which engagement gives the metaphor a diachronic, historical meaning. The metaphor argues that the place does not matter, but the allusion asserts that the time does.

I would like the last words to be given to Christ, whose figure does not always satisfy but who most clearly struggles to embody the human rhythm of revisionary repetition. After the cold repetitions of the Father ("By some false guile pervert; and shall pervert"), and the unyielding antitheses ("Sufficient to have stood, though free to fall") the voice of the Son reestablishes the revisionary mode of chiasmus:

O Father, gracious was that word which clos'd
Thy sovran sentence, that Man should find grace;
For which both Heav'n and Earth shall high extol
Thy praises, with th'innumerable sound
Of Hymns and sacred Songs, wherewith thy Throne
Encompass'd shall resound thee ever blest.

For should Man finally be lost, should Man
Thy creature late so lov'd, thy youngest Son
Fall circumvented thus by fraud, though join'd
With his own folly? that be from thee far,
That far be from thee, Father...
(III.144-54)

Justus Lawler, in a recent study of schemata such as chiasm, argues that this scheme is "primarily representative of the intersection of the infinite and the finite,"[25] and if this metaphysics of rhetoric has any validity, it is here in the signature of Christ, the mark of the divine upon human history. Milton's Christ is always defined by the chiastic structure: he is "Love without end, and without measure Grace," a phrase that encloses the infinite (without end, measure) within the more accessible language of love and grace. The chiasmus, even in the form of Satanic parody, seems to embody for Milton that repetition which does not merely reflect the distance and terror of the Father's authority. We can only regret that the figure of Christ, the crossing of man and god, is not as great a poetic as he is a political success in the world of *Paradise Lost*. Critical conscience dissuades us from exalting him into the model of authority. That Milton struggles so hard to accommodate this figure, to find in him once again the resolution of history, suggests to me that authority is finally messianic, even the less urgent authority of literature. Poetic authority is difficult to understand just because it seems to "move" us without provoking that resistance we feel to the omnipresence of power. But *Paradise Lost* declares that literature is not exempt from these worldly vicissitudes, that it should move us even to resistance; and is this not another way of pointing to the poetic success of Satan? Milton's readers have either resisted him, or resisted with him. Inscribed in these versions of "filial freedom" is the conflict of literature and history, their false divorce and false reunion. If there were a sense in which we could "believe" in the messianic model, would that belief not signify the recovery of literature's idealized images for the world of history? Our agnosticism defers this apocalypse, but does not discover in the fact of duration an alternative to the sacred text. We remember that Shelley called time itself a redeemer, an even more inescapable Messiah.

CONCLUSION

The Strength of Usurpation

> But let us not be betrayed from a defense into a critical history of poetry and
> its influence on society. Be it enough to have pointed out the effects of poets,
> in the large and true sense of the word, upon their own and all succeeding
> times.
>
> Shelley, *A Defense of Poetry*

Inspiration, conceived as a "literal" event in the invocation to Book III,
seems to be a sufficient defense of Milton's authority, and yet the language
of even that single insistence upon the literal is difficult to purify of its
figurative alloy. The structure of the invocation moves through chiasmus
toward the assertion of literal vision, but the poem ultimately affirms the
tropological status of the chiastic structure. Not even Milton is able to
sustain an absolute faith in his own inspiration, and this fact has literary
historical consequences of great importance. I want to associate the preeminence of the revisionary mode over the visionary with the much noted
transition from vision to voice at the beginning of Book XII. This transition can be regarded as an event that is always taking place in Milton's
poetry. The invocational mode evolves into the *vocational*, which describes
the major difference between Milton's epic and its two successors, *Paradise
Regained* and *Samson Agonistes*. The plea for vision corrects itself as the plea
for voice. Milton's last invocation, at the beginning of *Paradise Regained*, is
curiously perfunctory, and I do not think this records merely my own
perception of a tone compatible with my argument. The opening paragraphs of this poem are intensely concerned with voices, as is the whole of
the brief epic. The "Father's voice" (I.32) speaks only once to the Messiah,
declaring Jesus his "beloved Son," and all other voices in the poem are
mired in the perplexities of interpreting this phrase. Jesus must interpret

the meaning of the "Son of God" without further words of divine origin. With *Samson Agonistes* the problem of voice (or "vocation") wholly consumes the thematic interest of the play, since Samson in his blindness is surrounded only by voices, no one of which ever declares itself to be divine. I take this growing concern with voice to be an indication of Milton's recognition that the loss of vision is a kind of incorrect trope for the much more serious absence of a divine voice. This situation is paradigmatic for any quest in post-Miltonic poetry to find the true ground of the poet's authority, and I want to conclude this study with some observations of a more specific nature on the literary historical significance of this event.

Again, I will take as a model the experience of Samson. He does not recover his sight, nor does he return to the language of invocation. He cannot invoke God to speak through him as he was once able to do. He does, however, recover the strength to act, in lines that are perhaps Milton's greatest revision of a biblical text:

At length for intermission sake they led him
Between the pillars; he his guide requested
(For so from such as nearer stood we heard)
As overtir'd to let him lean a while
With both his arms on those two massy Pillars
That to the arched roof gave main support.
He unsuspicious led him; which when Samson
Felt in his arms, with head a while inclin'd,
And eyes fast fixt he stood, as one who pray'd,
Or some great matter in his mind revolv'd.
                              (1629-39)

Where Milton gives us a choice between alternatives that must necessarily remain undetermined (prayer *or* some great matter), the Authorized Version gives us a complete and barbaric invocation of the deity:

And Samson called unto the Lord, and said, O Lord God, remember me I pray thee, and strengthen me, I pray thee, only this once, O God, that I may be at once avenged of the Philistines for my two eyes. (Judges 16:28)

The text may be suppressed from *Samson Agonistes* for a number of reasons, but there is a crudity of a specifically poetic sort over which this poet is finally triumphing. He will not pray for the restoration of his vision, nor for the voice of God to compensate him for the earlier loss. Here, where Milton might have found the harshest model of "sanctified bitterness," where his personal loss would most compel him to invoke his deity, he marvelously declines. Milton and Samson make of their own voices a *vocation*, and this is the sense of Samson's "rousing motions." We might understand in this climactic union of motion and motivation the very "intimate impulse" that must have led Milton to choose so regressive a biblical text, a story so full of the presence of God, when both Samson and the poet suffer from an absence. The choice is an act of courage.

To elect oneself is, if not an impossibility, at least a scandal in the religious life. Yet the notion of "self-begetting" loses some of its thoroughly Satanic resonance with the death of Samson. I still find as much of Satan as of Christ in the figure of Samson, but in this world, good and evil are "two twins cleaving together." And Samson is a better model for the modern poet than either Satan or Christ. The new context for self-begetting emerges quite explicitly in the last great simile of the poem, comparing Samson's destruction of Dagon's temple to the rebirth of the phoenix:

So virtue giv'n for lost,
Deprest, and overthrown, as seem'd,
Like that self-begott'n bird
In the Arabian woods embost,
That no second knows nor third,
And lay erewhile a Holocaust,
From out her ashy womb now teem'd,
Revives, reflourishes, then vigorous most
When most unactive deem'd,
And though her body die, her fame survives,
A secular bird ages of lives.
                    (1697-1707)

There are many returns working here, most obviously perhaps a revision of that earlier phoenix image in the descent of Raphael. There, we recall, the phoenix is a figurative "type" of Raphael, who expresses in his metamorphic descent the mode of accommodation. Geoffrey Hartman, whose essay is the best guide on this subject, takes the phoenix back to fundamental significations of the sun in *Paradise Lost*. Raphael, he says, "interprets the sun."[1] I would add that he interprets the Son of God as well, prefiguring in his descent the much greater coming of the Messiah. The phoenix of *Samson Agonistes* might be associated with Christ also (as it was traditionally), but I suspect that the image is detaching itself from a theological context, that it is really becoming a "secular" image. Milton has oddly altered the cyclical point of the myth by letting the "body die" and the "fame" survive. What does this mean? The existence of the phoenix, after all, is a fable, and not a wholly acceptable emblem for Christ (neither is Samson). Is the myth "dead," and does the meaning survive? There is no resurrection of the body for the phoenix, nor for Samson, but something does survive.

The return to pagan myth works toward the same end as the obsolescence of the Samson story, and in part allows us to understand Milton's generic choice, at this late date, of Greek drama. "Fame" is derived from a Greek word meaning "to sound, or to speak," and in this context we should consider the fact that Samson's life and death are *reported*. None of us is eyewitness to either. I would read this circumstance as emblematic of the situation of both the hero and the poet writing his story: the simile argues that speech survives, or voice, when vision is lost, and this is truer though more hidden than the figure of "inward eyes illuminated." The latter phrase points to a figure of compensation, to be sure, but voice is something more, neither wholly internalized, nor declaring itself of divine provenance. I believe it is the compensation itself. The return to the form of Greek drama is minutely reflected in the wording of the allusion. The offstage catastrophe has become for us the offstage epiphany, as close as we shall come to the "superior power" directing Samson in his final moments.

My last comment concerns the later history of "self-begetting," which was associated at the beginning of this essay with imagination, and which goes by that name more and more after Milton. Much of this book has been devoted to the long recession of inspiration, the resistance of poets to the secularization of their texts. The subsequent ascendance of imagination is easy to observe, but very difficult to locate at a putative moment of birth in any Renaissance text. I have argued that the antagonism of Spenser and Milton to the notion of imagination has to be confronted by literary historians in any study of poetic authority, and that this antagonism has intimately to do with the meaning of imagination as a mode of poetic self-begetting. If this is what imagination means to poets, its later history as a synecdoche for poetic power becomes inevitable. Obviously mental image-making is not the essence of poetry; poets give us first of all, *words*. That poets cling to this trope indicates a desire for continuity with an archaic poetic self, the vatic figure who really *saw* the thing he sang about; and this desire coexists with a contradictory "Satanic" impulse to ground the poem wholly in the self, to deny an origin that is prior or other. I am asserting, then, that what Milton writes about as a loss of vision becomes for subsequent poets the birth of imagination, because this loss throws the poet back upon an inner resource: Samson's "inward eyes." Milton did not rest here, but the concept of imagination preserves for literary history the moment of polarized consciousness, of a desire for both the external, authorizing origin, and the internal, "self-begetting" source. I find this tension between the senses of imagination epitomized most interestingly by Wordsworth, Milton's truest heir, at his great moments of visual blindness:

> Imagination! lifting up itself
> Before the eye and progress of my Song
> Like an unfather'd vapour; here that Power,
> In all the might of its endowments, came
> Athwart me; I was lost as in a cloud,
> Halted, without a struggle to break through.
> And now recovering, to my Soul I say
> I recognise thy glory; in such strength
> Of usurpation, in such visitings
> Of awful promise, when the light of sense
> Goes out in flashes that have shewn to us
> The invisible world, doth Greatness make abode,
> There harbours whether we be young or old...
>   (*Prelude* VI. 525-37; 1805 version)

Here again is the Renaissance usurper cutting off the vision of the literal "eye" to reestablish a vision within, but the ontological status of Words-worth's "invisible world" is uncertain. Is this Milton's "things invisible to mortal sight?" Wordsworth's "visitings" are perhaps permanently displaced into figuration, as vision here might be "only" a metaphor. Lingering rather cunningly within these lines is another usurper, the "unfather'd vapour" who rose from a river of Eden to tempt mankind to godhood. This is not so much an allusion to "Satan involv'd in rising Mist," but rather a very deep acknowledgment of something Satanic in the "strength of usurpation," a peculiar congruence in the representation of poetic origins. Imagination lifts itself up (self-raised by its own quickening power) and Wordsworth is shocked into an experience of the sublime. And this *is* the Miltonic sublime, even though Wordsworth's name for it is "Imagination."

We know, in fact, that among its many and complex deferrals, this passage defers a debt to Milton in the very event of its composition. These lines were interposed between two already finished paragraphs on the crossing of the Alps, the second of which ends with the famous "characters of the great Apocalypse," and a quotation from *Paradise Lost*: "Of first, and last, and midst, and without end." The earlier apocalyptic voice praises God, but the voice given by Wordsworth's imagination praises its own "Soul" in language hardly less apocalyptic. Wordsworth is as halted before the otherness of his own mind as Milton is before the mystery of the divine will.

If the word "imagination" misnames this experience, the mistake is preeminently a consequence of Milton's position in literary history. The imagination names what follows the loss of inspiration, or what follows Milton's obsolete names for poetic power. Milton did not make recourse to the concept (or did not finally name the *origin* of poetic power) because his tremendous strength carried him beyond the loss of vision, and beyond the frustration of the visionary longing. Poets do not easily give up the immemorial association of poetry with vision and prophecy, with sacred origins, and I have argued throughout this book that such resistance is fundamentally a consequence of anxiety about *authority*. Spenser withdraws with the departure of Dame Nature (whither no man wist) into an ironic revaluation of the secular. Milton moves in the silence of God to find a voice in this silence, and this is to have carried poetry "a little further on."

Perhaps we are only beginning to understand how far "a little further" really is. Poets are perennially concerned with the loss of vision, and we, their readers, are perennially perplexed about the authority of the poetic voice. These two facts speak directly to what is still an archaizing impulse in all of us. We want to believe that the words of the poet are spoken not only by him, but by "some superior power." And this is to admit that we do not, as yet, recognize an authority apart from some relation to the sacred, the original; we do not recognize the authority of the merely human.

Notes

Preface:

1. Stanley Cavell, "Knowing and Acknowledging," in *Must We Mean What We Say?* (Cambridge: Cambridge University Press, 1976), p. 263.

1. The Genealogy of Imagination

1. The existence of both Greek and Latin words for the same faculty of mind afforded numerous writers the opportunity to make distinctions between imagination and fancy. None of these distinctions, however, much affected the history of the idea and the great majority of writers before Coleridge (including Spenser and Milton) treat the terms as synonymous. Accordingly, I have not distinguished them myself anywhere in this book, since I believe that the synonymy of the two terms more truly reflects the state of Renaissance thought. The most general historical study of any length is by Murray Bundy, "The Theory of Imagination in Classical and Medieval Thought."

2. The major text is of course Aristotle's *De Anima*. For a number of reasons to be discussed later, I believe Bundy's interpretation of Plato unreliable, and I think it very doubtful that Plato had a "theory of imagination." Another useful survey, which emphasizes the post-Renaissance history of imagination, is by Jean Starobinski, "Jalons pour une histoire du concept d'imagination," in *La Relation critique*, pp. 174-95. The major twentieth-century philosopher to write on imagination is Jean-Paul Sartre, *L'Imaginaire*, translated by B. Frechtman as *Psychology of Imagination*. Edward S. Casey has recently produced a phenomenological study of imagination which contains some useful historical remarks as well: *Imagining: A Phenomenological Study*. My own approach owes much to Owen Barfield's essay, "Imagination and Inspiration." Some basic articles on the imagination in the English Renaissance are by William Rossky, "Imagination in the English Renaissance: Psychology and Poetic;" Murray W. Bundy, "Invention and Imagination in the Renaissance"; and J. L. Halio, "The Metaphor of Conception in Elizabethan Theories of Imagination." An important series of articles by Harry Berger, Jr., defines some of the issues to be confronted here. I will mention "The Ecology of Mind: The Concept of Period Imagination—An Outline Sketch," *Centennial Review*: (1964) 8:409-34; "The Renaissance Imagination: Second World and Green World"; and "L. B. Alberti on Painting: Art and Actuality in Human Perspective," *Centennial Review* (1966) 10:237-77. Too recently published to incorporate into my argument is James Engell's *The Creative Imagination: Enlightenment to Romanticism* (Cambridge: Harvard University Press, 1981). The period covered, however, does not overlap my own, and in fact, suggests that my own study can be regarded as a kind of prehistory. Much closer to my interests is the first chapter of Isabel G. MacCaffrey's *Spenser's Allegory: The Anatomy of Imagination*. I have tried here not so much to refine upon the concept of a period imagination, in which endeavor MacCaffrey's book exceeds even Harry Berger's careful studies, but rather to see the imagination genealogically, as the semantic field whose origin coincides with that of literature itself.

3. *The Advancement of Learning*, in Spedding, et. al. eds. *The Works of Francis Bacon*, 3:382.

4. See Bundy's chapter on Plotinus and the Neoplatonists in "The Theory of Imagination."

5. Aquinas, *Summa Theologica*, Fathers of the English Dominican Province, trans. 3 vols. (London: Burnes, Oates, and Washburne, 1916-25) II-ii. Q. 174. Art. 2.

6. Erwin Panofsky, "Artist, Scientist, Genius: Notes on the Renaissance Dämmerung," pp. 128 ff.

7. Charles C. Osgood, ed. and trans. *Boccaccio on Poetry, Being the Preface and the Fourteenth and Fifteenth Books of Boccaccio's "Genealogia Deorum Gentilium,"* p. 24. Also Boccaccio's *Life of Dante*, partially translated by Allan H. Gilbert in *Literary Criticism: Plato to Dryden*, p. 211.

8. On the Dante controversy, see Baxter Hathaway, *The Age of Criticism: The Late Renaissance in Italy*, pp. 66-67, and the chapters on Mazzoni and Bulgarini, pp. 355-90. Also Bernard Weinberg, *A History of Literary Criticism in the Italian Renaissance*, 2:819-911.

9. E. R. Curtius, *European Literature and the Latin Middle Ages*, p. 475.

10. *Ibid.*, p. 397.

11. *Ibid.*, p. 8.

12. See the discussion of this subject in Charles S. Singleton's *Dante's Commedia: Elements of Structure*.

13. *Boccaccio on Poetry*, p. 46.

14. Jacopo Mazzoni, *Della difesa della "Commedia" di Dante* (Cesena, 1688). Only the first book of Mazzoni's work was published in the sixteenth century. The passage is translated by Gilbert, pp. 386-87.

15. Hathaway, *The Age of Criticism*, p. 357.

16. Plato, *Sophist* 235e-236d. The significance of this distinction is discussed by Hathaway, pp.. 14-16, and in the chapters on Mazzoni. Since my argument hinges upon recognizing the extension of these terms into areas for which they were not originally devised, I must dissent from Bundy's thesis on the existence of an aesthetic "theory of imagination" in Plato. Bundy translates "eicastic imitation" as imagination and "phantastic" as fantasy, thus imposing upon Plato's text an early distinction between imagination and fancy that is very misleading. Francis M. Cornford, in his *Plato's Theory of Knowledge: The Theaetetus and the Sophist* (London: K. Paul, Trench, Trubner, 1935), translates eicastic imitation as "copymaking," which avoids the anachronism implicit in Bundy's use of the Latin term. It seems evident that Bundy has simply repeated Mazzoni's error. The subject of Plato's views on art is, to say the least, complicated, but a more reliable guide than Bundy is E. N. Tigerstedt in his article "Plato's Idea of Poetic Inspiration." Tigerstedt focuses upon the irony of Plato's presentation of the poet, and specifically upon the association of the poet's mania with his lack of knowledge about the meaning of his words. Tigerstedt follows Eric Havelock's *Preface to Plato* (Cambridge: Harvard University Press, 1963) in taking seriously Plato's condemnation of the poet, emphasizing with Havelock that the issue in Plato's dialogues is not the value or greatness of poetry (which Plato never really denies) but whether poetry is a form of knowledge. Plato's exaltation of the poetic mania, the poet's inspiration, is always accompanied by a disavowal of the poet's knowledge. It is doubtful that Plato ever changed his opinion on this subject, despite the high marks given the *phantasia* in the *Timaeus*. The fundamental issue for the early Greek philosophers was the authority of different kinds of discourse. They lived during a transition from poetic (oral) culture to philosophic (written)—a transition similar in significance to the one about which I am writing. Bundy's distortion of Plato reflects his own desire to enlist Plato on the side of imagination, as most Platonists who love art have tried to do.

17. An example would be a larger than life statue carved so that, when viewed from eye level, it would *look* proportional. In order to do this the sculptor would have to enlarge the upper portion of the statue.

18. Hathaway, p. 123.

19. Gilbert, p. 375.

20. Curtius, p. 398.

21. Puttenham, "The Arte of Englishe Poesie" in George Gregory Smith, ed., *Elizabethan Critical Essays*, 2:4. See also Meyer Abrams, *The Mirror and the Lamp: Romantic Theory and the Critical Tradition* (New York: Oxford University Press, 1953), pp. 272–85, for a history of the analogy of creation. Also Erwin Panofsky, "Artist, Scientist, Genius," pp. 171 ff.; Ernst Kantorowicz, "The Sovereignty of the Artist," in Millard Meiss, ed. *De Artibus Opuscula: Essays in Honor of Erwin Panofsky*, 2 vols. (New York: New York University Press, 1961); and Paul Kaufman, "Heralds of Original Genius," in *Essays in Memory of Barrett Wendell* (Cambridge: Harvard University Press, 1926). On words related to creation see Logan Pearsall Smith, "Four Romantic Words" in *Words and Idioms* (London: Constable, 1925) pp. 90–95; and Owen Barfield, *History in English Words* (New York: George H. Doran, 1926) p. 191.

22. Castelvetro, Scaliger, and Sidney are examples. For Castelvetro, see Gilbert, pp. 310–11. For Scaliger see Frederick Padelford, ed. and trans., *Select Translations from Scaliger's Poetics*.

23. See Barfield, *History in English Words*, pp. 191–96.

24. Torquato Tasso, *Discourses on the Heroic Poem*, p. 30.

25. *Ibid.*, p. 32.

26. For a general survey of this subject, see Russell Fraser, *The War against Poetry*.

27. Smith, ed., *Elizabethan Critical Essays*, 1:186.

28. *Ibid.*, 1:159.

29. *Ibid.*, 1:157.

30. *Ibid.*, 1:157–58.

31. *Ibid.*, 1:159.

32. *Ibid.*, 1:192.

33. On this subject see the essay by J. L. Harrison, "Bacon's View of Rhetoric, Poetry, and Imagination," p. 109.

34. Bacon, in Spedding et al., eds., 3: 382.

35. Harry Caplan, trans., *Gianfrancesco Pico della Mirandola on the Imagination* (New Haven: Yale University Press, 1930).

36. Bacon, *The Advancement of Learning*, Spedding et al., eds., 2:343.

37. *Ibid.*, 2:343.

38. It is important that the word "truth" be opposed to imagination here, rather than the word we would now use, "reality." The opposition between imagination and reality is very post-Cartesian. I would not consider Spenser, or most Renaissance thinkers, incapable of intuiting this distinction (obviously, Hobbes is already thinking at times on the other side of the Cartesian divide), but their notion of the real should not be confused with the concept of the "really existent." Phantasms, such as those which appear to Redcrosse in his demonically inspired dream, are *real* but not *true*.

39. John Smith, *Select Discourses* (1660, rpt. London, 1821) p. 190.

40. Calvin, *Institutes of the Christian Religion*, Ford Lewis Battles, trans., Jon T. McNeill, ed. 1:93–96.

41. See Rupert E. Davies, *The Problem of Authority in the Continental Reformers: A Study in Luther, Zwingli, and Calvin*, for a discussion of the issue.

42. An exemplary incident is recorded by Edmund S. Morgan in his *The Puritan Dilemma: The Story of John Winthrop*, pp. 147–53. Morgan recounts briefly the life of Anne Hutchinson, whose trial amusingly (if also a little disturbingly) discovers the greatest embarrassment of

Protestantism. Mrs. Hutchinson claimed that her heretical opinions were given to her by an "immediate revelation."

43. Davenant, in Joel E. Spingarn, ed., *Critical Essays of the Seventeenth Century*, 2:25.

44. Spingarn, 2:59.

45. Hobbes, *Leviathan*, ch. 2, "Of Imagination."

46. Spingarn, 2:59.

47. Hobbes, p. 410.

48. *Ibid.*, p. 426. See also Hobbes' definitions of *spirit, angel,* and *inspiration*, pp. 429 and 440.

49. Spinoza, *A Theologico-Political Treatise and A Political Treatise*, ch. 1, "Of Prophecy."

50. *Ibid.*, p. 167.

51. Smith, *Select Discourses*, p. 25.

52. *Ibid.*

53. Spinoza, p. 25.

54. Smith, *Select Discourses*, p. 183.

55. All quotations from the plays of Shakespeare are from the Pelican edition (Baltimore, 1969).

56. All quotations from Milton's poetry are taken from the edition by Merritt Hughes, *John Milton: Complete Poems and Major Prose.*

57. The best discussion I have found of Milton's relation to Shakespeare is by Leslie Brisman, *Milton's Poetry of Choice and its Romantic Heirs*, especially the discussion of this poem, to which I am much indebted.

58. Smith, ed., *Elizabethan Critical Essays*, 1:169.

59. On the relation of Spenser to Ariosto and Tasso, in the context of secular and sacred poetry, see Robert M. Durling, *The Figure of the Poet in the Renaissance Epic*, p. 234. It will be clear, in the course of my argument, that both Spenser and Milton retreat from their initial ambition to produce a kind of sacred text. This retreat is the burden of the later books of *The Faerie Queene*, and also (although less conspicuously) of *Samson Agonistes*. On the general background of English attempts to write sacred poetry, see Lily B. Campbell, *Divine Poetry and Drama in Sixteenth-Century England* (Cambridge: Cambridge University Press, 1959); and James H. Sims, "Milton and the Bible," in J. Max Patrick and Roger H. Sundell, eds., *Milton and the Art of Sacred Song* (Madison: University of Wisconsin Press, 1979), especially Sims, p. 15, on the period from Sidney to Cowley: "Though the Bible provides the best materials in the world for poetry, 'None but a good *Artist* will know how to do it: neither must we think to cut and polish *Diamonds* with so little pains and skill as we do *Marble*.' [Cowley, Preface to *Davideis*] Between Sidney and Cowley lie acres of diamonds of Scripture which are, in spite of imperfect cutting, given poetic settings in the continuing attempt to prove that divine poetry can replace secular poetry. Those who believe that divine and secular poetry are sister arts intended to benefit each other, like those who reject poetry of any kind, are in the minority."

60. A good example is the collection of essays edited by Joseph Anthony Wittreich, Jr., *Milton and the Line of Vision.*

2. A Critique of Origins: The Image of Source in *The Faerie Queene*

1. All quotations from the poetry of Spenser are taken from the Oxford edition, *Spenser: Poetical Works*, J. C. Smith and E. de Selincourt, eds.

2. Josephine W. Bennett, in *The Evolution of "The Faerie Queene,"* p. 174, argues that the marriage of the Thames and the Medway "was first planned and probably written as an experiment in 'English Versifying,' or classical meter, in 1580."

3. In *Spenser's Images of Life*, p. 115, C. S. Lewis remarks that all true poets love proper names.

4. Arendt, *Between Past and Future: Six Exercises in Political Thought*, pp. 121-22.

5. See Richard Neuse, "Milton and Spenser: The Virgilian Triad Revisited." I find Neuse more convincing on Spenser than on Milton.

6. Arendt, p. 121.

7. See the chapter on "The Pretext" (usually meaning "sacred pretext") in Maureen Quilligan's *The Language of Allegory*, especially the opening pages on the Bible as a pretext of allegory, and pp. 133 ff.

8. On the subject of romance in this and other Renaissance poems, see the study by Patricia Parker, *Inescapable Romance*.

9. Said, *Beginnings: Intention and Method*, passim.

10. *Ibid.*, p. 6.

11. *Ibid.*, p. 372.

12. James Nohrnberg, *The Analogy of the Faerie Queene*.

13. Redcrosse, of course, is already guilty of the sin of pride, which is nominally the true radical of all sin, including *accidie*. Nevertheless, I am more impressed at this moment by the fall into *accidie*, since this is the one sin to which all Spenserian questers, up to and including Calidore, are attracted. This skewing of the hierarchy of sin is determined, I would think, both by the narrative form of the quest (the necessity of continuous "travailing"), and by the vigilance of the Protestant ideology, its requirement of self-examination, the state of being "wary wise." So Spenser does not give us any correlative in the story of the Nymph to the sin of pride, but only tells us that the Nymph was "tyred."

14. Fletcher, *Allegory: The Theory of a Symbolic Mode*, p. 188.

15. Compare Coleridge in *Aids to Reflection* (1829): "No Natural thing or act can be called an originant, or be truly said to have an *origin* in any other. The moment we assume an Origin in Nature, a true *Beginning*, an actual first—that moment we rise *above* Nature and are compelled to assume a *supernatural* Power."

16. See Alastair Fowler, "The River Guyon" and James Nohrnberg, pp. 303-4.

17. The phrase is from a poem by Blake, of course, but I mean to acknowledge here also C. S. Lewis' *Spenser's Images of Life*, which contains a number of allusions to Blake. I want to make explicit a connection between desire and the visionary longing that must have reminded Lewis of Blake.

18. Michel Foucault, *The Archaeology of Knowledge*, pp. 106 ff.

19. Lewis, *The Allegory of Love: A Study in Medieval Tradition*, pp. 361-63; and "Genius and Genius."

20. On allegory as "outward show," and the play with inner-outer dichotomies, the best guide is A. Bartlett Giamatti, in his *Play of Double Senses: Spenser's Faerie Queene*. I doubt that Spenser is ever unaware that he must use the same set of terms to describe both the illusions of fantasy and the nature of allegory. The proems, especially the last, meditate on this uneasy congruity.

21. Although, for the sake of consistency, I have been using "fantasy," the alternative spelling "phantasy" is not insignificant. According to the *OED* the longer spelling "phantasy" came in after the revival of Greek learning, and this spelling is to be found largely in entries after the mid-sixteenth century. The meaning of the Greek etymon influenced the newer uses of the word. This is certainly what happens in Sidney's use of the word, and Spenser's orthographic choices might also be affected. (*Phantastes*, of course, takes us back to the Greek etymon, and is therefore suggestive of the newer meanings.)

22. See Paul de Man's discussion of allegory and irony in "The Rhetoric of Temporality,"

pp. 173-209. On the similitude of desire and fantasy, and the problem of determining origins, Spenser himself makes an explicit point in the Mask of Cupid, where *Fancy* and *Desyre* are marching side by side:

And him beside marcht amorous Desyre,
> Who seemd of riper yeares, then th'other swaine,
> Yet was that other swayne this elders syre,
> And gave him being, commune to them twaine.
>   (III.xii.9)

23. See Angus Fletcher's section on the "Biblical matrix" in *The Prophetic Moment: An Essay on Spenser.*

24. Lewis, *The Allegory of Love*, p. 332: "There is not a kiss or an embrace in the island."

25. A. C. Hamilton, in the recent Longman's edition (London, 1977), points to the convention in mythology and pagan literature of the warrior who lays aside his arms to take up with a mistress; but the word "instruments," as John Hollander has pointed out, echoes recent translations of the Bible, Psalm 137 ("By the rivers of Babylon...") The Douay-Rheims version gives, for the second verse, "On the willows in the midst thereof we hung up our instruments." See the series of English verse translations of the psalm in the Oxford anthology, John Hollander and Frank Kermode, eds., *The Literature of Renaissance England*, (New York: Oxford University Press, 1973) pp. 35-42. The biblical nuance hints at the greater loss in Verdant's behavior.

26. On the romance form, and its relation to the categories of the sacred and secular, see Northrop Frye's *The Secular Scripture: A Study of the Structure of Romance.*

27. Isabel G. MacCaffrey, *Spenser's Allegory*, p. 135.

28. Harry Berger, Jr., "A Secret Discipline: The *Faerie Queene*, Book VI," p. 73.

29. Elsewhere Berger and MacCaffrey adhere to a concept of the imagination in Spenser less mystified, or teleologically colored by a Stevensian poetic. The moment of anachronism is a measure both of how strong our mythology of imagination as origin really is, and of how intensely Spenser longs at this moment for an epiphanic source of both desire and poetry.

30. Although I am not sure that A. Bartlett Giamatti would agree with the extent to which I represent this visionary experience as subverted, I share with him a strong sense of the poet as excluded voyeur, and I owe to Giamatti my understanding of the conflict between *voyeur* and *voyant*. The distinction seems to me very deeply characteristic of Spenser's poetic longing. Humphrey Tonkin extends this paradigm to the encounter of the reader with the poem, *Spenser's Courteous Pastoral: Book VI of the Faerie Queene*, p. 141: "If Colin is the poet and the dance is his poetry, Calidore represents ourselves, the readers, in our fumbling efforts to understand the incomprehensible and our insistence on pat answers."

31. See especially Frye's essay "Myth, Fiction, and Displacement," in *Fables of Identity: Studies in Poetic Mythology*, pp. 21-38.

3. The Ground of Authority: The *Mutabilitie Cantos*

1. Arendt, *Between Past and Future*, p. 95.

2. For a general study, see A. Bartlett Giamatti's "Proteus Unbound: Some Versions of the Sea God in the Renaissance," in *The Disciplines of Criticism*, pp. 437-75.

3. On the subject see Lawrence Stone's *The Crisis of the Aristocracy, 1558-1641*, p. 16.

4. Barfield, "Imagination and Inspiration," in *Interpretation: The Poetry of Meaning*, p. 65.

5. *Ibid.*, p. 69.

6. The best article on this subject is by M. N. Holahan, "'Iamque opus exegi'; Ovid's

Changes and Spenser's Brief Epic of Mutability." See also William P. Cumming, "The Influence of Ovid's *Metamorphoses* on Spenser's 'Mutabilitie Cantos,' " *Speculum* (1931), 28:241-56.

7. Richard N. Ringler, "The Faunus Episode," *Modern Philology* (1965) 63:12-19, reprinted in *Essential Articles for the Study of Edmund Spenser*, A.C. Hamilton, ed. (Hamden, Conn.: Archon, 1972) pp. 289-98.

8. See the argument of Brooks Otis' *Ovid as an Epic Poet* (Cambridge: Cambridge University Press, 1970).

9. Ringler, *Essential Articles,* p. 295.

10. Alice Miskimin, *The Renaissance Chaucer,* p. 42.

11. *Ibid.,* p. 64. *The Complaint of Nature by Alain de Lille,* Douglas M. Moffat, trans. (New York: H. Holt and Company, 1908) p. 41.

12. Osgood translation, pp. 33-34.

13. See the persuasive argument of Sherman Hawkins, "Mutabilitie and the Cycle of the Months," in *Form and Convention in the Poetry of Edmund Spenser,* William Nelson, ed. (New York: Columbia University Press, 1961) pp. 76-102. I do agree with Hawkins that the cycle subsumes the fact of mutability into the order of constancy, though I see darker consequences of this fact.

14. Henri Frankfort, "The Emancipation of Thought from Myth," in *The Intellectual Adventure of Ancient Man,* p. 369.

4. "Some Superior Power": Spenser and Shakespeare in Milton's *Comus*

1. The Bridgewater *Comus* is reprinted in John Diekhoff's *A Maske at Ludlow: Essays on Milton's Comus.*

2. The "native Wood-notes wild" makes the same point about the natural, spontaneous quality of Shakespeare's verse as in "On Shakespeare." Consider also the lines from that poem, "Then thou our fancy of itself bereaving, / Dost make us Marble with too much conceiving."

3. Alan Rudrum, *A Critical Commentary on Milton's "Comus" and Shorter Poems* (London: Macmillan, 1967), p. 44. See also Thomas Warton's annotation in *Poems Upon Several Occasions ... by John Milton.*

4. Warton, p. 82.

5. On the general subject of Shakespeare and Milton, see G. Wilson Knight's essay, "The Frozen Labyrinth," in *The Burning Oracle: Studies in the Poetry of Action.* Also the work to which I am more fundamentally indebted, Leslie Brisman, *Milton's Poetry of Choice and its Romantic Heirs.* Still a useful and very perceptive essay is C. S. Lewis' "A Note on *Comus*," in *Studies in Medieval and Renaissance Literature* (Cambridge: Cambridge University Press, 1966) pp. 175-81.

6. *The Poems of John Milton,* John Carey and Alastair Fowler, eds., p. 171.

7. A. S. P. Woodhouse, "The Argument of Milton's *Comus.*"

8. Angus Fletcher, *The Transcendental Masque: An Essay on Milton's Comus,* pp. 142-43.

9. Fletcher, p. 205.

10. See the essay on "Cryptomnesia" in C. G. Jung's *Psychiatric Studies,* Bollingen Series 20 (Princeton: Princeton University Press, 1957). It might be possible to argue that some examples of allusion are actually produced by cryptromnesia.

11. I am relying upon Angus Fletcher's study of daemonic agents in *Allegory: The Theory of a Symbolic Mode.* I confine my discussion to the daemonic figures themselves in literature, in contradistinction to Fletcher's emphasis upon allegorical agents.

12. *Amend* is related by its Latin root to *mendax*: lying, false. The point is only tangential perhaps, but it reminds us of how complex a notion of representation is implied by Shakespeare's language. Theseus' "shadows," for example, is a rich ambiguity, to be read against all the problems of mimesis afflicting the mechanicals' play within the play.

13. My distinction between transfiguration and metamorphosis is intended to recall Christ's Transfiguration on Mount Tabor (Matt. 17), and the fact that the word is translated from the passive form of *metamorphoō*. Translation must surely have made it easier for theologians to distinguish between the event on Mt. Tabor and the pagan concept of metamorphosis.

14. The *Variorum* note says that these words are recorded by the *OED* as first used in *Comus*, although "imbodies" was already in use as a transitive verb. A. S. P. Woodhouse and Douglas Bush, *A Variorum Commentary on the Poems of John Milton* (New York: Columbia University Press, 1972), 2:(3)916.

15. Harry Caplan, ed. and trans., *Gianfrancesco Pico della Mirandola On the Imagination*, p. 43.

16. Details in *A Variorum Commentary*, 2:(3) 902.

17. William Empson, "Milton and Bentley," in *Some Versions of Pastoral*.

18. Virginity can be conceived in this context as the (temporary) embodiment of chastity, a distinction that respects the greater principle of chastity.

19. This sun is rising, of course, at the end of the "Nativity Ode," signifying also the recovery of pagan mythology as the matter of *allusion*.

20. Carey and Fowler, *The Poems of John Milton*, p. 213.

21. The relation is noted by G. Wilson Knight, *The Burning Oracle*, pp. 64–70; also Brisman, *Milton's Poetry of Choice*, ch. 1.

22. I am inclined to agree with Empson that for Milton "Elizabeth and her age counted as another paganism." *Some Versions of Pastoral*, p. 182.

23. See the *Variorum* commentary on these lines, especially the association of the Hesperides with the stars, 2:(3) 978.

5. The Visible Saint: Miltonic Authority

1. In some systems of rhetoric the terms are related to one another very closely, somewhat like metaphor and simile. Synecdoche can be regarded as the trope of representation itself, where the part "represents" the whole. Does the "crown" represent the "king"? The latter is usually called metonymy, and though I am maintaining this distinction, I recognize the difficulty in definition. Metonymy is also related etymologically to the concept of "name-changing," and I have often, following Milton's practice, taken the figure back to this original sense.

2. When Milton published "Lycidas" with his collected earlier poetry in 1645, he added the headnote in which he asserts that his poem "by occasion foretells the ruin of our corrupted clergy." The poem does not really do this, but the voice of the polemicist is speaking here. The headnote is a good example of Milton creating his authority by a retrospective reading of his life and work. For a general survey of his career as a pamphleteer, see Arthur Barker, *Milton and the Puritan Dilemma*.

3. Quotations from the prose are cited from the Yale edition, unless otherwise noted, and will be given parenthetically in the text. *Complete Prose Works of John Milton*, 1:869.

4. See Bloom, *A Map of Misreading*, pp. 98–99, which is also good on the linking of metonymy and hyperbole.

5. Burke, "Four Master Tropes," in *A Grammar of Motives*, p. 506.

6. Hill, *Milton and The English Revolution*. See the sections on Christian doctrine and the "great poems," especially pp. 356 and 403.

7. The scriptural analogue is again the kenosis of Christ; Milton empties himself in order to allow for the influx of authority, the recipient being immediately his text, and secondarily his name.

8. Kerrigan, *The Prophetic Milton*, p. 264.

9. Satan's modern defender, William Empson, focuses on the theologic eccentricity of the exaltation, although for the purpose of arguing one side of the controversy. I have abstracted the problem somewhat as a conflict between priority and secondariness, since I do not believe that Satan needs to be defended or attacked. See *Milton's God*, pp. 82 ff.

10. See Geoffrey Hartman's important comment on the coincidence of the Freudian prehistory with Milton's conception of Satan, *The Fate of Reading*, p. 54.

11. For example, William G. Riggs, *The Christian Poet in Paradise Lost*. Kerrigan is also very good on this subject in *The Prophetic Milton*, pp. 147 ff. See also Coleridge's comments in Joseph Anthony Wittreich, ed., *The Romantics on Milton*, pp. 270 and 277.

12. This connection has not been generally remarked. But see Jonathan Steadman's "Image and Idol: Satan and the Element of Illusion in *Paradise Lost*" and the chapter in *Milton's Epic Characters*, beginning on p. 227.

13. I refer in these comments not only to the Romantics but also to Milton's popularizers in the eighteenth century. It is an illusion of subsequent literary history that so many notions we have about Milton are Romantic. Dr. Johnson's powerful remarks on Milton's capacity to "crowd the imagination" contribute as much to the history of Milton's influence as the Romantic notion of imagination itself. The association had already been fixed by Addison in his series of *Spectator* essays on the imagination, from which Johnson derived the "sublime" conception of this faculty: "Our imagination loves to be filled with an object, or to grasp at anything that is too big for its Capacity." *Spectator*, no. 420.

14. Kerrigan, pp. 133 ff.

15. *The Ego and the Id*, Standard Edition, vol. 19 (London: The Hogarth Press, 1927): "The broad general outcome of the sexual phase dominated by the Oedipus complex may, therefore, be taken to be the forming of a precipitate in the ego, consisting of two identifications in some way united with each other. This modification of the ego retains its special position; it confronts the other contents of the ego as an ego ideal or super-ego."

16. Paul Ricoeur, *Freud and Philosophy*, p. 212.

17. *Ibid*, p. 222. From *The Ego and the Id*, p. 36: "The ego ideal is therefore the heir of the Oedipus complex, and thus it is also the expression of the powerful impulses and most important libidinal vicissitudes of the id."

18. "Mourning and Melancholia," Standard Edition, vol. 14.

19. Ricoeur, pp. 480 ff.

20. See *The Future of an Illusion*, Standard Edition, vol. 21, and *Totem and Taboo*, Standard Edition, vol. 13; also Ricoeur, pp. 230 ff., for comments on projection.

21. Ricoeur, p. 478.

22. See Kerrigan and Riggs, *passim*.

23. C. A. Patrides, "The Godhead in *Paradise Lost*: Dogma or Drama," in *Bright Essence: Studies in Milton's Theology*, W. B. Hunter et al., eds.

24. This is essentially William Riggs' position in the chapter titled "An Imitation of the Son." Also John T. Shawcross, "The Metaphor of Inspiration in *Paradise Lost*," in *Th'Upright Heart and Pure*, pp. 75–85.

25. The context of the division of the god (as representative of talents) is very interesting:

Ipse volens Phoebus se dispertire duobus,
  Altera dona mihi, dedit altera dona parenti,
  Dividuumque Deum genitorque puerque tenemus.
              (64–66)
Phoebus himself, wishing to part himself between us two, gave some gifts to me and
others to my father; and, father and son, we share the possession of the divided god.
              (Hughes' translation)
A much more radical division seems to be taking place in *Paradise Lost*.

26. The religious paradigm is the Hebraic suppression of God's name, which has some
effect on the Christian tradition of invocation. Milton is also remembering Spenser's suppression of the name of his muse, and these tactical indirections are intimately involved in the
"sacred" origins of the poetic text. Milton did, however, have the precedent of Cowley's
Davideis to consider, a poem that openly invokes Christ as its muse. I suspect that Milton
would have judged Cowley's openness a tactical error.

27. Richardson, *Explanatory Notes and Remarks on Milton's Paradise Lost*, p. 89.

28. A very intelligent discussion of the controversy, which I cannot rehearse here, can be
found in Jackson I. Cope's *The Metaphorical Structure of Paradise Lost*, pp. 149 ff. I will mention
William B. Hunter, who identifies Light with Christ in "The Meaning of 'Hail Holy Light,' "
MLN (1959) vol. 74. Hunter's essay is included in the anthology *Bright Essence*, the whole of
which is more than usually informed with a realization of the central significance of the Son,
poetic as well as theological.

29. Hartman, *The Fate of Reading*, p. 52.

30. Richardson, *Explanatory Notes*, p. 95.

31. Some meanings of "voluntary" from the *OED*: 1) arising or developing in the mind
without external constraint; having a purely spontaneous origin or character. 2) brought
about by one's own choice or deliberate action. 3) a musical piece or movement played or sung
spontaneously or of one's free choice, esp. by way of prelude to a more elaborate piece, song,
etc.

32. From Wordsworth's *Essay on Epitaphs*, in Wittreich, ed., *The Romantics on Milton*,
p. 122.

33. See Paul de Man, "Literary History and Literary Modernity," in *Blindness and Insight*.

34. I refer primarily to Bloom's *The Map of Misreading*, the chapter entitled "Milton and his
Precursors," which considerably advances the argument of the earlier *The Anxiety of Influence*.
Bloom remains committed, however, to the priority and exclusivity of the Protestant line
(Spenser-Milton-Wordsworth), and I think this has the effect of rendering the other, more
"Catholic" line (Chaucer, Shakespeare, Donne, Dryden, Pope) in some way extracanonical.

35. See *Allegory*, p. 241. Fletcher refers to Quintilian's definition of transumption (or
metalepsis) as "a change from one trope to another," and suggests that this is the mode of
Miltonic allusion. Fletcher's argument has been developed by Harold Bloom in *A Map of
Misreading*, in the chapter entitled "Milton and his Precursors." The history of the trope is
fully and very helpfully discussed by John Hollander, in his *The Figure of Echo: A Mode of
Allusion in Milton and After*.

36. I quote from Ernest Sirluck's note in the Yale edition, p. 516, which summarizes the
argument of his article, "Milton Revises the *Faerie Queene*."

37. Bloom, *A Map of Misreading*, p. 128.

38. *Ibid.*, p. 128, and Harry Berger, Jr., *The Allegorical Temper*, the chapter on "conspicuous
irrelevance."

39. See his note in the Oxford anthology, *The Literature of the Renaissance in England*, p. 771.

40. This is not to say that no great poet will attempt a drama (Wordsworth's *The Borderers* is a fine exception), but rather that the *poetic* drama is henceforth, inevitably, in the tradition of *Samson Agonistes* rather than Shakespeare. Poets tend to write "closet drama" while dramatists turn to prose. This seems to me much more astonishing than the supposed decline of epic.

41. Hartman, "Milton's Counterplot," in *Beyond Formalism*, p. 115.

42. *Ibid.*, p. 121.

43. On this subject, see the excellent article by Kingsley Widmer, who discerns a "counter-plot" in the Miltonic simile based upon a concept of renunciation: "The Iconography of Renunciation: The Miltonic Simile," in *Milton's Epic Poetry*, pp. 121-31.

44. The possibility of this allusion to *The Aeneid* was suggested to me by my student Joshua Kendall.

45. Bloom, *A Map of Misreading*, p. 141.

6. Ithuriel's Spear: History and the Language of Accommodation

1. See the suggestion of Harris Francis Fletcher in the Cambridge Edition, *The Complete Poetical Works of John Milton* (Cambridge: Harvard University Press, 1941), p. 173.

2. For example, Stanley Fish on the size of Satan's spear, in *Surprised by Sin*, pp. 22 ff.

3. Johnson, *Life of Milton* (1779), in *Lives of the English Poets* (London: Oxford University Press, 1973) 1:127-28.

4. Another example would be Adam's dream, which is less real than its fulfillment, but not "unreal." My reason for choosing Satan's shape-changing as an example will eventually be clear, though I think as a general principle that it is safe to say that not everything associated with Satan is satanic.

5. A recent and interesting example is Boyd M. Berry's *Process of Speech: Puritan Religious Writing and Paradise Lost*, especially pp. 123 ff.

6. Hill, *Milton and the English Revolution*, pp. 365 ff.

7. C. A. Patrides, in *Milton and the Christian Tradition*, discusses the doctrine of accommodation, with extensive reference to theological sources, pp. 7-14. See also his essays in Hunter et al., eds., *Bright Essence*. A less helpful discussion is to be found in Leland Ryken's *The Apocalyptic Vision in Paradise Lost*, pp. 7-24. The best analysis is by H. R. McCallum, "Milton and Figurative Interpretation of the Bible." Finally William Madsen, in *From Shadowy Types to Truth: Studies in Milton's Symbolism*, pp. 54-84. On the earlier history of "figural interpretation," there is the masterly essay of Erich Auerbach, "Figura," in *Scenes from the Drama of European Literature*.

8. I quote here from the Columbia University Press edition (New York, 1934), which is more literal than the Yale translation and preserves Milton's *accomodans* as the English "accommodating," 14:31.

9. Madsen, p. 74.

10. Kerrigan, *The Prophetic Milton*, p. 160.

11. Wittgenstein, *Zettel*, G. E. M. Anscombe and G. H. von Wright, eds., Anscombe, trans. (Berkeley: University of California Press, 1967), p. 42.

12. See Hans Frei, *The Eclipse of Biblical Narrative*, pp. 18 ff.

13. This was Tillyard's position in *Milton*, where he distinguished between "conscious" and "unconscious" meaning. See A. J. A. Waldock's critique, *Paradise Lost and Its Critics* (Cambridge: Cambridge University Press, 1947). To a certain extent both Lawrence Hyman's *The Quarrel Within* (Port Washington, N. Y.: Kennikat, 1972) and William Empson's *Milton's God* rely upon a notion of unconscious intention.

14. Let me recall parenthetically an obvious point of intersection with Spenser's *Mutabilitie Cantos*. Galileo and Spenser's Faunus have similar representational functions, although there remains an impressive difference in Milton's handling of the visionary longing.

15. It is worth remembering here that Milton probably read *Siderius Nuncius*, which was published in 1610, and had a wide reputation. Galileo's book reported on the first discoveries of the telescope.

16. Brisman, lecture, Yale University, 1977.

17. Geoffrey Hartman, "Adam on the Grass with Balsamum," in *Beyond Formalism*, p. 142.

18. Joseph Anthony Wittreich, Jr., *Visionary Poetics: Milton's Tradition and His Legacy*, p. 51.

19. Fletcher, *The Transcendental Masque*, p. 143. I am not referring here (and neither is Fletcher) to the fact of censorship, which would in any case have prevented Milton from openly protesting the restoration of the monarchy. He had rather a deeper failure in the Reformation itself with which to contend.

20. "To my Dear Friend Mr. Congreve, On his Comedy, call'd The Double-Dealer," *The Poems of John Dryden* (Oxford: Oxford University Press, 1958), 2:852.

21. McCallum, p. 407.

22. The seminal article is by Michael Fixler, "The Apocalypse within *Paradise Lost*," in Thomas Kranidas, ed., *New Essays on Paradise Lost*, (Berkeley: University of California Press, 1971). See also *passim*, Ryken, Kerrigan, and Wittreich.

23. Consider Frank Kermode's discussion of the distinction between *kairos* and *chronos* in *The Sense of an Ending: Studies in the Theory of Fiction* (London: Oxford University Press, 1966), p. 46.

24. Kant, in his "Analytic of the Sublime," makes recourse to the notion of *subreption*, a term from ecclesiastical law which means "a secret, underhanded, unlawful representation through suppression or fraudulent concealment of facts." This is the English definition, from the *OED*. I find this notion a good, if hyperbolical, description of Milton's accommodation of historical facts in *Paradise Lost*. Thomas Weiskel has commented on subreption and the sublime in *The Romantic Sublime: Studies in the Structure and Psychology of Transcendence*, p. 46, where the concept is explicated as the "attitude that leads to the representation of the supersensible in the world of appearances." That history is blocked from entry into the poem (history as "supersensible") while simultaneously saturating its rhetoric constitutes the sublimity of *Paradise Lost*. Or we might say that the rhetorical breaking through which is Milton's poem is possible only because England did not break through to its dreamed-of millennium.

25. Lawler, *Celestial Pantomime: Poetic Structures of Transcendence* (New Haven: Yale University Press, 1979), p. 53.

Conclusion: The Strength of Usurpation

1. Hartman, *Beyond Formalism*, p. 142.

Select Bibliography

Arendt, Hannah. *Between Past and Future: Six Exercises in Political Thought.* New York: Viking Press, 1961; rpt. Cleveland: World, 1963.

Auerbach, Erich. *Scenes from the Drama of European Literature.* Gloucester, Mass.: Peter Smith, 1973.

Bacon, Francis. *The Works of Francis Bacon.* James Spedding, Robert Ellis, and Douglas Heath, eds. 14 vols. New York: Garret Press, 1870.

Barfield, Owen. "Imagination and Inspiration." In *Interpretation: The Poetry of Meaning.* Stanley Romaine Hopper and David L. Miller, eds. New York: Harcourt, Brace, and World, 1967.

Barker, Arthur E. *Milton and the Puritan Dilemma, 1641-1660.* Toronto: University of Toronto Press, 1943.

Barthel, Carol Ann. "Milton's Use of Spenser: The Early Poems and *Paradise Lost.*" Diss. Yale University, 1974.

Battles, Ford Lewis, trans., and Jon T. McNeil, ed. *Calvin: Institutes of the Christian Religion.* 2 vols. Philadelphia: Westminster Press, 1975.

Bennett, Josephine W. *The Evolution of "The Faerie Queene."* Chicago: University of Chicago Press, 1942.

Berger, Harry, Jr. *The Allegorical Temper: Vision and Reality in Book II of Spenser's Faerie Queene.* New Haven: Yale University Press, 1957.

—— "The Prospect of Imagination: Spenser and the Limits of Poetry." *Studies in English Literature* (1961), 1:93-120.

—— "The Renaissance Imagination: Second World and Green World." *Centennial Review* (1965), 9:36-72.

—— "A Secret Discipline: The *Faerie Queene*, Book VI." In *Form and Convention in the Poetry of Edmund Spenser.* William Nelson, ed. New York: Columbia University Press, 1961.

Berry, Boyd M. *Process of Speech: Puritan Religious Writing and Paradise Lost.* Baltimore: Johns Hopkins University Press, 1976.

Bloom, Harold. *A Map of Misreading.* New York: Oxford University Press, 1975.

Brisman, Leslie. *Milton's Poetry of Choice and its Romantic Heirs.* Ithaca, N.Y.: Cornell University Press, 1973.

Broadbent, J. B. *Some Graver Subject: An Essay on Paradise Lost.* London: Chatto and Windus, 1960.

Bundy, Murray W. "Invention and Imagination in the Renaissance." *JEGP* (1930), 29:535–45.

—— "The Theory of Imagination in Classical and Medieval Thought." *University of Illinois Studies in Language and Literature* (1927), 12:1–289.

Burke, Kenneth. *A Grammar of Motives.* New York: Braziller, 1955.

Caplan, Harry, ed. and trans. *Gianfrancesco Pico della Mirandola on the Imagination.* New Haven: Yale University Press, 1930.

Carey, John and Alastair Fowler, eds. *The Poems of John Milton.* New York: Norton, 1968.

Casey, Edward S. *Imagination: A Phenomenological Study.* Bloomington: Indiana University Press, 1976.

Coolidge, J. S. *The Pauline Renaissance in England: Puritanism and the Bible.* Oxford: Oxford University Press, 1970.

Curtius, Ernst Robert. *European Literature and the Latin Middle Ages.* Willard R. Trask, trans. New York: Pantheon, 1953.

Davies, Rupert E. *The Problem of Authority in the Continental Reformers: A Study in Luther, Zwingli, and Calvin.* London: Epworth Press, 1946.

De Man, Paul. *Blindness and Insight: Essays in the Rhetoric of Contemporary Criticism.* New York: Oxford University Press, 1971.

—— "The Rhetoric of Temporality." In *Interpretation: Theory and Practice.* Charles S. Singleton, ed. Baltimore: Johns Hopkins University Press, 1969.

Diekhoff, John, ed. *A Maske at Ludlow: Essays on Milton's Comus.* Cleveland: Case Western Reserve University Press, 1968.

Durling, Robert M. *The Figure of the Poet in the Renaissance Epic.* Cambridge: Harvard University Press, 1965.

Empson, William. *Milton's God.* London: Chatto and Windus, 1965.

—— *Some Versions of Pastoral.* New York: New Directions, 1950, rpt. 1960.

Ferry, Anne Davidson. *Milton's Epic Voice: The Narrator in Paradise Lost.* Cambridge: Harvard University Press, 1963.

Fish, Stanley. *Surprised by Sin: The Reader in Paradise Lost.* New York: St. Martin's Press, 1967.

Fletcher, Angus. *Allegory: The Theory of a Symbolic Mode,* Ithaca, N.Y.: Cornell University Press, 1964.

—— *The Prophetic Moment: An Essay on Spenser.* Chicago: University of Chicago Press, 1971.

—— *The Transcendental Masque: An Essay on Milton's Comus.* Ithaca, N.Y.: Cornell University Press, 1971.

Foucault, Michel. *The Archaelogy of Knowledge.* A. M. Sheridan Smith, trans. New York: Harper and Row, 1972.

Fowler, Alastair. "The River Guyon." *MLN* (1960), 75:289-92.

Frankfort, Henri et al. *The Intellectual Adventure of Ancient Man.* Chicago: University of Chicago Press, 1946.

Fraser, Russell. *The War against Poetry.* Princeton: Princeton University Press, 1970.

Frei, Hans. *The Eclipse of Biblical Narrative.* New Haven: Yale University Press, 1974.

Frye, Northrop. *Fables of Identity: Studies in Poetic Mythology.* New York: Harcourt, Brace, and World, 1963.

—— *The Secular Scripture: A Study of the Structure of Romance.* Cambridge: Harvard University Press, 1976.

Giamatti, A. Bartlett. *Play of Double Senses: Spenser's Faerie Queene.* Englewood Cliffs, N.J.: Prentice-Hall, 1975.

—— "Proteus Unbound: Some Versions of the Sea God in the Renaissance." In *The Disciplines of Criticism.* Peter Demetz, Thomas Greene, and Lowry Nelson, Jr., eds. New Haven: Yale University Press, 1968.

Gilbert, Allan H. *Literary Criticism: Plato to Dryden.* American Book, 1940; rpt. Detroit: Wayne State University Press, 1962.

Greene, Thomas. *The Descent from Heaven: A Study in Epic Continuity.* New Haven: Yale University Press, 1963.

Halio, J. L. "The Metaphor of Conception in Elizabethan Theories of Imagination." *Neophilologus* (1966), 50:454-61.

Haller, William. *The Rise of Puritanism.* New York: Columbia University Press, 1938.

Harrison, J. L. "Bacon's View of Rhetoric, Poetry, and Imagination." *Huntington Library Quarterly* (1957), 20:107-25.

Hartman, Geoffrey. *Beyond Formalism: Literary Essays 1958-1970.* New Haven: Yale University Press, 1970.

—— *The Fate of Reading.* Chicago: University of Chicago Press, 1975.

Hathaway, Baxter. *The Age of Criticism: The Late Renaissance in Italy.* Ithaca, N.Y.: Cornell University Press, 1962.

—— *Marvels and Commonplaces: Renaissance Literary Criticism.* New York: Random House, 1968.

Hawkins, Sherman. "Mutabilitie and the Cycle of the Months." In *Form and Convention in the Poetry of Edmund Spenser.* William Nelson, ed. New York: Columbia University Press, 1961.

Hill, Christopher. *Milton and the English Revolution*. London: Faber and Faber, 1977.

Hobbes, Thomas. *Leviathan*. C. B. Macpherson, ed. Middlesex: Penguin Books, 1968.

Holahan, M. N. "'Iamque opus exegi': Ovid's Changes and Spenser's Brief Epic of Mutability." *English Literary Renaissance* (1976), 6:244–70.

Hollander, John. *The Figure of Echo: A Mode of Allusion in Milton and After*. Berkeley: University of California Press, 1981.

Hughes, Merrit Y., ed. *John Milton: Complete Poems and Major Prose*. New York: Odyssey Press, 1957.

Hughes, Merritt Y. et al. *A Variorum Commentary on the Poems of John Milton*. 4 vols. New York: Columbia University Press, 1970.

Hunter, W. B., C. A. Patrides, and J. H. Adamson, eds. *Bright Essence: Studies in Milton's Theology*. Salt Lake City: University of Utah Press, 1971.

Kerrigan, William. *The Prophetic Milton*. Charlottesville: University of Virginia Press, 1974.

Knight, G. Wilson. *The Burning Oracle: Studies in the Poetry of Action*. London: Oxford University Press, 1939.

Langdon, Ida. *Milton's Theory of Poetry and Fine Art*. New Haven: Yale University Press, 1924.

Lewis, C. S. *The Allegory of Love: A Study in Medieval Tradition*. London: Oxford University Press, 1936.

——"Genius and Genius." *Review of English Studies* (1936), 12:189–94.

——*Spenser's Images of Life*. Alastair Fowler, ed. Cambridge: Cambridge University Press, 1967.

MacCaffrey, Isabel G. *Spenser's Allegory: The Anatomy of Imagination*. Princeton: Princeton University Press, 1976.

McCallum, H. R. "Milton and Figurative Interpretation of the Bible." *University of Toronto Quarterly* (1961-62), 31:397–415.

Madsen, William G. *From Shadowy Types to Truth: Studies in Milton's Symbolism*. New Haven: Yale University Press, 1968.

Miller, Perry. *The New England Mind: The Seventeenth Century*. New York: Macmillan, 1939.

Milton, John. *Complete Prose Works of John Milton*. Don M. Wolfe, et al., eds. 7 vols. New Haven: Yale University Press, 1953-1974.

Miskimin, Alice. *The Renaissance Chaucer*. New Haven: Yale University Press, 1975.

Morgan, Edmund S. *The Puritan Dilemma: The Story of John Winthrop*. Boston: Little, Brown, 1958.

Neuse, Richard. "Milton and Spenser: The Virgilian Triad Revisited." *ELH* (1978) 45:606–39.

Nohrnberg, James. *The Analogy of the Faerie Queene.* Princeton: Princeton University Press, 1976.

Osgood, Charles G., ed. and trans. *Boccaccio on Poetry, Being the Preface and the Fourteenth and Fifteenth Books of Boccaccio's "Genealogia Deorum Gentilium."* Princeton: Princeton University Press, 1930, rpt. 1958.

Padelford, Frederick, ed. and trans. *Select Translations from Scaliger's Poetics.* New York: Holt, 1905.

Panofsky, Erwin. "Artist, Scientist, Genius: Notes on the Renaissance *Dämmerung.*" In *The Renaissance.* New York: Harper and Row, 1962.

Parker, Patricia. *Inescapable Romance: Studies in the Poetics of a Mode.* Princeton: Princeton University Press, 1979.

Patrides, C. A. *Milton and the Christian Tradition.* Oxford: Oxford University Press, 1966.

Quilligan, Maureen. *The Language of Allegory.* Ithaca, N.Y.: Cornell University Press, 1979.

Richardson, Jonathan. *Explanatory Notes and Remarks on Milton's Paradise Lost.* London: James, John, and Paul Knapton, 1734.

Richmond, Hugh M. *The Christian Revolutionary: John Milton.* Berkeley: University of California Press, 1974.

Ricks, Christopher. *Milton's Grand Style.* Oxford: Clarendon Press, 1963.

Ricoeur, Paul. *Freud and Philosophy.* New Haven: Yale University Press, 1970.

Riggs, William G. *The Christian Poet in Paradise Lost.* Berkeley: University of California Press, 1972.

Ringler, Richard. "The Faunus Episode." In *Essential Articles for the Study of Edmund Spenser.* A. C. Hamilton, ed. Hamden, Conn.: Archon Books, 1972.

Rossky, William. "Imagination in the English Renaissance: Psychology and Poetic." *Studies in the Renaissance* (1958), 5:49–73.

Ryken, Leland. *The Apocalyptic Vision in Paradise Lost.* Ithaca, N.Y.: Cornell University Press, 1970.

Said, Edward. *Beginnings: Intention and Method.* Baltimore: Johns Hopkins University Press, 1975.

Sartre, Jean-Paul. *Imagination: A Psychological Critique.* B. Frechtman, trans. Ann Arbor: University of Michigan Press, 1962.

Shawcross, John T. "The Metaphor of Inspiration in *Paradise Lost.*" In *Th' Upright Heart and Pure.* Amadeus P. Fiore, ed. Pittsburgh: Duquesne University Press, 1967.

Singleton, Charles S. *Dante's Commedia: Elements of Structure.* Baltimore: Johns Hopkins University Press, 1954.

Sirluck, Ernest. "Milton Revises the *Faerie Queene.*" *Modern Philology* (1950), 48:90–96.

Smith, George Gregory, ed. *Elizabethan Critical Essays.* 2 vols. Oxford: Oxford University Press, 1904.

Spenser, Edmund. *Spenser: Poetical Works.* J. C. Smith and E. de Selincourt, eds. London: Oxford University Press, 1912; rpt. 1969.

Spingarn, Joel E. *Critical Essays of the Seventeenth Century.* 3 vols. Bloomington: Indiana University Press, 1957.

Spinoza, Baruch. *A Theologico-Political Treatise and A Political Treatise.* R. H. M. Lewis, trans. New York: Dover, 1951.

Starobinski, Jean. "Jalons pour une histoire du concept d'imagination." In *La Relation critique.* Paris: Galimard, 1970.

Steadman, Jonathan. "Image and Idol: Satan and the Element of Illusion in *Paradise Lost.*" *JEGP* (1960), 59:640–54.

—— *Milton's Epic Characters.* Chapel Hill: University of North Carolina Press, 1959.

Stein, Arnold. *The Art of Presence: The Poet and Paradise Lost.* Berkeley: University of California Press, 1977.

Stone, Lawrence. *The Crisis of the Aristocracy 1558-1641.* London: Oxford University Press, 1967.

Tasso, Torquato. *Discourses on the Heroic Poem.* Mariella Cavalchini and Irene Samuel, trans. London: Oxford University Press, 1973.

Tigerstedt, E. N. "Plato's Idea of Poetic Inspiration." In *Commentationes humanarum literarum* of the *Societas Scientiarum Fennica* (1969), 44:(2)1–78.

Tillyard, E. M. W. *Milton.* London: Chatto and Windus, 1930.

Tonkin, Humphrey. *Spenser's Courteous Pastoral: Book VI of the Faerie Queene.* London: Oxford University Press, 1972.

Warton, Thomas, ed. *Poems Upon Several Occasions . . . by John Milton.* London: Printed for G. G. J. and J. Robinson, 1791.

Weinberg, Bernard. *A History of Literary Criticism in the Italian Renaissance.* 2 vols. Chicago: University of Chicago Press, 1961.

Weiskel, Thomas. *The Romantic Sublime: Studies in the Structure and Psychology of Transcendence.* Baltimore: Johns Hopkins University Press, 1976.

Widmer, Kingsley. "The Iconography of Renunciation: The Miltonic Simile." In *Milton's Epic Poetry: Essays on Paradise Lost and Paradise Regained.* C. A. Patrides, ed. Middlesex: Penguin Books, 1967.

Wittreich, Joseph Anthony, Jr. *Visionary Poetics: Milton's Tradition and his Legacy*. San Marino, Calif.: Huntington Library, 1979.

Wittreich, Joseph Anthony, Jr., ed. *Milton and the Line of Vision*. Madison: University of Wisconsin Press, 1975.

—— *The Romantics on Milton*. Cleveland: Case Western Reserve University Press, 1970.

Woodhouse, A. S. P. "The Argument of Milton's *Comus*." *University of Toronto Quarterly* (1941), 11:46–71.

Index